TEACHING AND BEHAVIOR SUPPORT FOR CHILDREN AND ADULTS WITH AUTISM SPECTRUM DISORDER

TEACHING AND BEHAVIOR SUPPORT FOR CHILDREN AND ADULTS WITH AUTISM SPECTRUM DISORDER

A Practitioner's Guide

Edited by James K. Luiselli

OXFORD
UNIVERSITY PRESS

Oxford University Press, Inc., publishes works that further
Oxford University's objective of excellence
in research, scholarship, and education.

Oxford   New York
Auckland   Cape Town   Dar es Salaam   Hong Kong   Karachi
Kuala Lumpur   Madrid   Melbourne   Mexico City   Nairobi
New Delhi   Shanghai   Taipei   Toronto

With offices in
Argentina   Austria   Brazil   Chile   Czech Republic   France   Greece
Guatemala   Hungary   Italy   Japan   Poland   Portugal   Singapore
South Korea   Switzerland   Thailand   Turkey   Ukraine   Vietnam

Published by Oxford University Press, Inc.
198 Madison Avenue, New York, New York 10016
www.oup.com

Oxford is a registered trademark of Oxford University Press

Library of Congress Cataloging-in-Publication Data

Teaching and behavior support for children and adults with autism spectrum disorder:
  a practitioner's guide/edited by James K. Luiselli.
        p. ; cm.
  Includes bibliographical references and index.
  ISBN 978-0-19-973640-9 (alk. paper)
  1. Autism spectrum disorders—Patients—Rehabilitation. 2. Life skills. I. Luiselli, James K.
  [DNLM: 1. Autistic Disorder—therapy. 2. Behavior Therapy—methods.
  3. Education, Special—methods. WM 203.5]
  RC553.A88T43 2011
  616.85'882—dc22

                                                                    2010028075

Printed in the United States of America
on acid-free paper

PREFACE

Many books have been written about autism spectrum disorder (ASD) in children and adults. There are useful volumes that discuss diagnosis, assessment, and treatment, most directed at an academic audience and students in training. Fewer books exist that are exclusively practitioner-focused. However, the demand for research-to-practice translation requires that evidence-based outcomes produce empirically supported procedures. Accordingly, the purpose of this book is to give practitioners essential "how-to" advice that is easy to understand and implement.

The topics I selected for the book represent critical areas in need of attention by any practitioner who provides services for a child or adult with ASD: how to conduct assessment, how to teach skills, and how to reduce problem behavior. There is an additional "how-to" section that considers other important implementation guidelines. In total, the book contains 24 chapters, each written by a recognized ASD expert with both clinical and research specialization.

The chapters in the book follow a similar format. First, there is an overview describing current knowledge about the respective topic as gleaned from the published literature and each author's philosophy and perspective. Next, the chapters present basic information about the principles that govern procedural application. Intervention guidelines form the bulk of each chapter, written explicitly with the practitioner in mind. Where applicable, the authors also include illustrative forms, charts, and summary tables. Finally, the chapters discuss adapting and modifying procedures to settings, different age groups, and practitioner training requirements. Each chapter concludes with several "take-home" points, suggested readings, and, as warranted, other resources such as training videos and Internet web sites.

My intent in having a uniform chapter format is to facilitate consistency and readability throughout the book. Knowing the layout of each chapter, readers should be able to move among topics with the same clarity and ease of comprehension. Ultimately, my objective is to give practitioners essential knowledge for conducting successful assessment, instruction, and intervention with children and adults who have ASD.

You also will find several consistent themes among the chapters, notably the need for conducting preference and functional assessments, direct measurement, care provider training, and outcome evaluation. One reason these areas are voiced so often is that they have strong empirical support. Furthermore, I did not want these and other critical areas to be missed by readers who may refer to some but not all of the chapters in the book.

I'm grateful to Oxford University Press for supporting the book and making every phase of the production process a pleasurable experience. All of the authors have my gratitude: they wrote as requested, responded professionally to revision recommendations, and produced wonderful chapters. I must acknowledge many of the settings where the book was conceived, written, and edited, including Middlesex School, The Thoreau Club, Dunkin' Donuts, Burlington Mall, and all the ice rinks associated with Colonial Figure Skating Club and Concord-Carlisle Youth Hockey. Finally, my wife, Dr. Tracy Evans Luiselli, and our children, Gabrielle and Thomas, continue to support and enlighten me in ways I can easily acknowledge but not so easily describe.

James K. Luiselli

CONTENTS

PART 4
OTHER HOW-TO GUIDELINES

CONTRIBUTORS

Keith D. Allen, Ph.D., BCBA-D
Munroe Meyer Institute
University of Nebraska-Lincoln
Lincoln, NE

Richard L. Azulay
Canton Public Schools
Dean S. Luce Elementary School
Canton, MA

Jennifer D. Bass, Psy.D., BCBA-D
Cincinnati Children's Hospital Medical
    Center
Division of Developmental and Behavioral
    Pediatrics
Cincinnati, OH

Wendy K. Berg, M.A.
The Center for Disabilities and Development
The University of Iowa
Iowa City, IA

Hayoung Choi, Ph.D.
Special Education Research Institute
Ewha Womans University
Seoul, South Korea

Robin S. Codding, Ph.D.
Department of Counseling and School
    Psychology
University of Massachusetts Boston
Boston, MA

Jaime A. DeQuinzio

Mark R. Dixon, Ph.D.
Rehabilitation Institute
Southern Illinois University
Carbondale, IL

Chaturi Edrisinha, Ph.D.
Educational Leadership and Community
    Psychology
St. Cloud State University
St. Cloud, MN

Terry Falcomata, Ph.D.
The Meadows Center for Preventing
    Educational Risk
The University of Texas at Austin
Austin, TX

Christina Fragale
The Meadows Center for Preventing
    Educational Risk
The University of Texas at Austin
Austin, TX

Mitch J. Fryling, Ph.D.
Department of Applied Behavior Analysis
The Chicago School
Los Angeles, CA

Patrick M. Ghezzi, Ph.D., BCBA-D
Director, UNR Early Childhood Autism
    Program
Department of Psychology
University of Nevada
Reno, NV

Jennifer M. Gillis, Ph.D., BCBA-D
Department of Psychology
Auburn University
Auburn, AL

Vanessa Green, Ph.D.
Victoria University at Wellington
Wellington, New Zealand

Gregory P. Hanley, Ph.D., BCBA
Psychology Department
Western New England College
Springfield, MA

Jay W. Harding, Ph.D.
Center for Disabilities and Development
The University of Iowa
Iowa City, IA

Nicole L. Hausman

Kathryn E. Jann

Heather J. Kadey

SungWoo Kahng, Ph.D., BCBA-D
Department of Behavioral Psychology
Kennedy Krieger Institute
Baltimore, MD

Megan L. Kliebert, M.A.
Department of Psychology
Louisiana State University
Baton Rouge, LA

Kimberly A. Kroeger, Psy.D.
Cincinnati Children's Hospital Medical
    Center
University of Cincinnati College of
    Medicine
Cincinnati, OH

Taira M. Lanagan, M.S., BCBA
Center for Autism and Related Disorders, Inc.
Tarzana, CA

Giulio E. Lancioni, Ph.D.
University of Bari, Italy

Marc J. Lanovaz

John F. Lee
The University of Iowa

Amanda Little, Ph.D., BCBA
The Meadows Center for Preventing
    Educational Risk
The University of Texas at Austin
Austin, TX

James K. Luiselli, Ed.D., ABPP, BCBA
May Institute
Randolph, MA

Autumn N. McKeel

Raymond G. Miltenberger

Adel C. Najdowski, Ph.D.
Center for Autism and Related Disorders, Inc.
Tarzana, CA

Mark F. O'Reilly, Ph.D., BCBA-D
Department of Special Education
The University of Texas at Austin, U.S.A.
Austin, TX

Yaniz C. Padilla
School Psychology Program
The University of Iowa
Iowa City, IA

John T. Rapp, Ph.D.
Educational Leadership and Community
    Psychology
St. Cloud State University
St. Cloud, MN

Derek D. Reed
Department of Applied Behavioral Science
University of Kansas
Lawrence, KS

**Florence D. DiGennaro Reed, Ph.D.,
    BCBA-D**
Melmark New England
Andover, MA

Joseph N. Ricciardi, Psy.D., ABPP, BCBA
Seven Hills Clinical Associates
Worcester, MA

Henry S. Roane, Ph.D.
Departments of Pediatrics and Psychiatry
SUNY Upstate Medical University
Syracuse, NY

Valerie R. Rogers

Hanna C. Rue, Ph.D.
May Center for Child Development
Woburn, MA
Kelly M. Schieltz
The University of Iowa
Iowa City, IA

Ralf W. Schlosser, Ph.D.
Department of Speech-Language Pathology
    and Audiology
Northeastern University
Boston, MA

Stacy B. Shaw

Rachel Shayne

Jeff Sigafoos, Ph.D.
School of Educational Psychology &
    Pedagogy
Victoria University of Wellington
Wellington, New Zealand

Kimberely Smith
Department of Psychology
Auburn University
Auburn, TX

Peter Sturmey, Ph.D.
Queens College and The Graduate Center
City University of New York
New York, NY

Jonathan J. Tarbox, Ph.D., BCBA-D
Center for Autism and Related
    Disorders, Inc.
Tarzana, CA

Bridget A. Taylor, Psy.D., BCBA-D
Alpine Learning Group
Paramus, NJ

Jeffrey H. Tiger, Ph.D., BCBA-D
Department of Psychology
Louisiana State University
Baton Rouge, LA

David P. Wacker, Ph.D.
Center for Disabilities and
    Development
University of Iowa Children's Hospital
Iowa City, IA

Michele D. Wallace, Ph.D., BCBA-D
Charter College of Education
Division of Special Education
    and Counseling
California State University,
    Los Angeles

Sara White, Ph.D.
Private Practice
Bellingham, WA

Susan M. Wilczynski, Ph.D., BCBA-D
National Autism Center
Randolph, MA

David A. Wilder, Ph.D., BCBA-D
School of Psychology
Florida Institute of Technology
Melbourne, FL

TEACHING AND BEHAVIOR SUPPORT FOR CHILDREN AND ADULTS WITH AUTISM SPECTRUM DISORDER

PART 1

HOW TO CONDUCT ASSESSMENT

CHAPTER 1

BEHAVIORAL OBSERVATION AND MEASUREMENT

Jonathan J. Tarbox, Adel C. Najdowski,
and Taira M. Lanagan

OVERVIEW: WHAT WE KNOW

The purpose of applied behavior analysis (ABA) is the improvement of behavior in meaningful and socially important ways. The primary method for assessing behavior change is through repeated observation, measurement, and visual inspection of graphed data. This practice makes it possible to determine when interventions are effective or ineffective so that effective interventions are maintained and ineffective interventions are not continued for extended periods of time. Practitioners of ABA-based assessment and intervention for individuals with autism spectrum disorder (ASD) will find that their day-to-day job will entail some sort of observation and measurement of what the individuals with whom they are working are doing. This chapter will describe the basic observation and measurement procedures that have proven useful to practitioners over decades and will provide a step-by-step guide for putting them into practice.

GETTING STARTED: BASIC PRINCIPLES AND APPLICATIONS

The basic rationale for collecting behavioral observation data is that anecdotal observation and opinion are simply not sufficiently accurate or reliable to use as the basis for making decisions about treatment effectiveness. Observation and objective measurement of behavior must be conducted during assessment and baseline periods, throughout intervention, and during follow-up. Prior to intervention, measurement is used for assessing the current status of an individual's behavior or skill, a period referred to as "baseline." This is a period of no intervention that allows practitioners to assess the individual's current level of the target behavior.

Following the collection of baseline, a chosen intervention is implemented. As data are collected, they are plotted on a graph, which allows practitioners to analyze the effectiveness of their interventions through visual inspection of the level and trend of the target behavior on the graph. When behavior changes in a desirable direction from baseline, the intervention is deemed effective and continues until it is no longer needed or can be faded out. When behavior does not change in a desirable direction from baseline, the intervention is considered ineffective, and a new component is added to the current treatment, or a new treatment is put in place of the current treatment.

GUIDELINES FOR CONDUCTING OBSERVATION AND MEASUREMENT

The basic steps to follow when observing and measuring behavior are described below. They are as follows: defining the behavior, choosing a measurement method, collecting baseline data, collecting intervention data, making data-based decisions, and collecting interobserver agreement data.

1. Define the target behavior. Before a behavior can be measured accurately, it must be operationally defined. An operational definition describes the target behavior so that more than one data collector can observe the same individual and record more or less the same data. Operational definitions must be objective, clear, and complete. Operational definitions must be *objective*, in that they refer only to what can be directly observed and do not infer anything that cannot be observed, such as an individual's emotions or intentions. Internal states are, of course, relevant to the individual's current well-being, but they are not directly observable and so defining a behavior based on them often results in different observers making different inferences, thereby making the data inconsistent across time and across observers. Operational definitions must also be *clear*, in that they are unambiguous in terms of what they specify and describe. A good test of whether an operational definition is clear is whether someone who has never observed the behavior can "act out" the behavior when given the definition. Operational definitions must be *complete*, in that they must identify what does and does not constitute an instance of the target behavior, as well as indicate when one instance of the behavior ends and when a new instance of the behavior begins (i.e., what separates one occurrence of behavior from the next). Adding a few examples and non-examples of the behavior to the definition often helps complete it.

2. Choose a method of measurement. The data collection method chosen must balance two often-conflicting priorities: (1) it must represent the occurrence of the behavior as accurately as possible, and (2) it must be practical to use on an everyday basis.

(a) *Frequency* recording involves counting the number of times a particular behavior occurs (see top panel of Figure 1.1 for sample data sheet and raw data). Frequency is appropriate for behaviors that have a clear beginning and end and is the preferred method of data collection when the number of times that a behavior occurs is of primary interest to the treatment team. Frequency data collection requires practitioners to observe the individual continuously, which may not be practical in cases where a practitioner is responsible for interacting with multiple individuals (e.g., a classroom teacher). Frequency can also be difficult to measure when the behavior occurs at particularly

Target behavior	Measurement:	Raw data	Conversion
Hitting	(FREQ) RATE DUR LAT	ЦНſ ЦНſ	10

Target behavior	Measurement:	Raw Data	Conversion
Social initiations	FREQ (RATE) DUR LAT	ЦНſ ЦНſ	10 behaviors / 10 minutes = 1 per minute

Target behavior	Measurement:	Raw data	Conversion
On-task	FREQ RATE (DUR) LAT	35 sec, 48 sec, 52 sec, 15 sec, 29 sec	Total dur = 179 sec Mean dur = 36 % of session = 179 sec / 600 sec = 30%

Target behavior	Measurement:	Raw data	Conversion
Responding to social questions	FREQ RATE DUR (LAT)	12 sec, 23 sec, 15 sec, 19 sec	12+23+15+19= 69 sec Mean latency = 69 s / 4 occurrences = 17.25 s

Target behavior	Measurement	Raw data					Conversion
Vocal stereotypy	Whole interval (Partial interval) Momentary time sample	+	−	+	+	−	Percent occurrence = 6 / 10 x 100 = 60%
		+	+	+	−	−	

FIGURE 1.1 Sample data sheets and raw data for frequency, rate, duration, latency, and interval recording.

high rates, due to the excessive time required for tallying behaviors. Another limitation to frequency recording is that it does not take into consideration the duration of the observation period. For example, if an individual is observed for a whole day and engages in three instances of aggression, versus is observed for one hour and engages in three instances of aggression, the implications for the overall amount of aggression that the individual actually engages in across daily life would be quite different. For this reason, frequency data should usually be converted into rate data, as described below.

(b)   *Rate* data collection involves recording the frequency of a particular behavior and then dividing that frequency by the duration of the observation period, thereby correcting for the potential problem of varying durations of observation, as described above. To determine the rate of a behavior, divide the frequency by the time period during which it was recorded (see second panel of Figure 1.1 for sample data sheet and data for a hypothetical 10-minute observation). Rate of behavior can be expressed as behaviors per minute, per hour, per day, per week, or per month. When calculating rate across successive observations, it is important that the frequency of the behavior is always converted into the same unit of time (e.g., minute, hour, day), so that the data from one observation can be compared to another and graphed over time.

(c)   *Duration* recording measures the length of time that a behavior occurs, from the time the behavior begins to the moment it ends. The most accurate way to measure duration is to use a stopwatch that is started as soon as the behavior begins and stopped as soon as it ends. When the episode ends, its duration is recorded on a data sheet, and the stopwatch is reset to zero in preparation for the next episode (see third panel of Figure 1.1 for sample data sheet and data). This procedure can be made easier by not recording the duration of each episode but, rather, simply starting the stopwatch each time the behavior starts and stopping it each time the behavior stops. This yields the total duration of all episodes of the behavior during the observation period and does not require frequent recording and resetting of stopwatches; however, it does not yield the number of episodes of the behavior. Duration data can be summarized and graphed as the total duration of time spent engaging in the behavior (by adding the durations of each episode of behavior during the observation period), as the percentage of the observation during which the behavior occurred (by dividing the total duration of episodes of the behavior by the total duration of the observation period and multiplying by 100), or as the mean duration of the behavior during an observation period (by dividing the total duration of the episodes of the behavior by the number of episodes).

(d)   *Latency* of responding measures the time that elapses from the occurrence of a stimulus to the occurrence of a response. In practical terms, latency is the amount of time from when an instruction, question, or prompt is delivered until the response occurs (see fourth panel of Figure 1.1 for sample data sheet and data). Latency may be the preferred measurement when the primary variable of concern is how fast a student responds (e.g., in encouraging a student to respond faster to a teacher's instructions or prompts). A stopwatch may be used to measure latency by starting it when the instruction occurs and stopping it when the response occurs. Latency can be summarized and graphed for each individual response over time, or as the mean latency to response during an observation period (by dividing the total of all latencies to those responses by the frequency of those responses).

(e)   *Partial-interval* data collection involves recording whether a behavior occurred at all during a predetermined time period. It is often a preferred form of data collection for high-rate behavior because it is easy to use. It is also preferred for behaviors that one is trying to reduce because it tends to overestimate the occurrence of behavior. Partial-interval recording can overestimate the occurrence of behavior because even if the behavior occurs for one instant during a long interval, the entire interval is scored as an occurrence for that behavior. To use partial-interval recording, an interval is selected, and data are taken on whether the behavior occurs at all during the interval (see bottom panel of Figure 1.1 for sample data sheet and data). Note that partial-interval data record the occurrence or non-occurrence of a specific behavior, not how many times the behavior occurred. For example, consider the target behavior of vocal stereotypy and an observation period of 10 minutes, which is then divided into 60 consecutive 10-second intervals. For each 10-second interval, record whether vocal stereotypy occurred during that interval. Determining the appropriate duration of intervals is a compromise between accuracy and practicality. The shorter the interval, the more accurate the estimate of the actual occurrence of the behavior will be, whereas the longer the interval, the less difficult it will be for the observer (e.g., less time spent looking up and down from the data sheet, less time thinking about which interval you are on, etc.). If an individual is observed for an entire day, intervals of 15 to 30 minutes in length might be appropriate, whereas if an individual is observed for only 10 minutes, intervals of 10 seconds might be appropriate. Partial-interval data are summarized and graphed as the percentage of intervals during which the behavior occurred.

(f) *Whole-interval* data collection involves recording whether a behavior occurred during the *entire* duration of an interval. It may be a preferred method for behaviors targeted for increase because it slightly underestimates the occurrence of behavior. Underestimation occurs because the target behavior must occur throughout the entire interval in order for it to be recorded; even if the behavior could have occurred for the majority of the interval, it is not counted unless it occurs during the *entire* interval. Data are summarized and graphed as the percentage of intervals during a given observation in which the behavior occurred for the whole interval.

(g) *Momentary time sampling* records whether an individual is engaged in the target behavior at the moment an interval ends—that is, the occurrence or non-occurrence of the behavior at the end of the interval is recorded. Momentary time sampling is a very indirect estimate of the occurrence of the behavior and therefore may not be sufficiently accurate, but this judgment must be made on a case-by-case basis. The major advantage of momentary time sampling is that it is relatively easy to do because it does not require continuous observation; it requires practitioners to observe only at the moment the interval ends. Therefore, momentary time sampling may be preferable in situations where data collection of any sort is going to be very difficult for practical reasons, and any estimate of the behavior is preferred over no data (e.g., when a teacher must collect multiple forms of data on multiple students simultaneously).

(h) *Percent correct* data are often used for data collection in skill acquisition or educational interventions. To collect percent correct data, each response that occurs is classified as either correct or incorrect (according to the operational definition for that intervention program), and the number of correct responses is divided by the number of correct plus incorrect responses, and the resulting decimal is multiplied by 100. Percent correct data should be used when the primary concern is whether or not an individual can perform a particular behavior accurately (e.g., answer the question, "What is your name?"), not when the primary concern is *how often* an individual performs a particular behavior (e.g., asking for a preferred item or activity, hitting someone else, self-initiating a trip to the bathroom). In other words, percent correct data do not ensure that an individual engages in a particular behavior on a regular basis, as an ongoing part of everyday life, but, rather, that he or she was able to do it correctly when accuracy was measured.

   3. Collect baseline data. After a measurement method is selected, baseline data are collected to assess the current status of the target behavior in order to provide a comparison for the data that will later be collected when the intervention is implemented. It is best if baseline data are collected until visual inspection of graphs demonstrates stability (i.e., the behavior is not going up or down overall, and it is not excessively variable); however, in the real world, this is not always possible. At a minimum, baseline data should be collected for as long as is necessary to demonstrate a need for intervention. Baseline data often surprise the treatment team by showing that the problem is far worse or far less serious than expected. The information gleaned from baseline data often makes intervention more effective, so this phase should not be overlooked.

4. Collect treatment data. Data are collected during treatment in an effort to determine if the intervention is effective. It is hard to overestimate the importance of these data because they are the basis upon which treatment decisions are to be made. In addition to collecting data throughout treatment, data should continue to be collected as the intervention is faded out and on an ongoing follow-up basis.

5. Make data-based decisions. Compare the status of the behavior during intervention to what it was during baseline. Consider the level, trend, and variability of the data when analyzing them. The top panel of Figure 1.2 illustrates two data paths that have an equal mean, but the data on the left are stable, whereas the data on the right are variable. It is generally more difficult to detect changes in variable data. The middle panel of Figure 1.2 illustrates data that are equal in mean value, but the data on the left illustrate an upward trend, whereas the data on the right illustrate a downward trend. When treatment results in an obvious change in behavior from baseline that is in a desirable direction (e.g., bottom panel of Figure 1.2), the treatment is likely effective and should be retained. If treatment results in no change or change in an undesirable direction, then the treatment is likely ineffective and may need to be changed or removed. As changes are made, continue to use visual inspection of the data to evaluate if and when the changes are effective. Decades of research and practice have proven that human judgment and expert opinion are less accurate than objective data collection, and critical treatment decisions should be made based on available data wherever possible. It is often necessary to abstain from judgment on a particular issue and to collect data that evaluate it for a few more observations before definitive decisions can be made.

6. Consider collecting interobserver agreement (IOA) data. IOA refers to the extent to which two observers agree on their scoring of the target behavior. Assessment of IOA ensures accuracy and consistency of data collection. The process of collecting and assessing IOA data is considered part of the "gold standard" approach to observation and measurement in ABA, but it is often not done in real-life settings. If additional staff are not available to collect IOA data on a regular basis, consider attempting to have any available staff conduct IOA "spot checks" whenever possible. Even infrequent assessment of IOA will make the data more accurate than not assessing it at all.

To calculate IOA, two or more clinicians independently observe and record data on the same behavior at the same time. IOA of 80% or greater is generally considered acceptable, although IOA above 90% is preferred. A simple way to calculate a percentage of IOA for interval data and percent correct data is to divide the number of agreements between the two observers by the number of agreements plus disagreements, and the resulting decimal is multiplied by 100. An agreement is defined as both observers recording the same data on a given opportunity (e.g., occurrence for a particular interval, correct for a particular response). For example, if Observer 1 and Observer 2 agreed on whether a behavior either occurred or didn't occur on 7 out of 10 intervals in an observation period, their IOA for that observation would be 70%. A simple way to calculate the percentage of IOA for duration, frequency, and latency data is to divide the smaller value recorded by the two observers by the larger value recorded, and multiply the resulting decimal by 100. For example, if Observer 1 recorded 33 minutes of tantrumming, and Observer 2 recorded 35 minutes, their IOA for that session would be 94% (33/35 × 100).

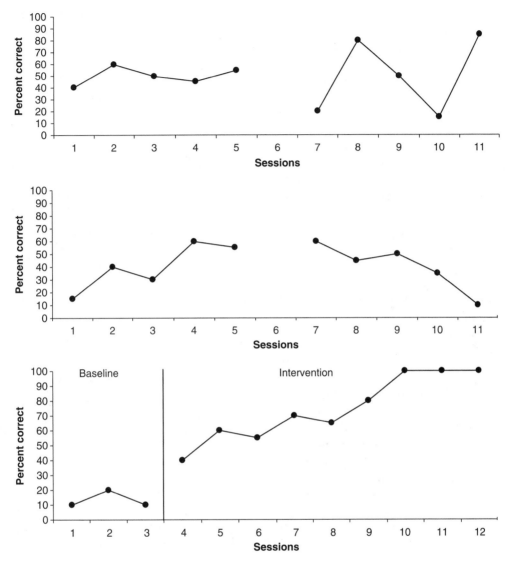

FIGURE 1.2 Sample graphs. Top panel illustrates stable versus variable data, both of which have the same mean. Middle panel illustrates upward versus downward trends, both of which have the same mean. Bottom panel illustrates a comparison of baseline to treatment, showing a hypothetical treatment that produces an increase in correct responding.

KEYS TO REMEMBER

1. Operationally define the target behavior.
2. Select a measurement method that will accurately represent the behavior and will be practical to use in the setting in which observations will take place.
3. Conduct observation and measurement under baseline conditions prior to implementing an intervention.

4. Continue to conduct observation and measurement when the intervention is in place and during follow-up.
5. Use visual inspection of graphed data to analyze the effectiveness of the intervention.
6. Make data-based decisions about how to continue the course of intervention.
7. Collect IOA data and assess agreement whenever possible.

SUGGESTED READINGS

Cooper, J., Heron, T., & Heward, W. (2007). *Applied Behavior Analysis* (2nd ed.). Columbus, OH: Merrill Publishing Co.

Johnston, J., & Pennypacker, H. (2009). *Strategies and Tactics of Behavioral Research* (3rd ed.). New York: Routledge/Taylor & Francis Group.

Kazdin, A. (1982). *Single-Case Research Designs: Methods for Clinical and Applied Settings.* New York: Oxford University Press, Inc.

Miltenberger, R. (2001). *Behavior Modification: Principles and Procedures* (2nd ed.).Belmont, CA: Wadsworth/Thomson Learning.

Sulzer-Azaroff, B., & Mayer, G. (1991). *Behavior Analysis for Lasting Change.* New York: Holt, Rinehart & Winston.

OTHER RESOURCES

1. Behavior Tracker Pro (available for download at http://store.apple.com/us) is an application available on iPhones and iPod Touch devices that has behavior tracking and graphing capabilities. Along with other features, this application supports frequency and duration data collection.
2. mTrial® software (available for purchase at http://www.mobilethinking.com/dtm/) is a program that allows users to record discrete trial and frequency data.
3. The MotivAider® (available for order at www.habitchange.com) is a device worn on the belt loop like a pager or in the pocket that vibrates as a prompt for students or as a prompt for practitioners to collect data. It can be set to operate automatically to vibrate at specific intervals.
4. The WatchMinder™ (available for order at www.watchminder.com) vibrates when the set interval is reached and can be programmed to display messages (e.g., "Pay attention" or "Follow the rules"). The WatchMinder™ is worn on the wrist and looks like a standard sports wristwatch.

CHAPTER 2

FUNCTIONAL BEHAVIORAL ASSESSMENT (FBA)

Derek D. Reed and Richard L. Azulay

OVERVIEW: WHAT WE KNOW

One of the core diagnostic criteria of ASD is a marked impairment in communication. Specifically, many individuals with ASD are unable to emit vocal language or have difficulties learning augmentative forms of communication. As such, individuals with ASD often communicate their wants and needs through motor behaviors. In many cases, these motor behaviors are socially inappropriate, coming in the form of aberrant behaviors such as stereotypy, aggressions, self-injury, or property destruction. Functional behavioral assessment (FBA) is a system of data collection of the environmental events both preceding and following a target behavior in an effort to understand its communicative intent.

We know that treating a behavior's function (i.e., a function-based intervention) results in the best clinical outcomes for the individual. In other words, when we can isolate the function of the behavior, we can better train the individual to appropriately request his or her wants or express his or her needs through more socially acceptable topographies of behavior. As an example, if your FBA reveals that an individual is engaging in aggression to elicit staff attention, providing the individual with dense amounts of attention when he is acting appropriately and ignoring aggressions will produce better outcomes than if you simply provided him with candy or toys for not acting aggressively. Thus, training a more efficient functionally equivalent replacement behavior while providing the desired consequence more frequently renders the problem behavior irrelevant. After such training, the individual will have acquired a new skill to allow him or her to access the desired function without needing to engage in problem behaviors in the future.

While many standardized instruments and tools are available to assist clinicians in assessing psychological or behavioral states and traits, FBA is a nominal term for the *process*—rather than a manualized procedure—of assessing behavioral function. Within the process of FBA, three principal approaches may be used conjointly or in isolation to collect the necessary data to determine behavioral function. These broad processes making up FBA are (1) indirect assessment,

(2) direct observation, and (3) functional analysis. This chapter will highlight both indirect assessment and direct observation (for information on functional analysis, see Chapter 3).

GETTING STARTED: BASIC PRINCIPLES AND APPLICATIONS

Functional behavioral assessment examines both the antecedents to (i.e., environmental conditions prior to) and consequences of (i.e., environmental conditions following) a target problem behavior. This approach to data collection derives from Skinner's operant view of behavior, which is explained by way of the three-term contingency of (1) a discriminative stimulus, (2) the response, and (3) the reinforcer. The discriminative stimulus is a specific form of an antecedent event that signals that reinforcement is available as a consequence, should the response be emitted. The reinforcer is a specific consequence event that subsequently increases the future probability of that response being emitted again in the future.

The three-term contingency is referred to as the "A-B-C sequence" in the FBA process. This sequence is not as precise as the three-term contingency, as it does not distinguish antecedent events as discriminative stimuli, nor consequences as reinforcers. This distinction is necessary, however, as simply conducting indirect assessments or direct observations of the target behavior cannot determine whether certain events do indeed *reinforce* the target behavior. One of the assumptions of FBA is that repeated pairings of particular antecedents and consequences will result in the individual learning to emit the response in the presence of the antecedent since he or she has discriminated that this antecedent signals reinforcer availability—in this case, the target behavior has become the "discriminated operant," or response, in the three-term contingency described above.

Due to the ability of antecedents and consequences to govern the emission of behavior, the goal of the FBA process is to filter the antecedents and consequences associated with the target behavior. Repeated demonstrations of certain antecedents and consequences occurring together with the behavior suggests a possible A-B-C chain. As these correlations become more apparent, the behavior analyst can build better hypotheses of the kinds of environmental events that control the target behavior. As the astute reader may realize, simply demonstrating a correlation between antecedents/consequences and behavior does not imply a valid functional relation between the two. Thus, the FBA process builds hypotheses to test via systematic manipulations to isolate the function of the behavior. In such manipulations, the behavior analyst constructs situations to purposefully activate and deactivate the target behavior in a repeated fashion, thereby demonstrating control over the response (i.e., a functional relation). For more on this technique, see Chapter 3. All FBAs should include some kind of manipulation to verify the functional relationship.

Similar to any operant behavior, target behaviors assessed within the FBA process are sensitive to both positive and negative reinforcement. Positive reinforcement is any consequence that was previously withheld from the individual but delivered contingent upon the response, increasing its future probability. Much research in operant learning has identified the following possible positively reinforcing functions of behavior: (1) attention, (2) access to preferred items or activities (i.e., tangibles), and (3) sensory input or "automatic reinforcement." A fourth possible function of behavior is negative reinforcement in the form of escape of avoidance of some aversive event present in the environment. In this case, emitting the response cancels the aversive event, subsequently increasing the likelihood that this individual will learn to engage in this behavior when presented with the aversive antecedents in the future. It is recommended that all four consequence types (i.e., attention, tangibles, sensory, and escape/avoidance) be evaluated as possible functions in the FBA process.

GUIDELINES FOR IMPLEMENTATION

INDIRECT ASSESSMENTS

Indirect assessments are procedures that are used in the FBA process to help identify antecedents and/or consequences associated with the client's target behavior but that do not require face-to-face contact with or direct observation of the client. Many questionnaires and rating scales are commercially available for this process. However, many of these scales, while time efficient and relatively inexpensive, lack adequate psychometric properties (e.g., reliability across time/raters, validity). Moreover, closed-ended scales such as these may lead to inaccurate conclusions regarding behavioral function, and thus wholly inappropriate interventions may be designed from these faulty data. With these caveats in mind, we recommend the use of record reviews and open-ended behavioral interviewing to better extract relevant information to help guide the FBA process. The FBA process should never end at the indirect assessment stage. Rather, the clinician should consider the indirect assessment stage a necessary but insufficient component of the FBA process.

Record Reviews

During the first phase of any FBA process, the clinician should examine the client's case folder to ensure that no medical issues may be eliciting the behavior and/or masking the function of the behavior. Moreover, record reviews may provide a history of the kinds of behavioral assessments—and possibly past FBAs or functional analyses—and their outcomes. Information such as this will help the clinician rule out confounding variables and aid in the efficiency of the subsequent FBA. Should previous accounts of FBAs be found, the clinician may consider replicating these procedures to assess the generality of the assessment across time or settings.

Behavioral Interviewing

Following a preliminary record review, the clinician should be equipped with better information regarding the client's clinical and medical history. The clinician should then engage in open-ended behavioral interviewing with a caregiver or guardian who has intimate knowledge of the client's behavioral repertoire and experience with the client's target behaviors. Proper behavioral interviewing is paramount in generating hypotheses of the behavioral function, as well as isolating particular antecedent events to examine more closely during subsequent direct observations. Successful interviewing will aid the clinician in ruling out functions and will increase the efficiency of the FBA by determining what to look for and when and where the behavior is most likely to occur.

When beginning the interview, first work with the interviewee to isolate the single most challenging behavior. The clinician should do his or her best to lead the dialogue and keep the interview focused. Begin with an open-ended question such as, "What behavior do you think would be most important to target in an intervention?" While the interviewee may list several topographies of problem behavior, the clinician should guide the interviewee to arrive at one specific behavior to target first. Once one behavior has been identified as the most problematic, the clinician should ask the interviewee to describe what the behavior looks like with an open-ended question such as, "If you had to teach me to engage in [problem behavior] the same way that [client's name] does, what things would you teach me to do?" The clinician should guide the conversation with the interviewee to arrive at an adequate operational definition of the target behavior that is both observable and measurable.

With a definition generated, the clinician should then ask the client to describe the intensity of the behavior and to estimate how frequently the behavior occurs. Finally, the clinician should ask the interviewee about possible antecedents and consequences to the behavior. Within this stage of the interview, the clinician should be sure not to ask leading questions or to unintentionally influence the responses. Thus, the clinician should ask open-ended questions regarding antecedents such as, "What sorts of things in the environment are reliable triggers for [client's name]'s [problem behavior]?" or "If you wanted to make sure that [client's name] engaged in [problem behavior], what would you arrange in the environment to make it happen?" To arrive at hypotheses of consequences, the clinician should ask open-ended questions such as, "What do you do when [client's name] engages in [problem behavior]?" or "From [client's name]'s perspective, what does [he or she] get from engaging in [problem behavior]?" The clinician should ask follow-up questions to any of the interviewee's responses to hone in on possible antecedents and consequences.

DIRECT OBSERVATION

Scatter Plot Analysis

When assessing the function of a behavior, the clinician would benefit from analyzing temporal patterns of behavior. A scatter plot analysis allows for a quick view of the pattern of a behavior within a determined period of time. Once a pattern is identified, this information can be compared to known variables, and hypotheses regarding the potential function of behavior may be developed.

If a variable that may provide insight into a potential function is unidentifiable at a particular time of day, scatter plot analysis may also lead the clinician to target a particular time of day for further direct observation. Once a potential function is identified, the clinician is again reminded to further assess this hypothesis through functional analysis, as described in Chapter 3.

A scatter plot datasheet consists of a grid of squares, with two axes. The x-axis labels the session (e.g., date) and the y-axis labels time increments or intervals (e.g., 8:15, 8:30) within the identified sessions (Worksheet 2.1). The clinician may choose shorter time intervals for more meticulous analysis or longer intervals for ease of data collection, which may also increase reliability of data collection.

The operational definition of the targeted behavior or multiple behaviors should be identified. A code is identified for recording occurrences of identified behavior(s). This code could be as simple as shading a cell if the target behavior occurred during the interval, or it may be made more complex—for example, marking or shading different percentages of the box to indicate different frequencies (e.g., place an "X" in the box for a single occurrence, shade half of the box for two to five occurrences, and shade the entire box for more than five occurrences). The scatter

Worksheet 2.1: Sample Recording Form—Scatter Plot

Client Name: _____   Behavior:_____
Operational Definition:_____

Set recording interval by inserting equal interval times in the first column. Insert dates of assessment in first row.
Shade in block if behavior occurs during that interval or tally frequency of behavior occuring during that interval.
In "Total" row and column record total intervals scored, or total frequency of behavior

Date

Time																	Total	Conditional Probability
																	/ =	
																	/ =	
																	/ =	
																	/ =	
																	/ =	
																	/ =	
																	/ =	
																	/ =	
																	/ =	
																	/ =	
																	/ =	
																	/ =	
																	/ =	
																	/ =	
																	/ =	
																	/ =	
																	/ =	
																	/ =	
																	/ =	
																	/ =	
																	/ =	
																	/ =	
																	/ =	
																	/ =	
																	/ =	
																	/ =	
																	/ =	
Total																	/ =	

plot may be as simple or complex as the clinician determines is warranted, given the nature of the referral question or the clinical profile of the client. Furthermore, the clinician is encouraged to consider the burden on data collectors when choosing a coding system and the value of the information being gathered. Data collectors may code occurrences of a behavior as a partial-interval count (i.e., the behavior occurred at least once during the interval), or there may be a more sensitive coding system developed for showing ranges of frequencies within identified time intervals (e.g., shade half a box for fewer than five occurrences, shade entire box for more than five occurrences).

When several sessions of data have been collected, the clinician should carefully review the data. If a pattern of behavior is readily identified, it may be an opportunity for a treatment decision. If no pattern is apparent, data collection may continue or may be adjusted as necessary. Some patterns may not be clear unless the clinician is aware of variability within daily schedules, including events that may occur at scheduled times but not daily. If the behavior is present during the majority of intervals, the interval length may require adjustment, or scatter plot analysis may not be appropriate. Once the data have been reviewed, the clinician may choose to conduct further analysis. This may involve continued or adjusted scatter plot analysis, or the use of other tools such as A-B-C charts.

To provide additional layers of quantitative analysis to the scatter plot data, the clinician may wish to compute conditional probabilities of the behavioral event given certain times of day or during particular environmental situations correlated with the time of day. To calculate a conditional probability, simply sum the number of occurrences during that interval or time increment, and divide by the total number of observations made during that interval or time increment. Higher probabilities suggest a greater likelihood that the behavior will be emitted during that time. Identification of such temporal patterns permits more efficient use of subsequent direct observations and may flag certain periods of the day for more intense data collection (i.e., A-B-C charts, described below) to capture the nuances of those times of day. Moreover, subsequent functional analyses may be designed to replicate the situational factors associated with these times of day to best arrive at a function for the target behavior.

A-B-C Charts

A-B-C charts are a direct measure that attempt to identify the three-term contingency (Antecedent—Behavior—Consequence) surrounding an identified behavior. A-B-C charts are narrative accounts of environmental events that occur before, during, and after the occurrence of the behavior (Worksheet 2.2). When developing an A-B-C chart, the operational definition of the behavior should be carefully considered. Even with the behavior clearly defined via operational definitions, data collectors will still be expected to provide a clear description of each occurrence of the behavior.

Data collection involving antecedents should include a description of all relevant events preceding the occurrence of the behavior. Such assessment includes variables that may affect motivating operations, potential discriminative stimuli for the occurrence of the behavior, as well as potential precursor behaviors exhibited by the student. The time of day, activity, location, behavior of peers, and behavior of the client are some of the pertinent variables to code. An example of thorough data collection with respect to antecedents could be as follows: "At 12:15 pm, after having refused morning snack, seated at lunch table across from peer A, who was crying. Staff B directed Client to take a bite of his sandwich and gestured toward the sandwich. Client stated that he did not want his sandwich. Staff B directed him to sandwich with an additional gestural prompt."

When recording data specific to the behavior observed, the data collector should include a clear description of the behavior, including topography and frequency. An example of thorough data collection with respect to the behavior could be as follows: "Client reached right hand up 8 inches and moved hand with closed fist toward upper arm of Staff B, making contact with arm 3 times." This description of the behavior should be within the operational definition, and it may help to either develop a new operational definition or enrich an existing definition.

Data collection surrounding consequences should include all relevant variables that occur following the behavior, including but not limited to staff response, peer response, and client

Worksheet 2.2: Sample Recording Form—A-B-C Chart

Client Name: _____   Behavior: _____

Operational Definition: _____

_____

Antecedent Potential motivating operations, discrimitive stimuli, or precursor behaviors	Behavior Topography and frequency of behavior	Consequence Staff reaction, Peer response, Client response

response. An example of thorough data collection with respect to the consequences could be as follows: "Staff B stated that lunch was finished, and removed sandwich from table. Peer A laughed and threw his milk carton at Staff B. Client laughed and then made a vocal request for cookies. Staff B rolled eyes and told client he needed to knock it off."

If the clinician must recruit others (e.g., caregivers or teachers/staff) to assist with data collection, the training of these assistants should be thorough, using practice sessions to ensure reliability. If possible, the clinician should observe data collectors in the environment and assist, or use methods such as written scenarios or videos for training sessions. Data collectors should be trained to consider all environmental variables, including any motivating operations or potential discriminative stimuli. When training data collectors to complete A-B-C charts, it is essential to convey the importance of reporting all events that occur, even if they are inconsistent with a client's treatment plan. Data collectors should provide an accurate account of all events surrounding the target behavior. The level of feedback and support should be consistent throughout data collection, with no additional or atypical corrective feedback delivered if discrepancies in treatment procedures are identified. This is of particular importance when data collectors may need to record the consequences they deliver that may be in contrast to expected contingencies (i.e., those prescribed in behavior intervention plans). Thus, data collectors must not fear reprisal from the clinician for documenting deviations from behavior change protocols due to emergency or atypical procedures or situations.

When assessing the data, the clinician must carefully consider the information gathered and whether these findings contribute toward the identification of potential functions. For example, the presence of an academic demand during the school day may not necessarily identify the function of the behavior to be escape, as it may simply be that the probability of work being presented to the student is high during the academic day. In addition, multiple antecedents may be identified that could lead toward different functions. A work task presented by a preferred teacher may present the opportunity for escape, or the opportunity for access to attention from a preferred person. Tallying frequencies of common antecedents and consequences, as well as antecedent–consequence pairings, will provide information toward a hypothesis of function. Once a potential function is identified, the clinician is again reminded to further assess this through functional analysis as described in Chapter 3.

KEYS TO REMEMBER

1. Behavior is not random. Behaviors are emitted for some meaningful (i.e., functional) reason for the individual. The FBA process helps identify these reasons.
2. Functional behavioral assessment is a process, not a single procedure, of indirect assessments and direct observations, as well as functional analyses, aimed at determining the environmental events associated with the target behavior.
3. Interventions based upon the behavior's function are more likely to be maintained over time than interventions not based on function.
4. During the FBA process, the behavior analyst analyzes antecedents and consequences, as well as antecedent–consequence pairings, to identify the function of the behavior.
5. The behavior analyst should evaluate attention, tangibles, sensory, and escape/avoidance consequences as possible functions for the target behavior.
6. In isolation, indirect and direct observations merely demonstrate correlations between the environment and behavior. Only when a functional analysis is conducted within the FBA process may the function be verified.
7. Always begin with record reviews to identify possible medical conditions or to review previous behavioral assessments.
8. When doing behavioral interviewing, use open-ended questions to drive hypothesis formation of possible antecedents and consequences to the behavior to increase the efficiency of the FBA process.
9. When developing data collection methods for direct observation, the clinician should consider both convenience and strength of the method to allow for ease of use by data collectors, while collecting the most information.

10. Provide adequate training to data collectors without the introduction of atypical corrective feedback procedures for errors in treatment that are identified through accurate descriptive data collection.

SUGGESTED READINGS

Bijou, S. W., Peterson, R. F., & Ault, M. H. (1968). A method to integrate descriptive and experimental field studies at the level of data and empirical concepts. *Journal of Applied Behavior Analysis, 1,* 175–191.

Drasgow, E., & Yell, M. L. (2001). Functional behavioral assessments: Legal requirements and challenges. *School Psychology Review, 30,* 239–251.

Gresham, F. M., Steuart Watson, T., & Skinner, C. H. (2001). Functional behavioral assessment: Principles, procedures, and future directions. *School Psychology Review, 30,* 156–172.

O'Neill, R. E., Horner, R. H., Albin, R. W., Sprague, J. R., Storey, K., & Newton, J. S. (1997). *Functional Assessment and Program Development for Problem Behavior: A Practical Handbook.* Pacific Grove, CA: Brooks/Cole.

Touchette, P. E., MacDonald, R. F., & Langer, S. N. (1985). A scatter plot for identifying stimulus control of problem behavior. *Journal of Applied Behavior Analysis, 18,* 343–351.

C H A P T E R   3

FUNCTIONAL ANALYSIS

Gregory P. Hanley

OVERVIEW: WHAT WE KNOW

Children and adults diagnosed with an autism spectrum disorder (ASD) often engage in severe problem behavior (SPB; e.g., self-injury, aggression, extended tantrums). SPB can be effectively treated *without* considering why it occurs in the first place by making changes to the environmental events occurring prior to and following SPB (this action is consistent with the practice of behavior modification). However, a sound understanding of the prevailing events that serve to reinforce SPB (called maintaining reinforcers), signal the availability of the reinforcers for SPB (called discriminative stimuli), and potentiate the value of those reinforcers (called establishing operations) is now favored prior to developing treatments for SPB. This understanding is possible and most probable following effective design and implementation of a functional analysis (FA) of SPB. Table 3.1 outlines several reasons why a functional analysis is currently favored as a pretreatment assessment of SPB for persons with ASD.

FA involves direct observation and measurement of SPB under different conditions in which some environmental event, thought to be relevant to the SPB, is manipulated. FA has allowed hundreds of clinical researchers and practitioners to understand the factors responsible for the occurrence of most types of SPB exhibited by persons with ASD and to design precise, effective, and humane treatments for these behaviors.

GETTING STARTED: BASIC PRINCIPLES AND APPLICATIONS

There are three general reinforcement contingencies that have been repeatedly shown to be responsible for the continued occurrence of various types of SPB: social-positive reinforcement, social-negative reinforcement, and automatic reinforcement. *Social* refers to conditions in which the reinforcing event is mediated by another person, whereas *automatic* refers to conditions in which the reinforcement is not socially mediated but is instead a direct result of the SPB (i.e., it

Table 3.1 Seven Reasons Why a Functional Analysis is Favored as
a Pretreatment Assessment.

	Practical Reasons
1	Hundreds of studies have shown that FAs allow for effective, precise, and individualized interventions to be developed.
2	FAs provide stable and sensitive baselines of SPB from which treatment effects can be verified.
3	FAs allow interventionists of SPB to know why SPB changes and when it is likely to change, in addition to how to change it.
	Humanistic Reasons
4	FAs are dignifying in that they essentially involve "asking" the person engaging in the SPB why he or she is doing it, and then allowing that person to have his or her wants or needs met in more socially appropriate ways.
5	FAs foster humility by requiring an interventionist to understand more about a person's relevant history before intervening.
	Scientific Reasons*
6	Essential characteristics of science in general (e.g., objectivity, tentativeness, parsimony) and behavior analysis in particular (e.g., direct observation of behavior, repeated measurement, single-subject experimental design) are inherent to FAs.
7	The essential goals of science (e.g., description, prediction, *and* control) are also realized with FAs (i.e., the assessment goes beyond interview and observation).

*Note: There is little difference between the science and the practice of applied behavior analysis, the field from which FA procedures were developed. Nevertheless, the scientific rationale is partitioned here to isolate the special commitments to a scientific and behavior analytic approach when one conducts functional analyses in the treatment of SPB.

provides a preferred sensory experience). The *positive* and *negative* in the contingency descriptions refer to whether the events are presented or removed, respectively, following occurrences of SPB.

Social-positive reinforcers often take the form of attention, toys, foods, or activities presented by caregivers, teachers, or peers. Periods of time without these interactions or items make them valuable, and the presence of those who provide access to them signals their availability. Social-negative reinforcers often take the form of breaks from or postponement of events such as classroom instructions or hygiene routines; their value is established through the mere presentation of the non-preferred or aversive event (e.g., an instruction), and proximity to those who provide breaks from the instructions, routines, or other aversive event often signals their availability. Types of automatic reinforcers are inferred from the form of the SPB (e.g., head hitting vs. hand mouthing), and maintenance via automatic reinforcement is implicated by the persistence of the SPB when social consequences and associated social cues are absent from the contexts in which the SPB occurs (i.e., if the SPB persists when alone).

The goal of the functional assessment process is to identify an individualized treatment for problem behavior. Treatment is predicated on the type(s) of contingencies influencing SPB, and these contingencies are detected in the FA. FAs may involve multiple conditions to test for all three general contingencies or to test for unique contingencies. FAs may also be conducted more than once, with changes in the conditions occurring across analyses. In other words, FAs can be iterative and can be complicated; I will expand on these conditions in the next section. FAs may, however, be as simple as that which is portrayed in the following scenario.

As noted earlier, an FA involves at least two distinct conditions. The first may involve an adult repeatedly providing teacher-nominated academic instructions to a young child with ASD about every 30 seconds for a short period of time (these periods are called observations or sessions and usually last between 5 and 15 minutes). During this same time period, the teacher may allow the child to briefly escape from the instructions following an occurrence of self-injury (i.e., the teacher stops prompting the child and removes the task-related materials). This set of sessions is referred to as a *test* condition because a contingency between self-injury and escape is arranged (i.e., escape is provided when and only when self-injury occurs). During other distinct periods of time, escape from instructions may be (a) available continuously by not issuing any instructions, (b) prevented from occurring following self-injury, and/or (c) provided according to time (and thus provided independent of self-injury). This latter set of sessions is referred to as the *control* condition because the contingency involving escape is absent (it should be evident from this example that there are multiple effective ways to design a control condition). Test and control sessions would be implemented in alternation (e.g., test, control, test, control) until at least three of each had been implemented. Self-injury would be observed and instances counted (or the duration of self-injury measured) by another adult. The data from each session would be converted into a rate (or a percentage of the session) and depicted on a line graph. A comparison of the level of self-injury in the test and control conditions conveys whether self-injury is sensitive to (in this example) escape from instructions as reinforcement. Evidence supporting the assertion that self-injury is sensitive to escape from instructions (i.e., maintained by social-negative reinforcement) is provided if self-injury is consistently higher in the test than in the control condition.

Other FA tools provide hints as to which contingencies to arrange in test conditions and whether more than one test condition should be included in the FA. These other tools are open-ended indirect and descriptive assessments (DAs), and they are important because they inform the design of multiple aspects of an FA (see Chapter 2). Indirect assessments do not involve any direct observation of behavior; instead, reports regarding the events responsible for SPB result from interviews or questionnaires. DAs involve direct observation of SPB, but there is no manipulation of environmental events during these observations. By specifying the use of *open-ended* assessments, I am emphasizing that caregiver interviews should involve more than questions regarding mundane events (e.g., delivery of attention, escape) and/or questions that require a "yes" or "no" sort of response. Interviews should involve questions that allow caregivers or teachers to "open up" and describe the conditions under which SPB occurs from their perspective and without forced responses or imposed context.

Open-ended interviewing is important for building a relationship with the caregivers and teachers of the child engaging in SPB, and it also allows for the identification of idiosyncratic antecedent (e.g., "self-injury is likely whenever I speak to another child") and consequent events (e.g., "self-injury stops whenever I sit close to and speak softly to him"). By "idiosyncratic," I mean events that are unique to a particular child and that you would not have typically included in an FA. In essence, this information from open-ended interviews can be used to determine (a) how to construct your test and control conditions and (b) how many test conditions to construct. For instance, using the information from the above example, I would recommend conducting one test and one control condition. In the test condition, I would arrange for an adult to sit away from the child with the history of self-injury and speak to another child throughout the session. The presence of the adult should signal that social-positive reinforcement is available and having the adult sit away and talk to another child should establish its value. As an aside, I would also be sure that developmentally appropriate but not highly preferred toys were available to both children during both test and control sessions. Nevertheless, the most important element of this test condition is to have the adult move close to and speak softly to the child with the history of SPB following each instance of self-injury (for about 30 seconds) and not do so following any other behavior. By contrast, in the control condition, I would have both children and the adult present, but I would have the adult sit close to the child with the history of SPB for the entire session and speak softly to him at least every 30 seconds. The hypothesis, derived from the open-ended interview, that the child's self-injury was maintained by social attention in the form of adult proximity and soft conversation and that this reinforcer was made valuable when it was observed being provided to another child would be supported if self-injury occurred consistently in the test condition and not very often in the control condition. Teaching the child alternative behaviors to recruit this sort of adult attention, not allowing this sort of adult attention to be provided following SPB, and teaching the child to tolerate progressively longer periods without this sort of attention would be critical elements to a function-based treatment for this child.

An open-ended interview guide to inform the conduct of an FA is provided at the end of the chapter. I do not recommend conducting an FA without administering this assessment because it should allow you to build a relationship with the caregivers and teachers and provide you with the necessary information to design an efficient, informed, and a safe analysis. DAs may also be useful here, but because DA implementation can be time-consuming and DA data analysis complicated, I recommend that they be considered only when the caregiver's report is highly inconsistent or when an FA based on the open-ended interview provided does not yield conclusive results. If you do choose to conduct a DA, it too should be open-ended so that qualitatively rich information regarding unique variables can be identified and incorporated into an FA. In essence, open-ended indirect (or descriptive) assessments and FAs are *both* valuable to the process of understanding behavioral function prior to treating SPB. Because indirect assessments rely on verbal reports of others, which may or may not allow for valid inferences regarding behavioral function, and because descriptive assessments convey only the *prevalence* of environmental events and, due to their correlational nature, cannot provide any evidence of an event's *relevance* to SPB, these assessment types cannot replace FAs. Rather, they are complementary to FAs. The open-ended indirect or descriptive assessments allow you to *discover* unique events that may be influencing the occurrence of SPB, whereas FAs allow you to *demonstrate* the importance of those discoveries. Furthermore, the informed FA will allow you to establish a stable and sensitive baseline of SPB from which to determine whether your treatment is effective.

GUIDELINES FOR IMPLEMENTATION

Proper and effective functional analysis of SPB requires a working partnership between people who have an extended history with the person who is engaging in the SPB (e.g., caregivers and teachers) and an expert in functional assessment (e.g., a certified behavior analyst). FAs should proceed only after appropriate consent from caregivers or guardians is provided and an open-ended interview is conducted. The open-ended interview will first help to identify the types of SPB that are of concern (e.g., hitting others, yelling, head hitting, or hand mouthing; see Question 1 of the Interview). If caregivers report that the child engages in multiple topographies (forms) of problem behavior, it is important to identify those of greatest concern, and arrange consequences to occur in your test conditions only for one or two types of problem behavior (see Questions 2 and 3 of the Interview). The likelihood of an *undifferentiated* analysis—one in which no information is provided regarding the events responsible for the occurrence of SPB due to substantial overlap between levels of SPB in the test and control conditions—increases with each distinct topography of behavior targeted in the FA.

Once the types of SPB that will be functionally analyzed are identified, safeguards for the child and the adult conducting the sessions of the FA should be considered (see Question 4 of the Interview). For instance, the adult conducting the FA should consider wearing a thick sweat-shirt, a baseball cap, or protective padding under his or her clothing if scratching others, hair pulling, or punching, respectively, are to be the types of aggressive behavior to be analyzed. Conducting an FA as part of an interdisciplinary team including medical personnel is strongly recommended when functionally analyzing severe forms of self-injury (e.g., head banging, eye gouging, head punching). It is important to agree as a team on criteria to terminate sessions based on either the amount of self-injury (e.g., 50 head hits) or on the products of self-injury (e.g., redness with any swelling). It may also be important to consider short session durations when the behavior to be analyzed poses high risk to either the child or adult (5 minutes per session is often sufficient). Although somewhat counterintuitive, lower rates and intensities of SPB are most likely when the reinforcers for the SPB are provided immediately and for each and every response. Thus, a schedule of immediate reinforcement for every response should be arranged in FA test conditions to maintain the safety of the person with ASD. Risky alternatives to providing possible reinforcers immediately and consistently following SPB include *not* providing reinforcers for problem behavior during FAs (this is sometimes referred to as "ante-cedent only" or "structural" analyses) or providing reinforcers on some intermittent schedule. These practices are likely to increase the frequency and intensity of SPB and are therefore not recommended.

If it is deemed too risky to allow for the occurrence of even low rates of the SPB, then conducting FAs of milder forms of problem behavior that are reported to reliably occur prior to or clustered with the SPB is a good option (see Question 5 of the Interview, and see procedures outlined in Smith & Churchill, 2002). In this arrangement, both the severe and mild forms of problem behavior are measured throughout the assessment and treatment evaluation, but consequences are arranged only for the milder forms of problem behavior in the FA.

It is important that the events being tested as possible reinforcers for SPB are valuable at the time of their availability in the test sessions of the FA. Not allowing or minimizing access to these events just prior to sessions may help establish their value, as well as not providing them unless SPB occurs within each session. Other situations may also establish their value (as in the example in which attention was important only when it was being provided to a same-aged peer), and these unique situations can be identified through informal observations of the person with the history of SPB or via the open-ended interview; these same situations can then be arranged in the FA test conditions (see Questions 6–10 of the Interview).

To illuminate the possible reinforcers for the SPB that may be arranged as consequences in the test condition(s) of an FA, questions regarding typical caregiver or teacher responses to SPB are often helpful (see Questions 11–13 of the Interview). To determine how many test conditions to conduct, at least initially, it is prudent to ask caregivers and teachers why they think SPB is occurring (see Questions 14–16 of the Interview). Clear and consistent reports implicating a single reinforcer should lead to the design of an efficient test/control analysis (i.e., one test condition). If there is any indication that the SPB appears to directly produce its own reinforcers (i.e., is self-stimulating), then observations of the child when he or she is alone (test condition) versus when he or she is in an enriched environment containing stimulating toys and activities (control condition) would be important to arrange first. The reader should consult the publications at the end of the chapter for more information about conducting typical FA conditions to identify general reinforcement contingencies maintaining SPB, as well as additional best practices for conducting FAs.

It may seem that FAs would be obviated and descriptive assessments most appropriate when assessing the function of low-rate, extremely dangerous, or covert (i.e., difficult to observe) SPB. However, FAs have been successfully applied with (a) low-rate SPB by conducting sessions of long duration, (b) extremely dangerous behavior by arranging for the consequences to follow milder forms of problem behavior that reliably precede SPB, and (c) covert SPB by applying the hypothesized reinforcers to an arbitrary response such as microswitch presses.

There are conditions under which it seems that the reinforcers for SPB are constantly changing, and FAs are not capable of identifying this "moving target." This is often a concern when assessing the SPB of persons with ASD who possess strong verbal skills. However, often the child specifies the reinforcer by identifying it in a request prior to engaging in SPB. In other words, SPB is occasioned when the child's requests are denied. By arranging a test condition in which an adult complies with the child's requests only following instances SPB (and a control condition in which all requests are reinforced), this "moving target" function can be identified. This sort of analysis capitalizes on the fact that the various events evoking SPB are often specified by the child with ASD immediately prior to SPB, and allows for effective treatment to be prescribed (an example of an effective treatment would be to *not* reinforce requests following SPB, to reinforce reasonable requests that occur without SPB, and to teach the child the types of requests that will and will not be reinforced).

Finally, those implementing FAs should be careful to strike a balance between the experimental integrity of the analysis (i.e., arranging the test and control conditions in such a way that any difference in the level of SPB between the two conditions is a result of the hypothesized contingency and not some other confounding event) and the ecological validity of the analysis (i.e., arranging contingencies in test conditions that are consistent with those experienced by the person with ASD outside of the assessment sessions). Attempts to increase the ecological validity of the FA by conducting sessions in the "natural environment" or by having teachers or caregivers implement the contingencies in the test and control conditions is laudable and may be useful, but only when experimental integrity can be maintained in the natural environment and only when parents and teachers can implement the contingencies with fidelity (and express an interest in being involved in the analysis). Instead of, or perhaps in addition to, these inclusion tactics, I recommend that the design of FAs always be informed by open-ended interviews or observations to increase the ecological validity of the FAs and that experts in contingency management and safe behavioral assessment (e.g., certified behavior analysts) conduct the FAs in contexts in which only planned differences in test and control conditions can be guaranteed.

KEYS TO REMEMBER

1. FAs are scientifically valid, practical, and humane, and thus integral to developing treatments for persons with ASD who engage in SPB.
2. There is no standard FA; however, the necessary features of an FA include direct observation and measurement of SPB under at least two different conditions in which some environmental event, thought to be relevant to the SPB, is manipulated.
3. Partnerships between people who have a relevant history with the child engaging in SPB and an expert in FA and contingency management are essential for designing

effective FAs. High-risk SPB also necessitates an interdisciplinary approach and consideration of special safeguards tailored to the intensity and specific form of the SPB.

4. Indirect and descriptive assessments cannot replace FAs for identifying the variables influencing SPB. Open-ended indirect or descriptive assessments are essential complements to FA, and by designing FAs based on the information from open-ended complementary assessments, experimentally and ecologically valid results are most likely.

5. If an initial FA does not yield useful information, the analysis should be redesigned based on additional information provided by open-ended indirect or descriptive assessments.

SUGGESTED READINGS

Hanley, G. P., Iwata, B. A., & McCord, B. E. (2003). Functional analysis of problem behavior: A review. *Journal of Applied Behavior Analysis, 36,* 147–185.

Iwata, B. A., & Dozier, C. L. (2008). Clinical application of functional analysis methodology. *Behavior Analysis in Practice, 1,* 3–9.

Iwata, B. A., Wallace, M. D., Kahng, S., Lindberg, J. S., Roscoe, E. M., Conners, J., Hanley, G. P., Thompson, R. H., & Worsdell, A. S. (2000). Skill acquisition in the implementation of functional analysis methodology. *Journal of Applied Behavior Analysis* 33, 181–194.

Smith, R. G., & Churchill, R. M. (2002). Identification of environmental determinants of behavior disorders through functional analysis of precursor behaviors. *Journal of Applied Behavior Analysis,* 35, 125–136.

Wallace, M. D., & Knights, D. J. (2003). An evaluation of a brief functional analysis format within a vocational setting. *Journal of Applied Behavior Analysis, 36,* 125–128.

QUESTIONS TO INFORM THE DESIGN OF A FUNCTIONAL ANALYSIS

OPEN-ENDED INTERVIEW GUIDE

To develop objective definitions of observable problem behaviors:
1. **What are the problem behaviors? What do they look like?**
    To determine the problem behavior(s) to be targeted in the functional analysis:
2. **What is the single most concerning problem behavior?**
3. **What are the top three most concerning problem behaviors? Are there other behaviors of concern?**
    To determine the precautions required when conducting the functional analysis:
4. **Describe the range of intensities of the problem behaviors and the extent to which the child or others may be hurt or injured from the problem behavior.**
    To assist in identifying precursors to dangerous problem behaviors that may be targeted in the functional analysis instead of more dangerous problem behaviors:
5. **Do the different types of problem behavior tend to occur in bursts or clusters and/or does any milder type of problem behavior typically precede the more dangerous problem behavior?**

To determine the antecedent conditions that may be incorporated into the functional analysis test conditions:

6. Under what conditions or situations are the problem behaviors most likely to occur?
7. Do the problem behaviors reliably occur during any particular activities?
8. What seems to trigger the problem behavior?
9. Does problem behavior occur when you alter routines or interrupt activities? If so, describe.
10. Does the problem behavior occur when it appears that the child won't get his or her way? If so, describe the things that the child often attempts to control.

To determine the test condition(s) that should be conducted and the specific type(s) of consequences that may be incorporated into the test condition(s):

11. How do you and others react or respond to the problem behavior?
12. What do you and others do to calm the child down once he or she has engaged in the problem behavior?
13. What do you and others do to distract the child from engaging in the problem behavior?

In addition to the above information, to assist in developing a hunch as to why problem behavior is occurring and to assist in determining the test condition(s) to be conducted:

14. What do you think the child is trying to communicate with his or her problem behavior, if anything?
15. Do you think this problem behavior is a form of self-stimulation? If so, what gives you that impression?
16. Why do you think the child is engaging in the problem behavior?

C H A P T E R   4

STIMULUS PREFERENCE ASSESSMENT

Jeffrey H. Tiger and Megan L. Kliebert

OVERVIEW: WHAT WE KNOW

Children with autism often present with marked deficits in their verbal, social, and self-help repertoires that are commonly targeted by behavior analysts through direct-instruction techniques. In other words, a target skill is selected, a prompting procedure is implemented to ensure the occurrence of that behavior, and a putative reinforcing consequence is delivered following that behavior such that the behavior will be more likely to occur under similar conditions in the future. The success of this approach is predicated, in large part, on the ability of a behavior analyst to identify a valued event or stimulus to deliver as reinforcement; however, identifying reinforcers for children with autism can be challenging in many instances.

Autism is characterized in part by restricted interests and a decreased involvement in the social world. Said another way, individuals with autism appear to be less sensitive to common social reinforcers (e.g., praise) than their typically developing peers and may have limited sensitivity to non-social sources of reinforcement (i.e., lack of engagement with common age-appropriate toys). Sensitivity to particular forms of reinforcement appears to emerge as a result of some biological predispositions (e.g., sensitivity to food as reinforcement), personal experiences (e.g., conditioning histories), and the immediate context (e.g., establishing operations and the availability of competing sources of reinforcement), resulting in idiosyncrasies in what will serve as reinforcement for any given individual at any given moment.

Given the importance of identifying effective reinforcers for behavioral programming, researchers have developed a number of direct assessment strategies for identifying potential reinforcers. These strategies, commonly referred to as preference assessments, are direct in that they rely on the observation of an individual's behavior in relation to a particular stimulus rather than upon the verbal report of a caregiver alone (e.g., "I think he likes chocolate"), which frequently has been shown to be relatively non-predictive of reinforcer strength.

GETTING STARTED: PRINCIPLES AND APPLICATIONS

The general philosophy of conducting preference assessments is based upon the assumption of the trans-situationality of reinforcement, meaning we predict that a stimulus that serves as a reinforcer in one situation will also serve as a reinforcer in another situation. Although this assumption as a guiding principle is not without shortcomings (i.e., the efficacy of any stimulus as a reinforcer is determined based upon the relative amount of that reinforcer consumed and other reinforcers available in the immediate environment), it offers a starting point for identifying potential reinforcers and has proven useful in clinical and educational programming. In a typical preference assessment, a putative reinforcer is presented either by itself or in an array with other potential reinforcers and is delivered contingent upon a simple response (e.g., an approach response such as reaching towards the stimulus or engagement with the stimulus). Across repeated presentations, stimuli that occasion the most approach responses will typically serve as the most potent reinforcers for strengthening other, more complex, desirable behaviors (e.g., social and verbal behavior). There are several different formats for conducting preference assessments that will be described below.

GUIDELINES FOR INTERVENTION

The first phase of conducting any preference assessment is to identify potential stimuli or activities to evaluate as reinforcers. This task is typically accomplished through interviewing caregivers who are familiar with the consumer or by directly observing the consumer in his or her natural environment. In particular we recommend a structured interview tool by Fisher and colleagues known as the Reinforcer Assessment Interview for Individuals with Severe Disabilities (see Suggested Readings below) that specifically prompts the interviewer to ask questions regarding individual preferences for food items, toys, and a variety of other sensory experiences. This step is valuable in that it may help to identify powerful reinforcers that would not otherwise have occurred to a therapist (e.g., we have served children whose most preferred reinforcers were green olives, dill pickles, and after-dinner mints).

After identifying the stimuli to be included in the preference assessment, the therapist should consider whether consumption of each reinforcer is a discrete or prolonged event. In other words, some events, such as eating a piece of dry cereal, require relatively little time. Other events, such as watching a video or playing a game, will maintain reinforcing properties only if available for longer durations. Thus, reinforcer consumption time must be programmed into each trial of a preference assessment. We recommend keeping the magnitude (amount) of reinforcement equivalent across trials (e.g., one small bite of each food or 30 seconds of access to each leisure item). In addition to scheduling the time relevant to conduct a preference assessment, such decisions will likely also affect how one collects data during each assessment.

The next step in conducting a preference assessment is to determine the appropriate stimulus presentation format. Broadly, there are three common presentation formats: single stimulus, paired stimulus, and multiple stimulus arrays. Each format has its relative advantages and disadvantages that will be discussed.

SINGLE STIMULUS ASSESSMENTS

During a single stimulus assessment each stimulus is presented individually across trials. In other words, a trial will begin by placing a single stimulus (e.g., a raisin) in front of a consumer for a period of time (e.g., 10 seconds). If the consumer approaches and consumes the item, the therapist would then score that that item was consumed. If the consumer did not approach the item, the therapist would remove the item at the end of the trial, score the non-consumption of the item, and then initiate the next trial (e.g., present a carrot). For items that might sustain more prolonged engagement (e.g., light-up toys, videos), a therapist might collect data on the amount of interaction or engagement observed during each trial. During each assessment, each item should be presented repeatedly (e.g., 5–10 times per item). The results of this assessment would then be tabulated by scoring the percentage of trials an item was approached (or the duration of time engaged with each item) and then rank-ordering items based upon these percentages. The items ranked the highest are the most preferred and therefore the most likely to support other behaviors (Worksheet 4.1).

This assessment method has the benefit of not requiring individuals to possess a scanning repertoire (i.e., to browse among an array of other items) or to make selections between stimuli; however, this method is limited in its ability to produce a preference hierarchy. In other words, it is common to have multiple stimuli with similar selection percentages or time-engaged per-centages, and thus this format is relatively insensitive to differences in reinforcer value.

PAIRED STIMULUS ASSESSMENTS

During a paired stimulus assessment, each potential reinforcer is presented in a paired array with each other potential reinforcer at least one time. For instance, if we were conducting a pref-erence assessment between carrots, raisins, and popcorn, Trial 1 might consist of a carrot versus a raisin, Trial 2 of a carrot versus a piece of popcorn, and Trial 3 of a raisin versus a piece of popcorn. During each trial, the consumer would have the opportunity to select and consume one of the available items; attempts to select both items need to be blocked. The results of this assessment would then be determined by calculating a selection percentage (i.e., the number of trials each item was selected divided by the number of trials it was presented), and each stimulus would be rank-ordered by its selection percentage (Worksheet 4.2).

This assessment method holds the benefit of placing each potential reinforcer in direct com-petition with every other reinforcer and thus creates a much more defined preference hierarchy. The downside of this assessment format is that it can be relatively time-consuming, depending upon the number of stimuli included and the reinforcer-access duration. For instance, if 10 lei-sure items were assessed with 1 minute of access to each item, completing the total assessment would require 45 trials and would likely last over 1 hour (allowing therapist time to reset each pair of items and record data).

MULTIPLE STIMULUS ASSESSMENTS

As opposed to the paired format, in which only two stimuli are presented simultaneously, all assessed reinforcers are presented simultaneously in a multiple stimulus array format. In other words, all materials or activities being assessed are presented simultaneously and placed equidis-tant from the consumer, who is then permitted to select from among the options.

Worksheet 4.1 Single Stimulus Assessment Data Sheet

Date:_____

Participant ID:_____

Item	Trial 1	Trial 2	Trial 3	Trial 4	Trial 5	% Selected	Item Rank
1.	Y N	Y N	Y N	Y N	Y N		
2.	Y N	Y N	Y N	Y N	Y N		
3.	Y N	Y N	Y N	Y N	Y N		
4.	Y N	Y N	Y N	Y N	Y N		
5.	Y N	Y N	Y N	Y N	Y N		
6.	Y N	Y N	Y N	Y N	Y N		
7.	Y N	Y N	Y N	Y N	Y N		
8.	Y N	Y N	Y N	Y N	Y N		
9.	Y N	Y N	Y N	Y N	Y N		
10.	Y N	Y N	Y N	Y N	Y N		
11.	Y N	Y N	Y N	Y N	Y N		
12.	Y N	Y N	Y N	Y N	Y N		

Instructions: List the included items in the column on the far left. Present one item during each trial. If the consumer interacts with or consumes the item, score (Y)es. If the consumer does not interact with or consume the item, score (N)o. Repeat the assessment up to 5 times. Summarize the results of these assessments calculating the percentage of trials presented in which the item was interacted with or consumed and rank order each item based upon these percentages from largest to smallest.

There are a few variations of the multiple stimulus format. In the simplest format the consumer selects an item from an array and the remaining items are removed while the selected item is consumed. After this consumption time is completed, the array is re-presented with the remaining non-selected items. This format is commonly referred to as a multiple stimulus format without replacement (MSWO) (Worksheet 4.3). An alternative version of this format, called a free-operant format, involves allowing access to multiple items simultaneously (Worksheet 4.4). Unlike the other formats, in which one item is selected to the exclusion of the other items on any given trial, in the free-operant assessment a consumer may change activities or materials at any given moment. Restriction criteria may then be put into place in order for the development of a preference hierarchy (e.g., when an item is associated with at least 2 minutes of engagement more than any other item, that item will be restricted).

Worksheet 4.2 Paired Stimulus Assessment Data Sheet

Date:_____

Participant ID:_____

Item	Trials Selected	Rank	Item	Trials Selected	Rank
A.)			G.)		
B.)			H.)		
C.)			I.)		
D.)			J.)		
E.)			K.)		
F.)			L.)		

Item	A	B	C	D	E	F	G	H	I	J	K
B	A B	— —	— —	— —	— —	— —	— —	— —	— —	— —	— —
C	A C	B C	— —	— —	— —	— —	— —	— —	— —	— —	— —
D	A D	B D	C D	— —	— —	— —	— —	— —	— —	— —	— —
E	A E	B E	C E	D E	— —	— —	— —	— —	— —	— —	— —
F	A F	B F	C F	D F	E F	— —	— —	— —	— —	— —	— —
G	A G	B G	C G	D G	E G	F G	— —	— —	— —	— —	— —
H	A H	B H	C H	D H	E H	F H	G H	— —	— —	— —	— —
I	A I	B I	C I	D I	E I	F I	G I	H I	— —	— —	— —
J	A J	B J	C J	D J	E J	F J	G J	H J	I J	— —	— —
K	A K	B K	C K	D K	E K	F K	G K	H K	I K	J K	— —
L	A L	B L	C L	D L	E L	F L	G L	H L	I L	J L	K L

Instructions: Assign each item to a letter. Identify the item pairs by randomly selecting a cell in the above grid. Score the selected item by circling the corresponding letter. Summarize the assessment using the table above the grid.

Multiple stimulus assessment formats have the benefits of creating a preference hierarchy and are relatively brief when compared to paired item assessments. For instance, assessing preferences for 10 items using the MSWO procedure with 1-minute reinforcement consumption periods would require only about 10 minutes. Due to their brevity, multiple stimulus assessments can be conducted frequently to "update" the results of preference assessments (i.e., the most preferred available reinforcer can be identified daily or prior to each instructional activity).

Worksheet 4.3 Multiple Stimulus Without Replacement Assessment Data Sheet

Date: _____

Participant ID: _____

Item	Order Selected	Order Selected	Order Selected	Order Selected	Order Selected	Mean Rank
1.)						
2.)						
3.)						
4.)						
5.)						
6.)						
7.)						
8.)						
9.)						
10.)						
11.)						
12.)						

Instructions: Each column of this sheet corresponds to one complete assessment. Assign each item to a number. During each assessment, record the order in which the consumer selected each item (i.e., first receives a 1, second receives a 2, etc.). Conduct up to 5 assessments. Summarize the assessments in the far right column by calculating the mean ranking of each item.

Multiple stimulus formats require the most developed scanning and selection repertoires among participants; if unclear preference patterns result after repeated administrations, it is likely worth considering smaller arrays.

ADAPTATIONS AND MODIFICATIONS

Some potential reinforcers, such as a toy or a small piece of food, lend themselves easily to preference assessments in that they can be presented to a consumer on a tabletop and removed easily. Some activities are not quite as simple, such as playing basketball or going for a walk outside. Recent advances in preference-assessment methodology have allowed for the assessment of these more protracted events using a concurrent-chains schedule of reinforcement. Despite the complicated name for this procedure, it is relatively simple. The first step of this procedure is to create a simple stimulus to pair with engagement in an activity. Some researchers have used colored cards or stickers; others have used photographs of the individual engaging in the activity. Each of these stimuli can then be presented to the consumer in any of the aforementioned preference assessment formats, with the exception that after selecting the picture or card (technically called the initial-link stimulus) the consumer would then gain access to a period of the selected activity (e.g., 3 minutes of access to playing basketball, in what is technically called the terminal link of the chain). Therapists should expect a learning period for consumers to learn the relation between selecting a particular initial-link stimulus and accessing an event as a result of that selection (especially if novel stimuli such as colored cards are used).

Worksheet 4.4 Free-Operant Assessment Data Sheet

Date: _____

Participant ID: _____

Item/ Interval	A	B	C	D	E	F	G	H	I	J	K	L
1: 0:00–0:10	A	B	C	D	E	F	G	H	I	J	K	L
2: 0:11–0:20	A	B	C	D	E	F	G	H	I	J	K	L
3: 0:21–0:30	A	B	C	D	E	F	G	H	I	J	K	L
4: 0:31–0:40	A	B	C	D	E	F	G	H	I	J	K	L
5: 0:41–0:50	A	B	C	D	E	F	G	H	I	J	K	L
6: 0:51–1:00	A	B	C	D	E	F	G	H	I	J	K	L
7: 1:01–1:10	A	B	C	D	E	F	G	H	I	J	K	L
8: 1:11–1:20	A	B	C	D	E	F	G	H	I	J	K	L
9: 1:21–1:30	A	B	C	D	E	F	G	H	I	J	K	L
10: 1:31–1:40	A	B	C	D	E	F	G	H	I	J	K	L
11: 1:41–1:50	A	B	C	D	E	F	G	H	I	J	K	L
12: 1:51–2:00	A	B	C	D	E	F	G	H	I	J	K	L
13: 2:01–2:10	A	B	C	D	E	F	G	H	I	J	K	L
14: 2:11–2:20	A	B	C	D	E	F	G	H	I	J	K	L
15: 2:21–2:30	A	B	C	D	E	F	G	H	I	J·	K	L
16: 2:31–2:40	A	B	C	D	E	F	G	H	I	J	K	L
17: 2:41–2:50	A	B	C	D	E	F	G	H	I	J	K	L
18: 2:51–3:00	A	B	C	D	E	F	G	H	I	J	K	L
19: 3:01–3:10	A	B	C	D	E	F	G	H	I	J	K	L
20: 3:11–3:20	A	B	C	D	E	F	G	H	I	J	K	L
21: 3:21–3:30	A	B	C	D	E	F	G	H	I	J	K	L
22: 3:31–3:40	A	B	C	D	E	F	G	H	I	J	K	L
23: 3:41–3:50	A	B	C	D	E	F	G	H	I	J	K	L
24: 3:51–4:00	A	B	C	D	E	F	G	H	I	J	K	L
25: 4:01–4:10	A	B	C	D	E	F	G	H	I	J	K	L
26: 4:11–4:20	A	B	C	D	E	F	G	H	I	J	K	L
27: 4:21–4:30	A	B	C	D	E	F	G	H	I	J	K	L
28: 4:31–4:40	A	B	C	D	E	F	G	H	I	J	K	L
29: 4:41–4:50	A	B	C	D	E	F	G	H	I	J	K	L
30: 4:51–5:00	A	B	C	D	E	F	G	H	I	J	K	L
Total												
Rank Order												

Instructions: Write the name of each item into a cell in the top row. Mark each 10-second interval in which the participant engages with each item by circling its letter. Total the number of intervals of engagement with each item in the bottom row and rank order.

KEYS TO REMEMBER

1. For preference assessments to provide an accurate representation of an individual's preferences, it is important that his or her selections be honored. Do not simply ask a consumer to select between two activities; he or she must be allowed to experience the activity.
2. The effectiveness of a stimulus as a reinforcer will change across time and repeated exposure. What was a reinforcer today may not be a reinforcer in one month or even at the end of the day. Preference assessments should be updated frequently to ensure that high-quality reinforcers are being delivered.
3. A highly preferred stimulus will not necessarily be an effective reinforcer. Rankings among stimuli in a preference assessment are simply that: rankings. A high-preference stimulus is preferred relative to the other stimuli in that assessment, but it may be that none of those stimuli will serve as adequate reinforcers, and additional stimulus identification may need to be conducted.
4. A low-ranking stimulus may not necessarily be a poor reinforcer. Again, all preference assessment rankings are relative. If you were to experience a preference assessment for $100, $50, $20, and $10 bills, the $10 bill would likely be the least preferred. However, the contingent delivery of $10 bills would likely still serve as a powerful reinforcer for your behavior!

SUGGESTED READINGS

DeLeon, I. G., & Iwata, B. A. (1996). Evaluation of a multiple-stimulus presentation format for assessing reinforcer preferences. *Journal of Applied Behavior Analysis, 29,* 519–533.

Fisher, W. W., Piazza, C. C., Bowman, L. G., & Amari, A. (1996). Integrating caregiver report with a systematic choice assessment to enhance reinforcer identification. *American Journal on Mental Retardation, 101,* 15–25.

Fisher, W., Piazza, C. C., Bowman, L. G., Hagopian, L. P., Owens, J. C., & Slevin, I. (1992). A comparison of two approaches for identifying reinforcers for persons with severe and profound disabilities. *Journal of Applied Behavior Analysis, 25,* 491–498.

Hanley, G. P., Iwata, B. A., & Lindberg, J. S. (1999). Analysis of activity preferences as a function of differential consequences. *Journal of Applied Behavior Analysis, 32,* 419–435.

Pace, G. M., Ivancic, M. T., Edwards, G. L., Iwata, B. A., & Page, T. J. (1985). Assessment of stimulus preference assessment and reinforcer value with profoundly retarded individuals. *Journal of Applied Behavior Analysis, 18,* 249–255.

CHAPTER 5

INTERVENTION INTEGRITY ASSESSMENT

Florence D. DiGennaro Reed and Robin S. Codding

OVERVIEW: WHAT WE KNOW

The term *intervention integrity* has been used synonymously with treatment integrity, procedural fidelity, and implementation integrity. Regardless of the exact terminology used, the concept generally refers to consistent and accurate implementation of a treatment procedure in the way it was designed. Researchers have demonstrated that practitioners often fail to implement treatments within a short time following training (i.e., within three to five sessions). This is concerning given that decisions to continue or modify treatment are based on the assumption that the treatment is being fully implemented. Thus, measuring intervention integrity is important in order to draw valid conclusions that observed positive outcomes are due to the treatment procedures and are unrelated to other factors. If intervention integrity is not assessed and desired outcomes are not observed, practitioners are unable to evaluate whether a different intervention is necessary or if the designed intervention was poorly implemented.

Research has shown that client problem behavior is lowest when practitioners accurately implement function-based behavioral interventions (see Chapter 2 for information regarding functional assessment to guide intervention planning). Moreover, findings also support that high levels of intervention integrity are associated with positive client outcomes for academic-related behavior. These findings have been replicated across a variety of participants and settings (e.g., public schools, private schools, and therapy sessions), which underscores the importance of measuring intervention integrity. Specifically, assessing this aspect of practitioner behavior and ensuring accurate treatment plan implementation increases the likelihood that the goals of treatment are realized.

Although intervention integrity is currently conceptualized as a multidimensional construct, the present chapter will describe different types of intervention integrity assessment as they relate to treatment adherence only. We will also highlight examples of empirically supported strategies that have been shown to be effective in improving the accuracy with which practitioners implement interventions. Examples of integrity assessment tools and a feedback form are provided at the end of the chapter.

GETTING STARTED: BASIC PRINCIPLES AND APPLICATIONS

A variety of intervention integrity assessment methods exist, such as (1) examination of permanent products, (2) direct observation, (3) self-report, and (4) use of manuals and treatment scripts.

PERMANENT PRODUCTS

Permanent product recording refers to examining a lasting product that results from implementation of an intervention step. Suppose, for example, a student who does not consistently turn in homework of high quality has the opportunity to earn a daily sticker for mathematics homework when he earns a grade of B or higher. Imagine this student is also able to exchange his stickers at the end of the week for a prize. One could examine several permanent products to indirectly assess intervention integrity, including the graded homework, stickers on a sticker chart, and tangible evidence of earning a prize (e.g., an opened package, the item in the student's possession). An advantage to this technique is that intervention integrity may be assessed at a time when the practitioner is not directly implementing the intervention with a client. Also, this type of recording produces little extra work for practitioners or their supervisors. However, it may not be possible to sample all intervention steps by using this form of assessment, and there is no way to verify that the practitioner implemented the intervention accurately, since implementation was not directly observed. Furthermore, some interventions do not result in permanent products, making this form of assessment inappropriate in those instances.

DIRECT OBSERVATION

Direct observation refers to observing the practitioner implement the intervention while simultaneously recording data on performance accuracy. This form of intervention integrity assessment is one of the most common forms of assessment studied in the scientific literature. We recommend finding an observer (e.g., consultant, supervisor, or colleague) who is not responsible for implementing the intervention at the time of the observation to collect these data. Although self-monitoring is an option, practitioners may find it challenging to record data accurately while also implementing the intervention. Individuals interested in using direct observation will first need to create a datasheet. Commonly, the steps of the intervention are operationally defined (i.e., a task analysis is generated) with detailed codes for recording performance accuracy. Next, a method for summarizing the performance data is specified. Percentage of intervention steps implemented correctly is a frequent summary statistic; however, more detailed analyses can also be calculated.

To aid readers of this book, sample integrity assessment recording forms are provided at the end of this chapter. Worksheet 5.1 is perhaps the simplest of all of the forms provided and may

Worksheet 5.1 Sample Integrity Assessment Recording Form

Intervention Plan Step	Performance
Hold up one color card and ask, "What color?"	
If student makes a correct response, deliver one token on token economy board and provide vocal praise.	
If student does not make a correct response, provide a vocal prompt without delivering a token or vocal praise.	
Record data.	
Hold up one color card and ask, "What color?"	
If student makes a correct response, deliver one token on token economy board and provide vocal praise.	
If student does not make a correct response, provide a vocal prompt without delivering a token or vocal praise.	
Record data.	
After student has earned two tokens, allow a 2-minute break in the play area.	
Percentage of Intervention Steps Implemented Correctly	%

Scoring Codes:

Record + if intervention plan step was implemented as designed.

Record – if intervention plan step was not implemented as designed.

Record NA for non-applicable steps at the time of observation.

Analysis:

Calculate percentage of intervention steps implemented correctly by using the following formula:

$$\frac{\text{Number of +}}{\text{Total number of intervention steps implemented}} \times 100$$

be the easiest to use for readers unfamiliar with integrity assessment. The steps of an abbreviated behavioral intervention are listed in the left column of the table, with a space next to each step for recording a plus sign (+) for correct implementation or a minus sign (–) for incorrect implementation. A formula for calculating the percentage of steps implemented correctly is provided at the bottom of the datasheet. Worksheet 5.2 provides repeated opportunities to observe intervention steps within an observation session and allows for more detailed recording of the types of errors made by the practitioner. Again, the intervention steps are provided in the left column of the table. The observer records performance on each step of the intervention by circling one of several codes, which are defined at the bottom of the form. A space is also provided below each intervention step for comments. An advantage to this form is that it allows for analysis of errors of omission and commission as well as correct implementation. The analysis table at the bottom of Worksheet 5.2 provides a space for these summaries. In Worksheet 5.3, another intervention integrity assessment recording form, the behavioral intervention is organized by strategy type (antecedent strategies and consequence strategies for appropriate or inappropriate behaviors). The observer may record whether the intervention step was implemented as written, if it was not implemented as written, or if there was no opportunity to observe this step.

Worksheet 5.2 Sample Integrity Assessment Recording Form

Hold up one color card and ask, "What color?"	EO EC CC CI NA	EO EC CC CI NA	EO EC CC CI NA	EO EC CC CI NA	EO EC CC CI NA	EO EC CC CI NA
Comments						
If student makes a correct response, deliver one token on token economy board and provide vocal praise.	EO EC CC CI NA	EO EC CC CI NA	EO EC CC CI NA	EO EC CC CI NA	EO EC CC CI NA	EO EC CC CI NA
Comments						
If student does not make a correct response, provide a vocal prompt without delivering a token or vocal praise.	EO EC CC CI NA	EO EC CC CI NA	EO EC CC CI NA	EO EC CC CI NA	EO EC CC CI NA	EO EC CC CI NA
Comments						
Record data.	EO EC CC CI NA	EO EC CC CI NA	EO EC CC CI NA	EO EC CC CI NA	EO EC CC CI NA	EO EC CC CI NA
Comments						

Definitions of Codes:

EO = error of omission (did not implement a necessary treatment step)

EC = error of commission (included an unnecessary treatment step or added an unapproved step)

CC = correct complete (fully implemented treatment step as designed)

CI = correct incomplete (partially implemented treatment step)

NA = not applicable

Errors		Correct	
Frequency EO =	Frequency EC =	Frequency CC =	Frequency CI =
% EO =	% EC =	% CC =	% CI =
Frequency Total Errors =		Frequency Total Correct =	
% Total Errors =		% Total Correct =	

Additional data-recording forms are also available in the suggested readings listed at the end of the chapter.

SELF-REPORTING

Self-reporting is a form of assessment that involves the practitioner recording his or her performance (i.e., intervention integrity) after implementing the intervention. Conceivably, this appears to be the easiest of the assessment types to complete; however, errors in underestimating and overestimating performance are common.

Worksheet 5.3 Sample Integrity Assessment Recording Form

Type of Procedure	Description of Plan Components	Implementation Rating (Indicate the level of integrity with which staff are implementing the procedure)
Antecedent Strategies	1. Student should carry communication book with him at all times.	❑ Implemented as written (every time) ❑ NOT implemented as written (sometimes or never as written) ❑ No opportunity to observe (teacher had no opportunity to exhibit)
	2. Teacher should honor functional communication, when appropriate.	❑ Implemented as written ❑ NOT implemented as written ❑ No opportunity to observe
	3. Before introducing an instruction, remind student of the upcoming reinforcer.	❑ Implemented as written ❑ NOT implemented as written ❑ No opportunity to observe
	4. Use transition warnings 5 minutes, 3 minutes, and 1 minute before transitioning from a more preferred to a less preferred activity.	❑ Implemented as written ❑ NOT implemented as written ❑ No opportunity to observe
Consequence Strategies: **Appropriate Behavior (Hands Appropriately Engaged)**	1. Deliver high levels of vocal praise for compliance and appropriate behavior (approximately every 2 minutes during work tasks and 5 minutes when on break).	❑ Implemented as written (every time) ❑ NOT implemented as written (sometimes or never as written) ❑ No opportunity to observe (teacher had no opportunity to exhibit)
	2. Once work schedule is complete, student should obtain reinforcer for appropriate behaviors during entire work session.	❑ Implemented as written ❑ NOT implemented as written ❑ No opportunity to observe
Consequence Strategies: **Noncompliance**	1. Implement least to most prompting hierarchy to ensure compliance to all instructions (Verbal, Gesture, Light Physical, Full Physical).	❑ Implemented as written (every time) ❑ NOT implemented as written (sometimes or never as written) ❑ No opportunity to observe (teacher had no opportunity to exhibit)
Consequence Strategies: **Aggression**	1. Physically block all attempts to aggress and position body in "ready" stance to promote safety.	❑ Implemented as written (every time) ❑ NOT implemented as written ❑ No opportunity to observe
	2. Limit attention for aggression (e.g., no vocal statements and minimal eye contact).	❑ Implemented as written (every time) ❑ NOT implemented as written ❑ No opportunity to observe

MANUALS AND TREATMENT SCRIPTS

A number of interventions and curricula contain manualized treatments and scripts, which facilitate the development of integrity assessment forms because the treatment components are clearly operationalized. Fortunately, many also include corresponding integrity assessment forms (e.g., Incredible Years Parent Training program).

GUIDELINES FOR INTERVENTION

Traditional in-service training has not translated into skill application, and we know that even after initial training consisting of modeling, coaching, and performance feedback, integrity is low within three to five sessions. There is ample evidence to suggest that practitioners require ongoing support to facilitate effective treatment implementation. Fortunately, there is a growing body of research supporting the use of several follow-up procedures that offer continued support to practitioners: (1) performance feedback, (2) written performance feedback, (3) directed rehearsal, (4) contingent meeting cancellation, and (5) dynamic fading and progress monitoring. In addition, video modeling may be used as an initial training technique to prevent integrity failures. Each of these procedures is described below.

PERFORMANCE FEEDBACK MEETINGS

One of the most commonly used follow-up procedures consists of one-to-one meetings between practitioners and a supervisor (or consultant). These meetings can take various forms; therefore we will describe procedures that we have used. The content of the feedback meeting is shaped from data collected on intervention integrity, either via permanent products or direct observations. Within the same day (e.g., 24 hours; preferably within an hour) as each observation or permanent product form is collected, the practitioner meets, where convenient, with the supervisor. At this time, components of the behavioral intervention are reviewed and feedback is provided on all of the components that were observed. Ensuring that a copy of the intervention protocol is present during the meeting for both parties is often helpful. Feedback includes providing praise for those intervention steps implemented as written as well as constructive feedback for those components that were inaccurate or omitted. Constructive feedback involves a discussion of ways to properly implement those components that weren't implemented accurately. Finally, practitioners should have an opportunity to ask questions before the meeting ends. The total time spent in these meetings is brief, ranging from 5 to 20 minutes, with an average of 10 to 12 minutes, in our experience. The meetings tend to require less time as practitioners increase the accuracy with which treatment plans are implemented. The frequency of these meetings can be daily, every other day, weekly, or every other week and can be gradually faded (see dynamic fading below). Typically, performance feedback meetings follow training procedures and are used to ensure proper implementation as practitioners become more fluent with the behavioral interventions. Material and setting requirements for this procedure include intervention integrity data, treatment plan(s), and a meeting space.

WRITTEN PERFORMANCE FEEDBACK

A time-efficient alternative to verbal performance feedback meetings is to provide practitioners with written feedback regarding intervention integrity. Often when providing written feedback, graphs depicting student performance on the target behavior(s) and practitioner's treatment integrity percentages are provided. The feedback form may contain praise statements for steps implemented as written and constructive recommendations for steps implemented incorrectly or omitted. The advantage of written feedback is that it can be left in practitioners' mailboxes or cubicles or sent via electronic mail. Material and setting requirements for this procedure include intervention integrity data, graphs, and written feedback forms (see Worksheet 5.4 at the end of the chapter for a sample form).

Worksheet 5.4 Written Performance Feedback Form

Teacher:_____   Student:_____   Date:_____

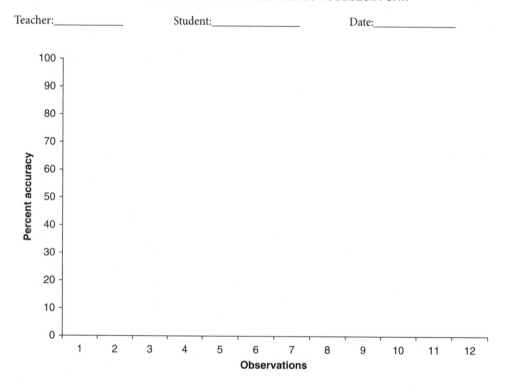

Key:
- • Teacher
- ° Student

Performance Feedback:

❑ Great job! You obtained 100% accuracy and implemented the intervention as written!

❑ Good effort. You obtained ___% accuracy and made errors on the following steps:

DIRECTED REHEARSAL MEETINGS

This procedure consists of scheduling one face-to-face meeting immediately (within 1–24 hours) after direct observation or permanent product data collection illustrates that practitioners did not achieve appropriate levels of intervention integrity (e.g., 80–100% of steps completed as written). During the meeting, the practitioner reviews and practices any missed or incorrectly implemented steps three consecutive times while his or her supervisor role-plays as the client. Therefore, this procedure is implemented contingent on low intervention integrity. Material and setting requirements for this procedure include intervention integrity data, treatment plans, and a meeting space.

CONTINGENT MEETING CANCELLATION

We have incorporated this element with directed rehearsal meetings; however, this may also be an effective strategy to use with general performance feedback meetings. Our research has illustrated that canceling directed rehearsal meetings contingent on perfectly accurate treatment implementation can serve as a negative reinforcer and increase future intervention integrity. Material and setting requirements for this procedure include intervention integrity data as well as a prescheduled meeting time and location.

DYNAMIC FADING AND PROGRESS MONITORING

We have found that an important element of follow-up support is thinning the schedule of performance feedback or directed rehearsal meetings. Following three consecutive sessions of acceptably accurate treatment implementation (e.g., in our work we strive toward 80–100% accuracy, with higher performance expected for less complex intervention plans), the meeting schedule can be gradually thinned. We have faded from daily meetings, to every other day, to weekly, to every other week. Meetings that begin on a thinner schedule, such as every other week, could be faded to once monthly. It is possible that meetings could be terminated following intervention integrity performance that consistently falls in the expected range. It is critical, however, for progress monitoring in the form of direct observation or permanent product data collection to continue. The schedule of data collection could be thinned, particularly if an entire agency is conducting observations across all staff, to once monthly. Continued collection of permanent product data tends to be easier to manage; however, not all treatment plans lend themselves to permanent product samples. Should treatment integrity performance fall below the expected level at any time, booster sessions should be provided using one of the aforementioned strategies and/or the team may wish to modify the intervention plan. We recommend that the practitioner's performance be monitored more regularly following a booster session to ensure that consistent performance is resumed.

VIDEO MODELING

We have recently found video modeling to be an effective procedure that minimizes the personnel time devoted to training while also offering practitioners frequent opportunities to review accurate plan implementation before working with students. Video modeling requires practitioners to view a video of a model, often an experienced colleague, demonstrating accurate implementation of all individualized intervention steps with either the actual client or with an actor (e.g., an employee who volunteers to role-play). The video may also contain voice-overs and on-screen textual prompts that detail relevant aspects of the procedures. In our experience, videos that illustrate between 14 and 20 discrete steps can be viewed in as few as 4 to 7 minutes. We recommend that practitioners watch relevant videos a maximum of 45 minutes prior to working with the target student. Video modeling can be administered in isolation or can be conducted with performance feedback if using it as a follow-up procedure. When adding performance feedback, supervisors should pause the video during segments that depict plan procedures that were implemented inaccurately while prompting practitioners to attend to the upcoming demonstration. If no errors were committed, practitioners should be praised for accurate plan implementation and the video would be played without interruption. It may also be possible to generate videos that depict effective class-wide management strategies that serve as effective antecedent procedures for many students. Material and setting requirements for this procedure include video equipment, a viewing room, and a treatment plan.

KEYS TO REMEMBER

1. Use research-based training practices initially to reduce the likelihood that practitioners will exhibit low intervention integrity. These include reviewing intervention protocols, modeling the intervention for the practitioner, coaching the practitioner while he or she is implementing the intervention, providing immediate real-time feedback of performance, and using video models or visual cues to aid initial acquisition of the skill. Be sure the video contains client–practitioner interactions that model perfectly accurate intervention implementation. It is also helpful to ensure necessary arrangements have been made to allow time and a space for viewing the video.

2. Evidence suggests that outcomes of treatment are directly related to the degree to which a function-based treatment is implemented with competence. Thus, make a commitment to intervention integrity assessment by choosing between permanent product recording or direct observation and generating a data collection schedule. Initially, we recommend direct observation with systematic fading to weekly, biweekly, or monthly as the practitioner shows high levels of performance.

3. Incorporate empirically supported strategies to improve or maintain practitioner performance. Performance feedback is the most widely studied practitioner support tactic, and we strongly recommend using vocal, graphic, or electronic feedback within 24 hours following data collection. Provide specific praise to the practitioner for intervention components implemented as written followed by constructive feedback on components that were omitted or not implemented as written. Be sure there is time available for questions.

4. If intervention integrity is low despite feedback, the practitioner may be experiencing a skill deficit and might benefit from repeated practice in needed areas (e.g., directed rehearsal). Directed rehearsal involves asking the practitioner to practice each missed intervention step three times during a role-play meeting.

5. If intervention continues to remain low despite feedback and opportunities for practice, the intervention may be overly complex or rely on resources not currently available. In this instance, intervention integrity may improve if the plan is simplified.

SUGGESTED READINGS

Codding, R. S., Feinberg, A. B., Dunn, E. K., & Pace, G. M. (2005). Effects of immediate performance feedback on implementation of behavior support plans. *Journal of Applied Behavior Analysis, 38*, 205–219.

Gresham, F. M. (1989). Assessment of treatment integrity in school consultation and prereferral intervention. *School Psychology Review, 18*, 37–50.

Hagermoser-Sanetti, L. M., & Kratochwill, T. R. (2008). Treatment integrity in behavioral consultation: measurement, promotion, and outcomes. *International Journal of Behavioral Consultation and Therapy, 4*, 95–114.

Noell, G. H., Witt, J. C., Gilbertson, D. N., Ranier, D. D., & Freeland, J. T. (1997). Increasing teacher intervention implementation in general education settings through consultation and performance feedback. *School Psychology Quarterly, 12*, 77–88.

Wheeler, J. L., Baggett, B. A., Fox, J., & Blevins, L. (2006). Treatment integrity: A review of intervention studies conducted with children with autism. *Focus on Autism and Other Developmental Disabilities, 21*, 45–54.

CHAPTER 6

SKILLS ASSESSMENT

Hanna C. Rue

OVERVIEW: WHAT WE KNOW

Skill assessment is a critical component to the development of an effective intervention program for individuals with an autism spectrum disorder (ASD). In fact, federal law, the Individuals with Disabilities Education Act (Public Law 105–17; referred to as IDEA 1997), devotes an entire section to the necessity of assessment for children with special needs, including children with ASD. IDEA 1997 specifies that a variety of assessment measures should be used when evaluating students with special needs. However, the law does not identify specific instruments or skills assessments practitioners should use. IDEA 1997 provides guidelines to ensure appropriate education for children with special needs. As individuals with an ASD grow into adulthood, ongoing skills assessment remains a necessary component of program development.

The *Diagnostic and Statistical Manual of Mental Disorders* (DSM-IV-TR) provides practitioners with diagnostic criteria for the various ASDs. The diagnostic criteria describe skill deficits for each ASD, such as deficits in social skills and communication, among others. Although the DSM-IV-TR provides simple categorization of skill deficits, it is widely accepted by practitioners that skill deficits vary greatly among individuals with ASD. For example, two children of the same age and same diagnosis may have vastly different needs in terms of social skills training. One young person may be a verbal communicator yet avoid eye contact and lack the ability to tolerate people standing near him. Another young person may be a nonverbal communicator but initiate social interaction and physical contact from others. For school-aged individuals with ASD, thorough academic skills assessments are crucial for development of effective teaching programs. As individuals with ASD age, skill acquisition programs target vocational training, promoting independence, and development of appropriate leisure activities.

There are many standardized assessment tools available for professionals. Various measures of adaptive behavior provide standard scores and age-equivalence data for self-care, social, and communication skills. Standard scores are often explained in terms of an individual's general strengths and weaknesses in the various areas assessed. Although this type of information can be useful, practitioners are left with many unanswered questions when developing a skill acquisition program. For example, what behaviors does the individual need to acquire to become proficient at the identified activity? Or, was the individual's performance during the standard-ized assessment representative of his or her actual ability? There are also standardized measures available to assess academic performance. These measures can be lengthy and require attending skills and adequate communication skills. Some individuals with ASD are able to tolerate a stan-dardized testing situation; conversely, others are considered "not testable." For results to be valid when using standardized measures, the practitioner must adhere to a specific protocol. Often, the testing situation does not lend itself to identifying the individual's true abilities and deficits.

GETTING STARTED: BASIC PRINCIPLES AND APPLICATIONS

Empirical studies consistently identify applied behavior analysis (ABA) interventions as effec-tive in increasing adaptive behaviors and decreasing challenging behaviors displayed by indi-viduals with ASD. The science of behavior analysis evaluates the behavior of the individual. A well-rounded behavioral program for an individual with ASD is based on principles of rein-forcement and includes techniques such as prompting, shaping, chaining, and discrete-trial teaching. Decades of research in laboratory and applied settings have produced a massive amount of detail regarding the implementation of these procedures. Even something as simple as providing an edible reinforcer (e.g., piece of cookie) has decades of literature to guide the practitioner on when to provide the edible, how much to provide, and how to fade use of the edible. The same basic behavioral principles guide the development of assessment procedures employed by behavior analysts.

To individualize a skill acquisition program, practitioners must allocate sufficient time to skill assessment. Practitioners using behavior analytic methodology take an initial measure of behavior (i.e., prior to implementation of skill acquisition or behavior reduction interventions), referred to as a baseline measure. With some adaptation, a baseline measure of a specified skill can become an informal skill assessment. For example, a practitioner may be interested in teach-ing color identification to a child with ASD. The child may or may not have experience with color identification. As a baseline measure or informal skill assessment, the practitioner may present the child with ASD the opportunity to identify a variety of colors. It may be that the child with ASD can correctly identify blue, red, and black but is unable to identify yellow, orange, and purple. The practitioner would use the information from the initial measure to determine colors to be targeted for learning. Without this information, the practitioner may waste valuable time attempting to "teach" known material.

For years, behavior analysts have used informal skills assessments to guide the development of individualized skill acquisition programs for clients with ASD. In the 1960s and 1970s behav-ioral psychologists developed intensive behavioral interventions for individuals with ASD. In many studies, simple baseline measures of skill deficits were used prior to the development of skill acquisition programs. Over the years, the technology of skill assessment has evolved to incorporate some of the contemporary measures used in applied behavior analysis.

GUIDELINES FOR IMPLEMENTATION

A skill assessment is guided by the appropriate curriculum. It is recommended that the practi-tioner make use of many published curriculum guides available to professionals, as referenced at the conclusion of this chapter. Practitioners should carefully review the available curriculum guides to determine which is best suited for the individual client with ASD. Once the curriculum is identified, you can begin the skills assessment.

A general goal of skill assessment is to determine whether the individual with ASD is able to perform the skill or is simply not motivated to perform the skill. Initially, skill assessment may appear cumbersome and tedious, but as practitioners become experienced with implementation of the procedures, skill assessment becomes straightforward. Skill assessment is relatively quick, considering the amount of time many practitioners dedicate to teaching complex skills to individuals with ASD. The following steps provide instruction to complete a basic skill assessment.

1. Identify a starting point. Most curriculum guides identify prerequisite skills for each skill acquisition program. You should identify a starting point, which may be a prerequisite skill or an initial skill in the curriculum for each skill area to be addressed.

2. Define responses. Operationally define an acceptable correct response—that is, develop a specific description of what an independent correct response would look like. The response may be nonverbal (i.e., motor movement or material manipulation) or verbal.

3. Develop a data collection procedure. A simple way to code data is to record a plus sign (+) for independent correct responses, a minus (–) for incorrect responses, and NR for no responses.

4. Gather necessary materials. You will need datasheets, a pencil, and stimuli (e.g., flashcards) necessary for the skill acquisition program. Recommended stimuli are often listed in the curriculum guide. Identify a work space with minimal distraction.

5. The initial baseline measure. In the first phase of the skill assessment, present the instruction (e.g., "Show me your nose") and/or materials to the individual with ASD. Allow 5 to 10 seconds for a response. If the individual responds correctly within 10 seconds, mark a +. If the individual responds incorrectly, mark a –. Mark "NR" if the individual does not provide a response within 10 seconds (Worksheet 6.1). There is NO consequence provided for correct or incorrect responses or no responding during this phase. The instruction and opportunity to respond represent one trial. A minimum of 10 trials are provided during each session. Three to five sessions should be completed to ensure stable responding.

6. Data analysis. Upon completion of Step 5, you will have accumulated data that indicate correct and incorrect responding in the target skill area. Use simple percentages to calculate the number of correct responses given during all opportunities to respond for each target (i.e., correct responses/all recorded responses = percentage correct). If the individual with ASD is unable to maintain 80% correct responding over three consecutive sessions, the target is not mastered or known. You may consider different criteria depending on the probability of correct responding given chance alone and the individual's learning history.

7. Identify targets. Using the data analyzed in Step 6, compile a list of target behaviors or skills that may require teaching or instruction (i.e., those skills that the individual could not maintain 80% correct responding over three sessions). These items are "targets." Also, maintain a list of the mastered or known skills (i.e., skills the individual was able to respond to correctly during 80% of trials over three sessions).

8. Identify performance deficit or skill deficit. During the second phase of the assessment, target items are interspersed with mastered items during trials. Initially, the targets and mastered items are interspersed evenly (i.e., one-to-one ratio). If the individual with ASD demonstrates an increase in correct responding to the target over several trials, gradually decrease the number of mastered items provided during the session—that is, progress from a one-to-one

Worksheet 6.1 Sample Datasheet: Phase I

Client Name:	Target Skill:
Instruction:	
Correct Response:	

Circle appropriate response. + = correct response, - = incorrect response, NR = no response

	Phase I: No Reinforcement					
	DATE					
TRIAL						
1	+ - NR	+ - NR	+ - NR	+ - NR	+ - NR	+ - NR
2	+ - NR	+ - NR	+ - NR	+ - NR	+ - NR	+ - NR
3	+ - NR	+ - NR	+ - NR	+ - NR	+ - NR	+ - NR
4	+ - NR	+ - NR	+ - NR	+ - NR	+ - NR	+ - NR
5	+ - NR	+ - NR	+ - NR	+ - NR	+ - NR	+ - NR
6	+ - NR	+ - NR	+ - NR	+ - NR	+ - NR	+ - NR
7	+ - NR	+ - NR	+ - NR	+ - NR	+ - NR	+ - NR
8	+ - NR	+ - NR	+ - NR	+ - NR	+ - NR	+ - NR
9	+ - NR	+ - NR	+ - NR	+ - NR	+ - NR	+ - NR
10	+ - NR	+ - NR	+ - NR	+ - NR	+ - NR	+ - NR
11	+ - NR	+ - NR	+ - NR	+ - NR	+ - NR	+ - NR
12	+ - NR	+ - NR	+ - NR	+ - NR	+ - NR	+ - NR
13	+ - NR	+ - NR	+ - NR	+ - NR	+ - NR	+ - NR
14	+ - NR	+ - NR	+ - NR	+ - NR	+ - NR	+ - NR
15	+ - NR	+ - NR	+ - NR	+ - NR	+ - NR	+ - NR
16	+ - NR	+ - NR	+ - NR	+ - NR	+ - NR	+ - NR
17	+ - NR	+ - NR	+ - NR	+ - NR	+ - NR	+ - NR
18	+ - NR	+ - NR	+ - NR	+ - NR	+ - NR	+ - NR
19	+ - NR	+ - NR	+ - NR	+ - NR	+ - NR	+ - NR
20	+ - NR	+ - NR	+ - NR	+ - NR	+ - NR	+ - NR
% correct						

ratio (target presented to mastered item presented) to 2:1 and 4:1 ratio. Learning trials are presented in the same manner as in Step 5, but correct responses result in the presentation of an item that functions as a reinforcer. Specifically, present something (e.g., toy, edible, or activity) that would motivate the individual to continue to work. Activities such as looking through a book or listening to music should be presented for approximately 20 seconds. Reinforcers are presented following correct responses to mastered and target items. Collect data following each response. A minimum of 10 trials should be delivered during each session for a total of three to five sessions (Worksheet 6.2).

Worksheet 6.2 Sample Datasheet: Phase II

Client Name:		Target Skill:
Instruction:		
Correct Response:		

Circle appropriate response. + = correct response, - = incorrect response, NR = no response.

	Phase II: Reinforcement Provided					
	DATE					
TRIAL						
1	+ - NR	+ - NR	+ - NR	+ - NR	+ - NR	+ - NR
2	+ - NR	+ - NR	+ - NR	+ - NR	+ - NR	+ - NR
3	+ - NR	+ - NR	+ - NR	+ - NR	+ - NR	+ - NR
4	+ - NR	+ - NR	+ - NR	+ - NR	+ - NR	+ - NR
5	+ - NR	+ - NR	+ - NR	+ - NR	+ - NR	+ - NR
6	+ - NR	+ - NR	+ - NR	+ - NR	+ - NR	+ - NR
7	+ - NR	+ - NR	+ - NR	+ - NR	+ - NR	+ - NR
8	+ - NR	+ - NR	+ - NR	+ - NR	+ - NR	+ - NR
9	+ - NR	+ - NR	+ - NR	+ - NR	+ - NR	+ - NR
10	+ - NR	+ - NR	+ - NR	+ - NR	+ - NR	+ - NR
11	+ - NR	+ - NR	+ - NR	+ - NR	+ - NR	+ - NR
12	+ - NR	+ - NR	+ - NR	+ - NR	+ - NR	+ - NR
13	+ - NR	+ - NR	+ - NR	+ - NR	+ - NR	+ - NR
14	+ - NR	+ - NR	+ - NR	+ - NR	+ - NR	+ - NR
15	+ - NR	+ - NR	+ - NR	+ - NR	+ - NR	+ - NR
16	+ - NR	+ - NR	+ - NR	+ - NR	+ - NR	+ - NR
17	+ - NR	+ - NR	+ - NR	+ - NR	+ - NR	+ - NR
18	+ - NR	+ - NR	+ - NR	+ - NR	+ - NR	+ - NR
19	+ - NR	+ - NR	+ - NR	+ - NR	+ - NR	+ - NR
20	+ - NR	+ - NR	+ - NR	+ - NR	+ - NR	+ - NR
% correct						

9. Identify skills needing instruction. Following completion of Step 8, calculate the percentage of correct responding provided to target items. If the percentage of correct responding to target items is not maintained at 80% for three consecutive sessions, the target requires teaching or instruction.

10. Teach. Proceed with the appropriate teaching or instruction strategies (e.g., most-to-least prompting) for each target.

ADAPTATIONS AND MODIFICATIONS

The guidelines for implementation outlined above are appropriate for skills assessments conducted with children and adults. The type of skills and materials used may differ depending on the age and developmental level of the individual with ASD. It is ideal, yet not always feasible, to conduct a skills assessment in the environment in which the skill will be used or taught. Modifications to the assessment environment may be necessary.

For the adult client, a vocational skills assessment sometimes must be completed in a "simulated" environment or workshop area. A practitioner conducting a vocational skills assessment under simulated conditions should observe the actual work that is being performed, documenting the materials used, the space provided to complete the job, and the time it takes other employees to finish their work.

Skills assessments conducted for school-aged children may require simulation of the classroom environment. A practitioner attempting to simulate a classroom situation for a skills assessment should observe children in the typical classroom setting and meet with the classroom teacher to discuss where the student would be seated in each classroom situation.

KEYS TO REMEMBER

1. Practitioners should consider the individual's developmental level when identifying the appropriate curriculum guide.
2. Keep assessment sessions relatively short (e.g., approximately 10 minutes).
3. Practitioners should remain aware of any challenging behaviors the individual with ASD may display in an attempt to communicate distress, agitation, or fear. The practitioner should take time to develop a rapport with the individual with ASD or coach a familiar paraprofessional through the assessment procedure.
4. Be prepared with a variety of items that may function as reinforcers.
5. Be prepared to make adaptations to obtain a reliable measure of the individual's ability. For example, an individual may prefer a certain seating arrangement or find certain stimuli aversive, factors that should be considered when planning and implementing a skills assessment.

SUGGESTED READINGS

Duhon, G. J., Noell, G. H., Witt, J. C., Freeland, J. T., Dufrene, B. A., & Gilbertson, D. N. (2004). Identifying academic skill and performance deficits: The experimental analysis of brief assessments of academic skills. *School Psychology Review, 33*(3), 429–443.

Lerman, D. C., Vordran, C., Addison, L., & Kuhn, S. A. C. (2004). A rapid assessment of skills in young children with autism. *Journal of Applied Behavior Analysis, 37,* 11–26.

Noell, G. H., Freeland, J. T., Witt, J. C., & Gansle, K. A. (2001). Using brief assessments to identify effective interventions for individual students. *Journal of School Psychology, 39*(4), 335–355.

OTHER RESOURCES

Leaf, R., & McEachin, J. (1999). *A Work in Progress: Behavior Management Strategies for Intensive Behavioral Treatment of Autism.* New York: Autism Partnership.

Maurice, C., Green, G., & Foxx, R. (Eds.) (2001) *Making a Difference: Behavioral Intervention for Autism.* Austin, TX: Pro-Ed.

Maurice, C., Green, G., & Luce, S. (1996). *Behavioral Intervention for Young Children with Autism: A Manual for Parents and Professionals.* Austin, TX: Pro-Ed, Inc.

Partington, J. W., & Sundberg, M. L. (1998). *The Assessment of Basic Language and Learning Skills.* Pleasant Hill, CA: Behavior Analysts.

CHAPTER 7

OUTCOME ASSESSMENT

Susan M. Wilczynski

OVERVIEW: WHAT WE KNOW

Autism spectrum disorders (ASDs) are characterized by severe limitations in communication, social interaction, and range of interests, as well as behavioral excesses in stereotypy. The number of diagnosed cases of ASD seems to grow each time a prevalence study is published, with current estimates ranging from 1:91 to 1:110 in young children. Although considerable resources are dedicated to determining both the cause and treatment of ASD, many questions remain.

This chapter is intended to help practitioners better understand the importance of outcome assessment. Outcome assessment considers all relevant variables that should be measured in determining whether treatment has been successful. The assessment focuses on specific skills taught during treatment and more general effects that reflect changes in development trajectories. Indicators might be necessary at each of these levels of outcome analysis for the same skill domain. For example, in the communication domain, practitioners might measure specific skills such as the number of words spoken or objects correctly identified receptively. General development would be measured by a child's or adult's performance on a standardized test instrument.

Researchers have emphasized general development when examining the effectiveness of comprehensive treatment programs. Conversely, specific skills usually dominate outcome assessment when more focused treatment studies are conducted. However, scholars and practitioners alike must look beyond this restricted conceptualization of outcome assessment. Specifically, it is necessary to provide evidence that treatments produce socially meaningful improvements and that quality of life (QoL) indicators are given at least as much importance as other instruments used to measure change.

GETTING STARTED: BASIC PRINCIPLES AND APPLICATIONS

High-quality instruments are a foundation of meaningful outcome assessment. Measuring change with an instrument that does not accurately capture the target behavior or the construct produces inaccurate information. Furthermore, different quality criteria should be applied based on the type of measurement methods used to assess change (i.e., either direct behavioral observation or tests and checklists).

SPECIFIC SKILLS AND PROBLEM BEHAVIORS

Direct behavioral observation is the most frequently used method for evaluating specific skills or problem behaviors. The quality of direct observation is tied to a number of important indicators. First, target behaviors must have a clear operational definition. Second, measurement should capture all occurrences of target behaviors during an observation period, best achieved using continuous data collection. Third, two professionals using the same operational definitions and data collection system should simultaneously record the presence or absence of a target behavior as a measure of interobserver agreement (IOA). To derive IOA, you compare the agreements and disagreements between recorders. When agreement is high (e.g., >80% agreement), practitioners can be confident that the target behavior has been reliably recorded. It is best to collect IOA data across baseline and treatment conditions and to collect a sufficiently representative sample of behavior (e.g., 25% of recording opportunities). Chapter 1 describes in more detail how to conduct direct observation and measurement.

GENERAL DEVELOPMENT

Tests, scales, or checklists are used most frequently to measure general development. These instruments should be based on observations by a qualified practitioner and should be administered and scored according to a standardized format. If administration or scoring differs each time the instrument is used, significant variability could result in an unreliable and inaccurate representation of change. Tests and similar instruments also should be psychometrically sound, meaning that they have acceptable reliability and validity. Common methods to assess the reliability of a standardized instrument are test–retest, parallel forms, and internal consistency. Similarly, there are many validity assessment methods, such as content, construct, concurrent, and predictive validity. The process of establishing sufficient psychometric support requires publication of multiple studies.

SOCIALLY MEANINGFUL CHANGES

Outcomes based on specific skills, problem behaviors, and general development should always be compared against socially meaningful changes. For example, outcome assessment may show a statistically significant change from pretreatment to posttreatment, but a statistically significant change may not be socially significant. One approach for measuring social significance is to compare the skill level or development of a child or adult with ASD to that of a typically developing child or adult. Practitioners also can determine what level of performance would be necessary to increase independence and/or result in gains that improve opportunities in the natural environment. Social validity can also be measured to subjectively determine if people who share the lives of the child or adult with ASD perceive an important change in real-world settings.

Another way to measure socially meaningful change is QoL assessment. Some of the instruments historically used to measure improvement in large-scale studies, for example IQ tests, do not effectively predict QoL. Unfortunately, even when IQ falls in the average range, few individuals with ASD live completely independently, hold full-time jobs, or are socially engaged outside of their families. Increasingly, practitioners are evaluating treatment effectiveness based on community functioning within such domains as social support, preparation for satisfactory employment, family life, and self-determination, all valid QoL indicators.

GUIDELINES FOR IMPLEMENTATION

SPECIFIC SKILLS

At a minimum, practitioners should measure change using direct behavioral observations whenever their goal is to increase specific skills or decrease problem behaviors. They should evaluate the quality of their operational definitions, capture the most accurate and complete representation of the target behavior, and assess IOA.

GENERAL DEVELOPMENT

Practitioners should know the psychometric properties of instruments that will be used for outcome assessment. Table 7.1 presents psychometric support criteria, and Table 7.2 links these criteria to commercially available instruments that target cognitive, academic, social, communication, and adaptive functioning.

SOCIALLY MEANINGFUL CHANGES

As noted previously, practitioners can and should collect data on the frequency, intensity, or duration with which typically developing children and adults demonstrate a target behavior. Armed with this information, practitioners can then determine if treatment produced a change

Table 7.1 Psychometric Support Criteria

Solid Support	Two forms of reliability established at .90 or greater and two forms of validity reported
Sufficient Support	Two forms of reliability established at .80 or greater and two forms of validity reported
Adequate Support	One form of reliability established at .80 or greater and one form of validity reported
Modest Support	One form of reliability established at .80 or greater
Weak Support	One form of reliability established below .80
Unsatisfactory Support	Does not meet the criteria for weak support

Table 7.2 Commercially Available Instruments Used for Outcome Assessment

Test Name	Solid	Sufficient	Adequate	Moderate	Weak	Unsatisfactory
Adolescent and Adult Psychoeducational Profile (AAPEP)				X		
Asperger's Syndrome Diagnostic Interview (ASDI)				X		
Australian Scale for Asperger's Syndrome (ASAS)						X
Autism Behavior Checklist (ABC)				X		
Autism Diagnostic Interview-Revised (ADI-R)	X					
Autism Diagnostic Observation Schedule (ADOS)			X			
Autism Screening Instrument for Educational Planning-2		X				
Bayley Scales of Infant Development-III (BSID-III)		X				
Behavior Assessment System for Children (BASC)—Parent Rating Scale		X				
Behavior Assessment System for Children—(BASC) Self Report of Personality			X			
Behavior Assessment System for Children—(BASC) Teacher Rating Scale			X			
Behavior Observation Scale (BOS)						X
Behavior Rating Instrument for Autistic and Atypical Children (BRIAAC)						X
Brigance Diagnostic Inventory Early Development-II		X				
Cattell Infant Intelligence Test						X
Child Behavior Checklist (CBCL)			X			
Childhood Autism Rating Scale (CARS)		X				
Children's Communication Checklist (CCC)						X
Children's Social Behavior Questions (CSBQ)	X					
Clinical Evaluation of Language Fundamentals-III					X	
Developmental Assessment of Young Children	X					
Developmental Profile II					X	
Diagnostic Interview for Social and Communication Disorders (DISCO)					X	
Differential Abilities Scale		X				
Early Intervention Developmental Profile			X			
Expressive One Word Picture Vocabulary Test	X					

Table 7.2 (Continued)

Test Name	Solid	Sufficient	Adequate	Moderate	Weak	Unsatisfactory
Gilliam Autism Rating Scale (GARS)				X		
Handicaps, Behavior, and Skills Schedule (HBS)					X	
Leiter-International Performance Scale-Rev		X				
MacArthur Communicative Development Inventory		X				
Merrill-Palmer Revised Scales of Development		X				
Merrill-Palmer Scales of Mental Tests						X
Peabody Picture Vocabulary-III			X			
Personality Inventory for Children				X		
Pervasive Developmental Disorders Rating Scale (PDDRS)		X				
Preschool Development Profile						X
Preschool Language Scale		X				
Psychoeducational Profile-Revised (PEP-R) Total Score			X			
Psychoeducational Profile-Revised (Chinese version)	X					
Receptive One Word Picture Vocabulary Test	X					
Receptive Expressive Emergent Language-2	X					
Reynell Developmental Language Scale					X	
Rimland Diagnostic Form for Behavior-Disturbed Children (Form E-1)						X
Rimland Diagnostic Form for Behavior-Disturbed Children (Form E-2)						X
Social Communication Questionnaire						X
Social Responsiveness Scale (SRS)		X				
Stanford-Binet Intelligence Scales: Fifth Edition	X					
Systematic Observation of Red Flags (SORF)				X		
Vineland Adaptive Behavior Scales (VABS)-Classroom Edition			X			
Vineland Adaptive Behavior Scales (VABS)-Expanded Form		X				
Vineland Adaptive Behavior Scales (VABS)-Survey Form		X				
Wechsler Individual Achievement Test	X					
Wechsler Intelligence Scale for Children-IV	X					
Wechsler Preschool and Primary Scale of Intelligence		X				
Woodcock-Johnson Test of Achievement III		X				

that approximates normative performance. In contrast, when standardized tests are completed, practitioners can determine if the child or adult with ASD has developed skills consistent with peers in the general population. This can be done by examining the standard score and comparing it against what is typical. Information about the average range of performance can be found in testing manuals.

Socially meaningful improvements can still be demonstrated even when the individual does not attain the "average" level of function. Before implementing treatment, the practitioner can establish the level of performance that would be necessary to increase independence or access to opportunities at home, at school, or in the community. This criterion should be established with input from a team of people who share the lives of the individual with ASD and, whenever possible, with the individual with ASD. For example, with sufficient input, the practitioner may determine that for a child or adult who does not currently respond to any social bids from peers, responding to 50% of these bids would be socially meaningful. In this way, peers would be more likely to initiate at a higher rate (because they were reinforced to do so), and more opportunities to practice social skills in real-world settings would be available.

Finally, practitioners can interview parents, teachers, and other service providers to determine if they see a difference in real-world settings. For example, if a treatment goal is to teach employment skills such as filing materials in an office or stocking foods at a grocery store, a job placement employer can be asked to independently evaluate performance.

Little research has been conducted on QoL for individuals with ASD. Ideally, QoL indicators will be included more frequently when evaluating the effectiveness of autism treatment in the future. At a minimum, social support, preparation for satisfactory employment, family life, and self-determination should be considered when evaluating whether a treatment for ASD has produced important outcomes.

Social Support

Almost anyone familiar with ASD would agree that social skills should be targeted for improvement. However, there may be significant differences in the way these skills are assessed. For example, the effectiveness of social skills programs is often measured by determining if the individual with ASD acquires knowledge about social rules. Unfortunately, knowledge of social rules is a necessary but insufficient predictor of whether a child or adult with ASD follows the social rule in real-world settings. Furthermore, even if the social skills are demonstrated in real-world settings, what is the quality of the social relationship? Satisfaction or loneliness, for example, is not predicted by the number of social relationships a person with ASD may have but rather by whether he or she has a functional social network that results in similar opportunities experienced by typically developing peers (e.g., sleepovers, party invitations).

Employment

Practitioners must determine if adults with ASD have developed the structural skills necessary to be employed. However, these skills alone are not likely to lead to sustained employment and job satisfaction. It is important to know what variables are deemed important by employers. Practitioners can also identify variables that are relevant to employers in *their community* by observing other individuals who are successful in the job and then interviewing the employer.

Family Life

Certainly, the quality of family life is important for children and adults with ASD. Happiness, for one, depends on successful functioning of the family. Some families lack sufficient social support, face financial burdens, become stressed by the lack of knowledge or understanding they experience in their communities, are challenged by child care, and lack sufficient support from professionals or access to services in their communities. Accordingly, practitioners are advised to incorporate a family needs survey as one component of comprehensive outcome assessment.

Self-Determination

Self-determination is essential to long-term quality of life. Choice is one form of self-determination. Choice can be embedded in treatment occurring at home, at school, and in the community at virtually any age. As an example, children with ASD can be taught to make choices such as selecting the order in which activities are completed, which reinforcer they can obtain for successfully completing work, or which individuals they can interact with when working on social skills. Some adults can be involved in selecting treatment goals and/or the treatment approach that is adopted. Practitioners can not only facilitate this process but can also measure the extent to which it is occurring across treatment settings. Another influence on self-determination is increased independence in important areas of life functioning—something that can be addressed by teaching a person self-management skills.

KEYS TO REMEMBER

1. Always collect data to know if important improvements result from treatment.
2. When planning outcome assessment, ask the question, "Is this goal appropriate for this specific individual with ASD?"
3. Ideally, outcome measurement should include direct observation and standardized assessment methods.
4. Be aware of the psychometric properties of standardized assessment tests and instruments when selecting them for outcome assessment.
5. Incorporate social validity and QoL indicators in your outcome assessment.
6. Measure social validity by asking people who share the lives of a child or adult with ASD their opinions about treatment acceptability and satisfaction.

SUGGESTED READINGS

Burgess, A. F., & Gutstein, S. E. (2007). Quality of life for people with autism: Raising the standard for evaluating successful outcomes. *Child and Adolescent Mental Health,* 12(2), 80–86. DOI: 10.1111/j.1475–3588.2006.00432.x

Lord, C., Wagner, A., Rogers, S., Szatmari, P., Aman, M., Charman, T., et al.. (2005). Challenges in evaluating psychosocial interventions for autistic spectrum disorders. *Journal of Autism and Developmental Disorders,* 35(6), 695–708. DOI: 10.1007/s10803–005–0017–6

Matson, J. L. (2007). Determining treatment outcome in early intervention programs for autism spectrum disorders: A critical analysis of measurement issues in learning based interventions. *Research in Developmental Disabilities, 28,* 207–218. DOI:10.1016/j.ridd.2005.07.006

Matson, J. L., & Nebel-Schwalm, M. (2007). Assessing challenging behaviors in children with autism spectrum disorders: A review. *Research in Developmental Disabilities, 28,* 567–579. DOI: 10.1016/j.ridd.2006.08.001

National Autism Center. (2009). *National Standards Report: National Standards Project—Addressing the Need for Evidence-Based Practice Guidelines for Autism Spectrum Disorders.* Randolph, MA: National Autism Center, Inc.

OTHER RESOURCES

Matson, J. L., & Wilkins, J. (2009). Psychometric testing methods for children's social skills. *Research in Developmental Disabilities, 30,* 249–274. DOI: 10.1016/j.ridd.2008.04.002

Wolf, M. M. (1978). Social validity: The case for subjective measurement *or* how applied behavior analysis is finding its heart. *Journal of Applied Behavior Analysis,* 11(2), 203–214.

PART 2

HOW TO TEACH SKILLS

CHAPTER 8

TOILET TRAINING

Jennifer M. Gillis, Kimberely Smith, and Sara White

OVERVIEW: WHAT WE KNOW

Toilet training is one of the most important skills for individuals to attain. Most children begin toilet training around age 3 or 4 years old; however, for a variety of reasons toilet training is not always achieved this early for individuals with autism spectrum disorders (ASDs). In fact, it is estimated that over half of individuals with ASD have experienced difficulties with toileting, making it a common focus of intervention for individuals in this population.

The majority of toilet training interventions derive from the intensive behavioral toileting program developed by Nathan Azrin and Richard Foxx in the 1970s. Often referred to as Rapid Toilet Training (RTT), this program has been successful for many populations, including individuals with ASD. Research also indicates that both parents and school/residential staff can be trained to implement RTT procedures, which allows for increased maintenance and generalization of toileting behaviors across settings.

Although the majority of toilet training research has been done with young children, studies also have reported success with individuals as old as 28 years of age and in most cognitive functioning ranges. Studies also show that training can be successful across different environments, including home, school, and residential facilities. While a practical issue such as spending extended periods of time in the bathroom at school can be a concern, practitioners should not consider age, cognitive ability, or setting of intervention as limiting factors.

GETTING STARTED: PRINCIPLES AND APPLICATIONS

Principles of reinforcement and punishment are the foundation of toilet training programs. Taken from operant learning theory, reinforcement procedures are used to increase continence by providing or removing some preferred reward, respectively, contingent upon the desired behavior. As an example of positive reinforcement, an individual might receive praise when he or she initiates use of and voids in the toilet. Punishment procedures, such as overcorrection and positive practice, are also used in toileting programs. More recently, however, positive practice (described later in the chapter) has been incorporated into toileting programs instead of overcorrection.

Stimulus control is another important learning principle. One key to a successful toileting program is having toileting behaviors under the control of certain discriminative stimuli, such as the feeling of a full bladder. Frequently, toileting programs must focus not only on establishing stimulus control of toileting behaviors, but also transferring control across relevant stimuli. For example, some individuals may only void when they wear a diaper or similar protective brief. Although the diaper has stimulus control over voiding, transferring this control from the diaper to the feeling of a full bladder is a necessary objective of the toileting program.

GUIDELINES FOR INTERVENTION

Toilet training can be a daunting task for parents and teachers alike. The guidelines provided here are designed to assist you through the process of toilet training. Some of the components included in the guidelines may have to be modified to the training needs of the specific individual or setting.

There are four preliminary tasks that we strongly urge you to consider to maximize the effectiveness of any toilet training program. Other materials and considerations that are necessary before starting a toileting program are presented in the checklist at the end of the chapter (Table 8.1).

1. A physician should provide medical clearance before you begin a toilet training program with any individual. The issue here is to rule out any physical problems that would contraindicate training.
2. The individual should master the following prerequisite skills: (a) sitting on the toilet for 1 to 2 minutes without problematic behaviors occurring, (b) basic requesting skills using verbal language, (c) sign language or picture communication, (d) quickly pulling

Table 8.1 Checklist Before Starting a Toileting Program

✓	Necessary materials and considerations
____	Preferred liquids (to be used when increasing fluid intake)
____	Activities to do off the toilet when implementing the toileting program
____	Extra underwear (10–15 pairs per day)
____	Extra clothes (shirts, pants, socks)
____	Plastic bags in which to place soiled clothes (especially for settings outside of home)
____	Digital timer
____	Data collection sheet
____	Pencil/pen for data collection
____	Two chairs near the toilet (one for the trainer and one for the individual)
____	It may be helpful to place plastic sheeting or absorbent sheeting outside the bathroom door to minimize damage to carpeting or flooring.

pants up and down, and (e) quickly pulling underwear up and down. These skills should be taught during the weeks prior to toilet training if they are not yet present.

3. It is important to become familiar with two variations in toilet training procedures. The first procedure is commonly referred to as scheduled sits or "trip" training. This is a less intensive procedure that involves taking the individual to the toilet on a regular schedule and providing a reinforcer for any instance of voiding in the toilet. If an accident occurs, the individual should immediately be taken to the toilet because interrupting the accident may cause the individual to stop voiding, thus providing an opportunity for him or her to finish voiding on the toilet and receive reinforcement. Staff and parents should not comment or talk about the accident or scold the individual. Clothes should then be changed with minimal attention given. The second procedure, RTT, was highlighted earlier. Later in the chapter, we present detailed guidelines for implementing RTT.

4. Seek out family or social supports to assist with the training. Of course, all people assisting with toilet training should be trained to competency on the toileting procedure. It is critical that the toilet training procedure be implemented the same way with the individual throughout the day and across locations. If a Board Certified Behavior Analyst (BCBA) is working with you, monitoring of the toileting intervention, training, and follow-up should be provided to ensure that procedural integrity remains high.

The intensive toilet training program can be implemented once the above tasks and checklist are completed. The guidelines for implementation of this program are presented below.

BEGIN BASELINE DATA COLLECTION

Baseline data collection should begin 1 month prior to program implementation. During baseline, you record the frequency and patterns of voiding so that the sitting schedule can be tailored for the individual. A minimum of 2 weeks of data is recommended. For baseline, the individual should be placed in regular underwear and liquid intake should not be varied from its usual schedule. A baseline datasheet should be located near the bathroom that the individual will be using. Record the date and time of each in-toilet and in-pants voiding.

USE OF DATA COLLECTION SHEET FOR BASELINE AND INTERVENTION PHASES

Worksheet 8.1 is an example of a datasheet you can use during baseline and intervention phases. The datasheet should be kept with the trainer at all times. Only the first two columns are necessary in baseline; the remaining columns will be needed during intervention. In the first column, write the time an accident or scheduled toileting occurs. In the second column, fill in the appropriate condition according to the codes at the bottom. For the third column, latency (length of time from when the subject sits down on the toilet until urination occurs) is recorded using a stopwatch. The fourth column can be tailored to the needs of the individual—for example, the triggering of a urine alarm can be recorded here if it is used in training. Or, if maladaptive behavior frequently occurs (e.g., temper tantrums), it could be recorded here as "Y" for occurrence or "N" for non-occurrence. The last column is used to record whether the toileting trip was prompted by the trainer ("P") or self-initiated ("S"). The columns are then repeated on the

Worksheet 8.1 Sample Baseline and Training Datasheet

Date	Time	Phase	Latency	Urine Alarm/ Problem Behavior?		Self-Initiation?	
				Y	Y	P	S
				Y	N	P	S
				Y	N	P	S
				Y	N	P	S
				Y	N	P	S
				Y	N	P	S
				Y	N	P	S
				Y	N	P	S
				Y	N	P	S
				Y	N	P	S
				Y	N	P	S
				Y	N	P	S
				Y	N	P	S
				Y	N	P	S
				Y	N	P	S

Data Collection Codes

Code	Definition
W +	Urination on toilet
W -	Urination accident
W-/W+	Urination accident but finished on toilet
D+	Dry when checked
BM+	Bowel movement on toilet
BM -	Bowel movement accident
P	Prompted self-initiation
S	Spontaneous self-initiation

other half of the page to provide more space. Columns can be added or removed for other components that may need tracking, such as frequency of positive practice, urine alarm detections, and self-initiated toileting requests (verbal, sign, gestural, picture symbol).

CONDUCT A REINFORCER PREFERENCE ASSESSMENT

To reinforce voiding on the toilet, potential reinforcers must be identified. A preference assessment should be conducted to identify several foods, toys, or objects to be used as programmed consequences (reinforcers). These items should be easily accessible in the toileting area. The preference assessment can be conducted during baseline and must be completed before the toileting intervention begins. We also advise that you conduct periodic preference assessment during intervention, because the reinforcing effect of previously identified consequences can change over time.

ESTABLISH A SITTING SCHEDULE

After baseline data are collected, a sitting schedule should be followed similar to the one illustrated in Worksheet 8.2. If the individual has exclusive, uninterrupted access to a bathroom throughout the day, you may want to consider training without pants and underwear during the initial phases. This arrangement allows the trainer to easily see when an accident is occurring and avoids the delay caused by pulling down pants and underwear. Even though the void starts as an accident, a quick transfer from chair to toilet provides the trainer an opportunity to reinforce voiding on the toilet for that trial. If toilet training is occurring in a group home or school, a urine alarm should be used to alert the trainer to the occurrence of an accident. The urine alarm attaches to an individual's underwear and produces an audible sound when voiding occurs.

Worksheet 8.2 Example of a Sitting Schedule and Guidelines

Phase	Sitting Schedule	Dry Pants Checks	Increasing Individual's Distance from Toilet	Criteria for Moving to Next Phase
1	10 minutes on toilet; 5 minutes in chair	Every minute	Chair should be beside toilet.	3 consecutive urinations within 1 minute of sitting down on the toilet
2	10 minutes on toilet; 10 minutes in chair	Every 2 minutes	Chair should be 3 feet from toilet.	3 consecutive urinations within 1 minute of sitting down on the toilet
3	5 minutes on toilet; 15 minutes in chair	Every 3 minutes	After 3 consecutive successes, chair should be moved from 6 feet away from toilet, to 9, then 12.	Remain on Phase 3 until 3 consecutive successes occur at 12 feet
4	3 minutes on toilet; 30 minutes in chair or in natural environment near bathroom	Every 5 minutes	Remain outside bathroom unless excessive accidents occur; return to last successful distance.	Remain on Phase 4 until 3 consecutive self-initiated successes occur from outside the bathroom
5	1 minute on toilet; 45–60 minutes off toilet	Every 45–60 minutes	In classroom or natural environment near bathroom	Remain on Phase 5 until initiations are occurring several times daily from outside the bathroom

FLUID INTAKE AND DRY PANTS CHECKS

Once the toileting program begins, increase an individual's fluid intake as a way to occasion more frequent voiding. Be sure to check with a physician to determine the amount of liquid that can be appropriately increased. While the individual sits on the toilet and in the chair, sips of liquid should be offered every 1 to 2 minutes. When using the urine alarm and sitting on the chair, dry pants checks involve the trainer asking: "Do you have wet or dry pants on?" The trainer should simultaneously prompt the individual to feel the pants and communicate whether they are "dry" or "wet." If pants are dry, a preferred item (based on the preference assessment) and praise should be provided simultaneously. (If toilet training is occurring without pants, dry pants checks should begin once pants are reintroduced.)

POSITIVE REINFORCEMENT FOR SUCCESSES AND SELF-INITIATIONS

Preferred items and praise should be provided immediately after the individual's urine stream goes into the toilet. Self-initiations are a critical part of becoming independent with toileting and should be programmed at the start of training (see the component on communication training below). During the early phases of training, if the individual simply stands up from the chair and sits on the toilet, this behavior should be counted on the datasheet as an initiation and the trainer should give the most preferred item to him or her. The trainer also should continue to prompt appropriate communication. Once the individual meets the Phase 1 criteria, the most highly preferred reinforcers from the preference assessment should be given only if the success was self-initiated.

POSITIVE PRACTICE

Positive practice involves repeatedly performing appropriate behaviors that should occur after an accident. For example, the trainer walks the individual quickly back and forth between the location of the accident and the toilet, undresses, and sits on the toilet. The frequency of positive practice should be recorded to verify whether it results in fewer toileting accidents. Be careful that the extra attention given to the individual during positive practice does not serve as a reinforcer for accidents.

ADAPTATIONS AND MODIFICATIONS

It is not uncommon to adapt and modify toilet training programs because of the particular needs of individuals and settings. Below are some of the areas worthy of consideration.

URINE ALARM

If the individual wears pants during toilet training, a urine alarm should be used to alert the trainer that an accident is occurring. When an accident occurs, the trainer can state a reminder,

"No wet pants" or "We keep our pants dry." The individual should be taken to the toilet to sit for 1 to 2 minutes to finish urinating. If no further urination occurs on the toilet, positive practice should be implemented.

COMMUNICATION TRAINING

As mentioned earlier, it is critical to teach the individual how to request the bathroom when his or her bladder is full. Immediately before the individual sits down on the toilet or enters the bathroom, prompt him or her to say "toilet" or "potty," sign "toilet," or choose a picture of the toilet. The mode of communication chosen should be one that is most functional for the individual. Ongoing development of appropriate requesting should continue throughout toilet training to facilitate more rapid acquisition of appropriate self-initiations. This skill is not essential for the early stages of toilet training but will become increasingly important as you move towards self-initiation.

BOWEL TRAINING

Although bowel movements do not occur as frequently as urinating, bowel movement training should also involve the individual sitting on the toilet at "high probability" times in the day. Positive reinforcement should also be used during bowel training to increase the successes on the toilet. If the individual continues having bowel movements in a diaper or underwear around the same time, consider having him or her sit on the toilet wearing a diaper or underwear with a hole cut out of the back. The size of the hole can be gradually increased to eventually do away with the diaper or underwear altogether.

INTERFERING BEHAVIORS

If an individual has a high number of interfering behaviors, particularly self-injury and aggression, there could be a safety risk to the individual and the person conducting training. Because bathrooms are generally confined and have potentially dangerous objects or surfaces (hard tile floors, porcelain surfaces), interfering behaviors are more difficult to manage without injury. As such, if individuals display interfering behaviors to escape or avoid non-preferred situations, these behaviors should be addressed prior to undertaking an intensive toilet training program. Also, some individuals will have particularly strong avoidance responses to sitting on the toilet or traveling to the bathroom. Being able to travel to the bathroom and sit on the toilet without interfering behaviors should be an intervention objective before initiating formal toilet training.

GENDER-SPECIFIC TRAINING ISSUES

Although training with males typically begins with them learning to urinate while sitting on the toilet, eventually they should be taught how to void appropriately when standing. A procedure termed "toileting targets" can be effective for such a purpose. Specifically, a small but visually conspicuous object is fastened to a toilet bowl or wall urinal and the individual is shaped to direct his urine stream at the "target." Once successful, the object can be gradually reduced in size and eventually eliminated.

KEYS TO REMEMBER

1. Assess an individual's prerequisite skills and teach them accordingly before initiating a toilet training program.
2. Start collecting baseline data 1 month prior to program implementation.
3. Train the family or staff assisting with toilet training to competency on all procedures.
4. Establish a specific schedule for sitting on the toilet and for taking breaks off the toilet.
5. Increase fluid intake to occasion frequent voiding.
6. Positive reinforcement for successful urinations and self-initiations should be included in all toileting programs.
7. Select a procedure such as positive practice that will be followed when the individual has an accident.
8. Implement communication training (as needed) to teach appropriate requesting to use the bathroom.
9. Include programming that addresses generalization and maintenance of toileting skills.
10. Whenever possible, arrange for a BCBA or similar professional to supervise toilet training.

SUGGESTED READINGS

Foxx, R. M., & Azrin, A. H. (1973). *Toilet Training the Retarded: A Rapid Program for Day and Nighttime Independent Toileting.* Champaign, IL: Research Press.

LeBlanc, L. A., Carr, J. E., Crossett, S. E., Bennett, C. M., & Detweiler, D. D. (2005). Intensive outpatient behavioral treatment of primary urinary incontinence of children with autism. *Focus on Autism and Other Developmental Disabilities, 20,* 98–105.

Luiselli, J. K. (1996). A transfer of stimulus control procedure applicable to toilet training programs for children with developmental disabilities. *Child and Family Behavior Therapy, 18,* 29–34.

Kroeger, K. A., & Sorenson-Burnworth, R. (2009). Toileting training individuals with autism and other developmental disabilities: A critical review. *Research in Autism Spectrum Disorders, 3,* 607–618.

Wilder, D. A., Higbee, T. S., Williams, W. L., & Nachtwey, A. (1997). A simplified method of toilet training adults in residential settings. *Journal of Behavior Therapy & Experimental Psychiatry, 28,* 241–246.

OTHER RESOURCES

"Toilet Training for Everyone: It's Never Too Late" by Pat Mirenda, PhD, BCBA. This is an Autism Training Webcast available from Autism Community Training. The link is: http://www.actcommunity.net/webcast/2008/TTWB07WEB.html. There is a fee to access this training.

C H A P T E R   9

FEEDING

Jennifer D. Bass and Kimberly A. Kroeger

OVERVIEW: WHAT WE KNOW

Many individuals with autism spectrum disorders (ASDs) show unusual eating patterns, most commonly food selectivity and subsequent food refusal. In fact, aberrant eating patterns used to be considered part of the diagnostic criteria for autism. Individuals with food selectivity eat only a limited number of foods according to various characteristics such as type of food, texture, appearance, color, or brand, and refuse other foods. For example, an individual with food selectivity based on brand may eat chicken nuggets from a particular fast-food restaurant but may refuse to eat all other chicken nuggets.

Food selectivity is a common problem for many young children with and without special needs. Typically developing children who are described as "picky" eaters by their parents often "outgrow" their picky eating. Unfortunately, the selective eating patterns of children with ASD often do not change over time and may worsen as the individual ages, likely due to a number of factors. It has been estimated that children with ASD eat half as many different foods as typically developing children. Children with ASD often refuse foods from entire food groups, most commonly fruits and vegetables, and eat fewer foods from each of the food groups. In addition, they tend to prefer a greater number of foods from certain food groups.

Children with food selectivity often engage in challenging behaviors during mealtimes, especially when presented with non-preferred foods. These challenging behaviors may include minor disruptive behaviors such as crying, screaming, and tantrums or more serious behaviors including aggression or self-injury. Children with food selectivity may try to avoid the non-preferred foods by leaving the meal area, refusing to open their mouths when food is presented, swatting away or throwing the food, or knocking the food off the table. They may also gag or vomit at the sight of new foods or spit out bites if they taste them.

The long-term effects of food selectivity are numerous. From a nutritional standpoint, individuals with food selectivity may be at risk for nutritional deficiencies as a result of inadequate food intake. It is possible that more serious medical issues may develop, compromising an individual's overall health and development. The selective eating patterns of children pose various challenges for families, including the need for parents to cook separate meals so that their selective eater will at least eat *something*. Furthermore, families are often unable to go out to eat at a restaurant due to the fear that their child will not eat anything or will "cause a scene" in public if presented with a food he or she does not like. Selective eating may also lead to further social stigma for individuals with ASD who already present with multiple social deficits inherent to their diagnosis.

GETTING STARTED: PRINCIPLES AND APPLICATIONS

Individuals with ASD often have a need for sameness, leading to resistance toward new things. The restricted patterns of behavior, interests, and activities present in individuals with ASD have been speculated to extend to the food acceptance patterns in this population. It is possible that individuals with ASD present with "neophobia," a fear of new things, when it comes to trying new foods that are out of their restricted food repertoire.

Similar to the conditioning effects that take place with any other fear, fear of new foods likely leads to the individual avoiding any contact with new foods. For example, a child may avoid peas, a new food, by throwing them when they are presented on his plate. This scenario leads to an interaction between the child and his parents. One common result of the child's behavior is that his parents may remove the peas from his plate or resist putting them on his plate the next time the family is going to eat peas. In this scenario, negative reinforcement has occurred. The child rejects the new food and his parents respond by taking it away or not presenting it again, which in turn leads to a higher likelihood that the child will reject the novel food in the future. Whereas the child may initially avoid a novel food due to its "newness," the selective eating behavior appears to be maintained by operant conditioning in the form of negative reinforcement.

Much of the empirical literature addressing feeding problems has focused on children without ASD who have various medical conditions. While these interventions provide an invaluable framework, they may or may not generalize to treating children with ASD because the principles underlying feeding problems such as food selectivity in this population may be very different. Due to the principles underlying it, food selectivity in children with ASD has been found to be modifiable by manipulating environmental contingencies through the use of both antecedent and consequent procedures. Systematic intervention is necessary to appropriately address food selectivity in individuals with ASD by reducing the aversive qualities of new foods through graduated exposure and changing the contingencies during meals so that individuals can no longer avoid new foods.

GUIDELINES FOR IMPLEMENTATION

All individuals with ASD are different, so each approach to treating food selectivity must be tailored to the needs of the specific individual. Several interventions have been found to improve the selective eating patterns of children with ASD. Regardless of the specific intervention, most feeding interventions have many components in common, which will be discussed next.

ADDRESS MEDICAL CONCERNS

Many medical issues can have a direct impact on an individual's eating. These medical issues include constipation, diarrhea, food allergies, gastroesophageal reflux (GER), and dysphagia, as well as oral motor delays. Often these medical complications can be alleviated with medication, prescribed intervention, or surgery, which will then allow for the child to participate in appropriate feeding treatment. It is necessary to address medical concerns prior to beginning any intervention to work on feeding problems to ensure the safety of the individual. This may involve consultation with various pediatric specialists or a complete medical workup to ensure that the individual is cleared for feeding treatment. The medical assessment may include diagnostic procedures assessing oral motor functioning (e.g., sucking and chewing), swallowing, and digestion. When introducing new foods, as is the case when treating food selectivity, food intolerances and allergies must also be ruled out.

ASSESS CURRENT EATING PATTERNS
AND MEALTIME ROUTINES

Once the individual has been medically cleared for feeding intervention, it is necessary to assess various aspects of the individual's current eating patterns and mealtime routines. The extent of food selectivity must first be determined. The initial step often involves the completion of a diet record, commonly referred to as a *food diary*. A food diary is a record of all foods and drinks consumed during meals and snacks across a certain period of time, typically 3 days. Completion of a food diary allows identification of the volume of food eaten, as well as the number, types, textures, and brands of foods accepted prior to intervention. In addition to the assessment of foods accepted prior to intervention, it is also necessary to assess various aspects of the individual's mealtime routines. Some of the most important aspects to assess include the individual's meal and snack schedule, duration of meals, location of meals, presentation of foods, and materials used during meals. It is also important to be aware of the individual's behavior during meals, when both preferred and non-preferred foods are presented.

ASSESS PREFERENCES

An assessment of an individual's preferences should be conducted to identify items or activities that may function as positive reinforcement during the feeding intervention. Due to the individual's food selectivity, food items may or may not be identified as preferences. If food items do not seem like a viable option, it will be necessary to identify non-food items. For a child, such non-food items may include toys, videos, books, or activities that the child enjoys, as well as attention in the form of social praise from others. Many behavioral interventions involve providing a preferred item or activity when the target behavior, such as accepting new foods, has been demonstrated. The preferred items or activities are typically presented after each successful target behavior (e.g., after each accepted bite of new food) initially and are then presented on a more intermittent basis (e.g., after a designated number of accepted bites of new food) as the individual becomes more successful over time.

DEVELOP PROTOCOL AND IMPLEMENT INTERVENTION

Once the assessment of current eating patterns and mealtime routines has been completed and preferences have been identified, a protocol for a specific feeding intervention can be developed. First, it is important to address any of the mealtime routines that may impede the success of a feeding intervention. These factors may include such aspects as the schedule of meals and the structure of meals (e.g., duration of meals, location of meals, presentation of foods, and materials used during meals). For example, if a child snacks throughout the day, does not have structured mealtimes, and does not sit at the table when he eats, these aspects of the mealtime would be addressed prior to targeting food selectivity.

When developing a protocol to intervene with food selectivity, it is helpful to identify target behaviors that the child demonstrates when the food is presented. A *bolus* is the actual food bite presented to the child. A *refusal* occurs when a child does not accept the bolus. If the child allows the bolus into his mouth it is considered an *acceptance,* and if he subsequently swallows the bolus, it is justly termed *swallow.* If the child allows the bolus into his mouth but then spits the bite out, it is considered an *expulsion.* At any point in the feeding intervention, a child may *gag* where it appears that he is coughing and likely to vomit. The child may also engage in the aforementioned *challenging behaviors* during the session. Data collection is imperative to the sustained success of any given feeding intervention. Recording the target behaviors that occur in a feeding session provides information that guides future intervention. A sample datasheet for recording the target behaviors during a feeding session is presented at the end of this chapter (Worksheet 9.1).

It is important to set obtainable goals and to begin with short-term objectives that the individual is most likely to achieve when first intervening with food selectivity. Simply exposing the individual to novel foods does not necessarily lead him or her to accept new foods. Instead, only tasting new foods leads to higher acceptance. However, for a child with extreme food anxiety, simply exposing him to new foods and praising the tolerance of that food being present may be an appropriate place to begin.

Once the child tolerates the presence of the new food for longer than 15 seconds without challenging behaviors, targeting the actual consumption of new foods can begin. Begin food presentations where the new food is systematically presented to the child on a routine basis. Such feeding sessions should work with the child's natural appetite when the child is hungry and more likely to eat. Therefore, conduct feeding sessions at similar times of day, such as before meals. Ensure that the child has not eaten for at least 2 hours prior to a feeding session so that the child is more motivated to eat. Bring the child to the feeding area and have him sit appropriately. Present the novel food to the child and provide a simple verbal directive, such as "take a bite," when the child is calm and challenging behaviors are absent. If the child complies with the directive by accepting and swallowing, provide high, behavior-specific praise for the behavior and allow access to the child's assessed preferences.

If the child does not consume the food, respond with a neutral tone that another feeding session will occur at a later point in time (e.g., "We'll try again later"). Do not continue to verbally negotiate, plead, or engage otherwise around the refusal behavior to obtain a successful acceptance or bite. This only allows for the child to obtain continued attention for the undesired behavior of food refusal. Instead, remove the food and redirect the child to a neutral activity. Do not allow access to a highly preferred activity or foods as this can inadvertently reinforce the food refusal behavior. When removing the food, ensure that the child is calm and not currently engaging in any challenging behaviors. If the child engages in challenging behaviors and does not accept the new or previously accepted foods, it is best to withhold high-preference foods

Worksheet 9.1 Sample Datasheet

Child Name: _____	Date: _____	Session # _____
Feeder: _____	Start Time: _____	Stop Time: _____

Food	Bite Trial	Refusal	Accept	Swallow	Expel	Gag	Challenging Behavior	SR+
	1							
	2							
	3							
	4							
	5							
	6							
	7							
	8							
	9							
	10							
	11							
	12							
	13							
	14							
	15							
	16							
	17							
	18							
	19							
	20							

Food: Name of food presented to child during trial (e.g., noodle, carrot, turkey)

Refusal: Child does not accept the bolus into mouth (e.g., refuses to open mouth, turns head away, puts head down)

Accept: Child opens mouth and places bolus into mouth (self-feeder) or allows bolus into mouth (non–self-feeder) within 5 seconds of food presentation and verbal instruction to "Take a bite"

Swallow: Child swallows bolus to point of bolus no longer being visible

Expel: Child spits out the bolus, uses fingers to expel bolus, or removes bolus from mouth in some manner following acceptance of bolus into mouth

Gag: Child makes choking or retching sounds as if to vomit; or child tenses neck, opens mouth, or protrudes tongue from mouth without making such sounds

Challenging Behavior: Child engages in challenging behavior (e.g., cries, screams, tantrums, aggresses, engages in self-injurious behavior, swats away or throws food, knocks food off table, makes negative comments about food, or makes negative comments toward feeder)

SR+: Feeder provides child access to assessed preferences following designated target behavior between feeding sessions. This will help to prevent the reinforcement of food refusal behaviors that could occur when the child is allowed access to high-preference foods after refusing low-preference foods. Conduct up to three to five feeding sessions per day, but never less than one per day. Keep feeding sessions brief, ranging from 5 to 30 minutes.

Once objectives have been established and feeding sessions have been initiated, criteria to advance to the next step or move back to the previous step must be set. A common criterion used in feeding interventions is 80% or 90% success across three consecutive feeding sessions. In feeding interventions, this may involve increasing the criterion to the next level once the child is successful at any given level for three consecutive trials. For example, if you are targeting graduated exposure to the novel food and the child has touched the novel food three consecutive times with an absence of refusal behaviors, you would then require the child to taste the food before allowing access to his assessed preferences.

Continue to advance the child until he is accepting and swallowing the bolus presented. Begin with a small bolus size, such as a pea-sized bite, so that the child does not become over-whelmed with the amount of new food presented. Once the child is then eating the single bite presentation, increase the quantity of the novel food presented. Continue in this manner until the child is eating an age-appropriate portion of the new food, and then incorporate the new food into regular meals for the child. Continue to add new foods in this manner, gradually increasing the level of difficulty. Table 9.1 shows an example of a feeding protocol that may be used for graduated exposure to novel food.

When deciding upon initial target foods, begin with foods that are highly likely to be accepted based on similarities to the child's current food repertoire. For example, if a child accepts only one type of texture, target new foods initially within this accepted texture. If the child accepts only specific foods or specific food brands, begin with foods that are similar in taste, or even the same foods in a different brand. The closer the initial food targets are to the already accepted foods, the more likely the child is to be successful in adding new foods. This success initiates a behavioral momentum where the child associates trying new foods with positive outcomes and is more likely to try subsequent novel foods.

Continue with the intervention protocol until long-term goals are met. Common long-term goals in feeding interventions include increasing acceptance of a particular food or entire food group as well as increasing the overall variety or amount of food consumed. Long-term goals

Table 9.1 Example of Feeding Protocol for Graduated Exposure to Novel Food

Level	Behavior Criterion
1	Child tolerates presence of novel food
2	Child touches novel food with finger
3	Child touches novel food to lips
4	Child places or allows placement of novel food in mouth
5	Child swallows 1 bite of novel food
6	Child eats 2 bites of novel food
7	Child eats 3 bites of novel food
8	Child eats 4 bites of novel food
9	Child eats 5 bites of novel food
10	Child eats age-appropriate portion of novel food

should address acceptance of a minimum of five foods across the five food groups (i.e., fruits, vegetables, dairy, starch, and protein) for a nutritionally balanced diet. As much as possible, foods chosen as targets should match the family's diet in order to achieve the most socially meaningful outcomes. Remember, each individual's taste preferences are different. The child may need to taste the new food 10 to 15 times before it becomes a preference. If the child has not developed a preference for the new food after eating it for 2 weeks, it may be discontinued and a new food introduced.

ADAPTATIONS AND MODIFICATIONS

Although most of the research on feeding has focused on children, feeding interventions can be designed for individuals of any age with some adaptations and modifications. As mentioned earlier, the selective eating patterns of individuals with ASD often do not change over time and may even worsen as an individual ages. As a result, adults may require longer periods of intervention to change these well-ingrained eating patterns. One of the aspects that must be considered involves who is ultimately responsible for determining whether expanding the food repertoire of an individual is a worthy goal. When children are young, their diet and nutrition is ultimately their parents' responsibility. However, as an individual becomes an adult, the question arises as to who is responsible for ensuring that he or she has adequate nutrition and variety in the diet.

Another consideration involves the intervention setting. For children, interventions are often conducted first in a clinic setting and then generalized to their home, their school, and possibly to restaurants. For adults, the settings may include a clinic and then the individual's place of residence, vocational placement or workshop, and favorite restaurants.

Finally, practitioner training requirements and resources must be considered. Feeding interventions that use more sophisticated techniques require a higher level of training to be implemented with integrity. Similarly, more sophisticated interventions often require greater resources, including time and effort.

KEYS TO REMEMBER

1. Intervene as soon as possible once food selectivity behaviors are identified, as these behaviors often do not resolve themselves over time in individuals with ASD.
2. Address any medical concerns via appropriate evaluation prior to beginning any feeding intervention to ensure the safety of the individual.
3. Assess the individual's eating patterns and mealtime routines prior to intervention to determine the severity of the feeding problems.
4. Assess and subsequently select individual-specific preferences that can be used to reinforce appropriate feeding behaviors during intervention.
5. Tailor the feeding intervention to the needs of the specific individual, as all individuals with ASD are different.
6. Set appropriate and obtainable short-term objectives and long-term goals for intervention, eventually targeting a variety of foods across the five food groups that match the family's overall diet as much as possible.

7. Require the individual to taste new foods. This leads to higher acceptance than simply exposing the individual to novel foods.
8. Collect data by recording the target behaviors during feeding sessions to monitor the success of intervention over time.

SUGGESTED READINGS

Ahearn, W. H. (2001). Help! My son eats only macaroni and cheese: Dealing with feeding problems in children with autism. In C. Maurice, G. Green, & R. Foxx (Eds.), Making a Difference: Behavioral Intervention for Autism (pp. 83–96). Austin, TX: Pro-Ed.

Freeman, K. A., & Piazza, C. C. (1998). Combining stimulus fading, reinforcement, and extinction to treat food refusal. *Journal of Applied Behavior Analysis, 31,* 691–694.

Ledford, J. R., & Gast, D. L. (2006). Feeding problems in children with autism spectrum disorders: A review. *Focus on Autism and Other Developmental Disabilities, 21,* 153–166.

Luiselli, J. K. (2006). Pediatric feeding disorders. In J. K. Luiselli (Ed.), Antecedent Assessment and Intervention: Supporting Children and Adults with Developmental Disabilities in Community Settings (pp. 165–185). Baltimore, MD: Paul H. Brookes Publishing.

Williams, K. E., & Foxx, R. E. (2007). *Treating Eating Problems of Children with Autism Spectrum Disorders and Developmental Disabilities.* Austin, TX: Pro-Ed.

CHAPTER 10

SELF-CARE

Michele D. Wallace and Mitch J. Fryling

OVERVIEW: WHAT WE KNOW

Individuals with autism face a number of challenges in their day-to-day lives. Many of these challenges pertain to self-care activities, such as getting dressed, brushing their teeth, washing their hands, taking a shower, toileting, and similar activities. It goes without saying that self-care skills are essential components of independent living and have a significant impact on the lives of individuals with autism spectrum disorders (ASDs) as well as those who care for them. We know that individuals with deficits in self-care skills require increased assistance in activities of daily living, thereby reducing individual independence and the likelihood of accessing less intrusive environments. Ultimately, these deficits often have a comprehensive and prolonged impact on the quality of life for individuals with ASDs, affecting their educational, residential, family, social, and vocational aspects of life.

The development of self-care skills with individuals with ASDs frequently requires specific assessment and intervention efforts; such skills often do not develop "on their own." However, the acquisition of self-care skills can require a vast amount of persistence from teachers, therapists, and parents, and for this reason, well-intended caregivers may over-assist individuals with self-care tasks or "do it for them." In the short term, it is often easier for the caregiver to complete the task for the individual (it's quicker and involves less problem behavior), and thus it is not uncommon for caregivers to do so. Furthermore, caregivers may underestimate what the individual is capable of and, wanting to help, will immediately assist; indeed, assisting often seems like the most helpful thing to do. The outcome of this is that an individual may remain dependent on the help of others over the long term. A byproduct of this cycle is that both the individual with ASD and caregivers have reduced access to many reinforcers of daily living, decreasing the quality of life for both. Moreover, this cycle is likely to contribute to what is commonly called burnout in caregivers. As if these reasons weren't enough to underscore the importance of teaching self-care skills, human services practitioners are *ethically obligated* to design programs that promote independent behavior. Thus, teaching self-care skills is an essential area to consider when developing programs for individuals with ASDs.

Essential to teaching self-care skills to individuals with ASDs is (1) assessing their current skill level and (2) developing a systematic teaching plan to address identified deficits, all the while using direct measures to evaluate progress. Given the content of this book, the remainder of this chapter will focus on teaching self-care skills when their absence is due to a skill deficit rather than noncompliance. The reader is urged to review other chapters regarding how to conduct a skills assessment (Chapter 6) and a functional analysis (Chapter 3) and implement an intervention for noncompliance issues (Chapter 19), the latter two specifically when the self-care deficit is due to noncompliance.

GETTING STARTED: BASIC PRINCIPLES AND APPLICATIONS

Central to teaching self-care skills is the notion of behavioral chains. A behavior chain is a series of responses that are linked to a terminal reinforcer (e.g., taking out a piece of gum to chew it). Moreover, each response in the chain serves a dual function: both as a reinforcer for the previous response and as a signal for the next response. For example, pulling out a piece of gum from my pocket (one response in the behavior chain) serves as a reinforcer for reaching into my pocket (previous response) and signals that if I unwrap the gum (the next response) I will be able to place the gum in my mouth (terminal reinforcer). Importantly, most of the responses in behavioral chains are not naturally reinforcing, and become reinforcers only after they have been paired with existing reinforcers. Added to this, there is often a large delay between the initiation of a behavioral chain and the completion of a task for which the terminal reinforcer is obtained. For these reasons self-care behaviors are often extinguished or never learned in the first place. Thus, it is often the case that the acquisition of behavioral chains requires specific teaching techniques to establish components of the chain as conditioned reinforcers as well as for the behaviors to serve as signals for the next response in the chain.

For a self-care skill to become a functional behavioral chain, the skill must first be broken into teachable units, prompting must be incorporated to ensure that the responses of the chain will be conditioned to serve as reinforcers as well as signals for the next response, praise should be provided at each step (to serve as an additional conditioned reinforcer), and a terminal reinforcer must be identified and delivered for the completion of the self-care task (Table 10.1). It is important to make sure to insert both prompts and reinforcement at every step, and subsequently fade both as the individual demonstrates independence, so that stimulus control may be transferred to the natural environment.

The process described above has been demonstrated to be best practice when addressing self-care skill deficits. In fact, learning theorists have consistently demonstrated that skill deficits can be overcome by using this approach. Deficits in self-care skills are not likely to be overcome in the absence of a specifically programmed intervention, a data collection system, and ongoing assessment and evaluation.

While the behavioral literature has demonstrated that several teaching strategies may be effective with individuals with disabilities such as ASDs, including Basic Skills Training and Discrete Trial Training, self-care skills have generally been taught by breaking down the skill into its component steps, and either teaching all of these steps in sequence during each teaching session (Total Task Chaining [TTC]) or by mastering individual steps and moving on to the next step only after skill acquisition has been achieved (Forward Chaining [FC] or Backward Chaining [BC]).

Table 10.1 Example of Reinforcers and Signals in Behavioral Chains: Task Analysis of Hair Brushing

M0 Messy hair	Signal "Brush hair"	R1 Pick up brush	R2 Brush right side	R3 Brush left side	R4 Brush back	R5 Brush front	R6 Put brush away	Reward 10 min "Yo Gabba Gabba!"
	Signal	R1	SR (praise + access to R2)					
		Completion of R1 becomes signal 2 + prompt	R2	SR (praise + access to R3)				
			Completion of R2 becomes signal 3 + prompt	R3	SR (praise + access to R4)			
				Completion of R3 becomes signal 4 + prompt	R4	SR (praise + access to R5)		
					Completion of R4 becomes signal 5 + prompt	R5	SR (praise + access to R6)	
						Completion of R5 becomes signal 6 + prompt	R6	SR (praise + 10 min "Yo Gabba Gabba!")

Each response in the chain serves as a signal (combined with a prompt) for the next response, and as a reinforcer (combined with praise) for the previous response.

TTC involves going through each step of the chain in sequence, during each training trial, with the teacher providing prompts for steps that the individual does not complete independently. For example, the trainer might start the chain by stating "brush your teeth," and then proceed through each of the prespecified steps in the tooth brushing sequence. In FC and BC, individual steps in the chain are targeted repeatedly until they are mastered, and only then is the next step trained. In FC teaching starts with the first step, and once the first step is mastered the second step is trained; once the second step is mastered, the third step is trained; and so on. The reverse is so for BC. In BC the last step in the chain is targeted for training first, followed by the second-to-last step, and so on. Unique to BC is that training immediately involves the natural consequence of completing the task (e.g., having shoes tied). Therefore, the completion of the task is quickly conditioned as a reinforcer in BC, as the completion of the task is immediately paired with a preselected, highly preferred reinforcer. However, with both FC and BC the individual does not engage in the whole behavioral chain until all of the individual steps are mastered. Research has shown us that each of these chaining methods can be effective strategies to develop self-help skills. However, research has not yet shown us exactly when to use one strategy over another (some guidelines are presented below).

GUIDELINES FOR INTERVENTION

Again, it is important to first determine whether you are dealing with a shortcoming or noncompliance. After you have determined that the deficit in self-care is the result of a deficiency, the following steps should be implemented:

1. **Conduct a preference assessment.** Identify a number of highly preferred reinforcers to use as the terminal reinforcer during training. Be sure to condition social praise (e.g., "good job") as a reinforcer throughout training by pairing praise with the presentation of highly preferred reinforcers identified during the preference assessment.

2. **Develop a task analysis and data recording sheet.** One way to establish a task analysis is to observe the task and its component behaviors as someone is doing it and keep a running list of the steps it takes to complete. For example, if you were to observe someone brushing his teeth, you would notice the following steps: grab the toothbrush, turn on the water, run the toothbrush under the water, grab the toothpaste, open the toothpaste, squeeze the toothpaste onto the brush, and so on. A second way to develop a task analysis is to consult with an expert in the area, or someone who has achieved mastery in completing the task. This strategy might be particularly useful for very complex tasks, and less pertinent to our discussion of self-care. Another common approach is to develop a task analysis by performing the task yourself and writing down all the steps taken, possibly several times, to clearly specify the most important components of the task. In addition, some common, everyday task analyses are available on the Internet and can be obtained by conducting a search (e.g., searching "tooth brushing task analysis").

You might wonder how detailed you need to be when developing a task analysis. It is true that you could continue breaking component behaviors down into even smaller component behaviors, resulting in your task analysis getting exceedingly detailed. We have a couple of suggestions to help you with this situation. First, you need to break things down only until they are small enough behaviors that they may be easily taught. You should always consider the current skill level of the learner, realizing that some areas of the task analysis might need to be broken down into more steps than others. There are no hard-and-fast rules about how detailed a task analysis should be in the absence of considering the task and the individual characteristics of the learner.

Develop a datasheet specific to the self-care skill, making sure that the datasheet will render information that will be useful when evaluating progress (e.g., will allow you to make a graphical representation of behavior, identify level of performance, and also identify the level of prompting used). Your datasheet should include all of the steps in the task analysis, the date and time of the training session, the level of prompting needed to complete each step, and the terminal reinforcer used to reinforce the skill (see Worksheet 10.1 at the end of the chapter).

3. **Assess current skill level.** There are two general methods used to assess the individual's current skill level with respect to a particular self-care task. The first method is the single-opportunity method. In this method the individual is given the instruction to complete the task and continues through each step of the chain until he or she no longer completes the task independently. For example, an individual might grab the toothbrush (Step 1), turn the water on (Step 2), wet the toothbrush (Step 3), and grab the toothpaste (Step 4), but then fail to open the toothpaste in the absence of assistance. In this example, the individual would be given a + for Steps 1 through 4, and a – for the rest of the steps. Hence, the individual is given only a single opportunity to go through the task. Typically, this type of assessment would be conducted a few times, and only those steps that are completed independently for some prespecified amount of time (e.g., three probes) would be considered to be mastered.

A second method of assessing the individual's current skill level is the multiple-opportunity method. In this method the individual is again given the instruction to begin the task as in the single-opportunity method; however, when the individual does not complete a component of the task, the trainer completes it for him or her and the individual is permitted to continue on with the chain. Continuing with our tooth-brushing example, if the individual completed Steps 1 through 4 and then did not complete the next step, the trainer would complete this step for the individual and the individual would be permitted to continue on with the next step (Step 6, putting the toothpaste on the toothbrush). In this way, the individual is given multiple opportunities to complete the entire behavior chain. Again, the individual would be given a + for component skills that were completed independently, and a – for those that weren't. The goal of these assessments is not to teach but to determine the individual's current level of performance; thus, the trainer should not be teaching during these assessment probes. More specifically, if the individual does not engage in a particular component skill independently, the trainer should quickly complete the task/step for the individual rather than model or otherwise prompt the individual to complete the task/step.

The benefit of the single-opportunity method is that it is quick and is less likely to overestimate the individual's current skill level. However, it doesn't give a complete picture of the individual's abilities regarding all of the steps of the task. Alternatively, the multiple-opportunity method evaluates all of the component skills, providing a more complete picture of the individual's current level of performance, but may overestimate his or her current skill level (i.e., potential for teaching during assessment). In any event, both of these assessments will help you to determine the individual's current levels of performance as well as what chaining technique you should use.

4. **Select a teaching (chaining) technique.** While research has not yet shown us which teaching method works best in specific situations, it is logical to assume that TTC may be better suited

Worksheet 10.1 Tooth Brushing Task Analysis

Name: <u>Sam Doe</u>							
STEP Date/Time→	11/5 10 am						
1. Pick up toothbrush	+						
2. Turn on water	+						
3. Rinse toothbrush under water	M						
4. Grab toothpaste	M						
5. Open toothpaste	P						
6. Squeeze toothpaste and put on toothbrush	+						
7. Place toothbrush on outer side top-right teeth and brush up and down 5 sec (Praise)	P						
8. Place toothbrush on outer side bottom-right teeth and brush up and down 5 sec (Praise)	P						
9. Place toothbrush on outer side top-left teeth and brush up and down 5 sec (praise)	P						
10. Place toothbrush on outer bottom-left teeth and brush up and down 5 sec (praise)	P						
11. Place toothbrush on inner top-right teeth and brush up and down 5 sec (praise)	P						
12. Place toothbrush on inner bottom-right teeth and brush up and down 5 sec (praise)	P						
13. Place toothbrush on inner top-left teeth and brush up and down 5 sec (praise)	P						
14. Place toothbrush on inner bottom-left and brush up and down 5 sec (praise)	P						
15. Place toothbrush on outer side of front teeth and brush up and down 5 sec (praise)	P						
16. Place toothbrush on bottom of upper right teeth and brush back and forth 5 sec (praise)	P						
17. Place toothbrush on top of bottom right teeth and brush back and forth 5 sec (praise)	P						
18. Place toothbrush on bottom of upper left teeth and brush back and forth 5 sec (praise)	P						
19. Place toothbrush on top of bottom left teeth and brush back and forth 5 sec (praise)	P						
20. Rinse toothbrush (praise)	V						
21. Put toothbrush in holder (praise)	V						
22. Spit out toothpaste (praise)	+						
23. Grab cup (praise)	V						
24. Fill cup with water (praise)	M						

Worksheet 10.1 (Continued)

25. Take a sip and swish water in mouth (praise)	M						
26. Spit out water (praise)	+						
27. Put cup down (praise)	+						
28. Turn water off (praise)	V						
29. Pick up towel (praise)	V						
30. Dry mouth and hands with towel (praise)	M						

PROVIDE PREFERRED REINFORCER: _____

+ = independent, P = physical prompt, M = model prompt, V = verbal prompt

when the individual has an imitative repertoire, if the task is not very long or complex, or when the individual can already perform many of the responses in the chain and just needs to learn them in sequence. Alternatively, if the individual can complete a number of the skills in the chain in order, we might consider using FC. BC might be preferred when there are large skill deficits within the chain, and when components of the chain need to be more thoroughly conditioned as reinforcers. Again, by starting with the final step in the chain, the completion of the chain is immediately paired with highly preferred reinforcers, and thus is immediately conditioned as a reinforcer itself. As training progresses, completions of earlier steps are also conditioned as reinforcers and are linked to the completion of the chain throughout. Selection of a teaching technique should always be based on individualized assessment information, the specific characteristics of the task, and other unique contextual factors (e.g., staffing skill and ratio, amount of time to dedicate to training).

After you have chosen a specific teaching technique, begin to plan how that technique will be used to teach the self-care task you are targeting; in other words, conduct a task analysis of the training session (develop a step-by-step routine). Stick with the chosen method until the skill is mastered; it is ill advised to switch chaining methods (e.g., switch back and forth between TTC and BC) during acquisition.

5. Prompting. After deciding on which chaining method you will employ, decide what kind of prompts you will use to ensure the learner engages in the correct behavior. Decide how you will prompt the learner via response prompts (i.e., your behavior that will serve to evoke the desired response) and/or whether you will incorporate additional stimuli to serve as prompts. The most common response prompts used are verbal, gestural/modeling, and physical prompts (i.e., tell, show, do). It is common to use all three prompts when teaching new skills. After you decide what will serve as your verbal, gestural/model, and physical prompt, the next thing to decide is in which order you will present the prompts (i.e., from most intrusive to least intrusive [MTL]—physical to verbal, or from least intrusive to most intrusive [LTM]—verbal to physical). Again, there is no hard evidence for one method over the other; however, with MTL you can avoid errors, while with LTM you can avoid prompt dependency. Like choosing the training method, it is important to stick with the chosen prompting method and not to change in the middle of training.

Irrespective of the prompting hierarchy, it is important to understand how you will transfer stimulus control via fading from the start. During fading, a prompt is removed gradually across learning trials until it is no longer provided or needed. If MTL prompts are used, fading requires gradually fading the prompt (e.g., gradually using fewer and fewer physical prompts; instead of hand-over-hand guiding the learner to pick up the toothbrush, you place the learner's hand on the toothbrush and lightly prompt his hand around the toothbrush). With LTM prompts, the most common method of fading is to insert a time delay. For example, if I gave the prompt to pick up the toothbrush I would wait 5 seconds before moving on to the next prompt of modeling, picking up the toothbrush, to allow the learner the opportunity to respond.

With respect to adding stimuli to prompt the individual to engage in the self-care skill, the most common forms include the use of picture schedules and video modeling. In picture schedules, photos of the learner engaging in each step are taken and placed in the corresponding order. Then, when engaging in the task, the individual is prompted to see what the next step is by highlighting the corresponding picture. The hope is that the picture schedule will help the learner engage in all the responses of the behavioral chain in the correct order. Picture schedules are extremely useful when the learner can independently engage in each step, just not necessarily in the correct order. When combined with self-management techniques (see Chapter 14), picture schedules can result in increased autonomy in self-care.

With video modeling (Chapter 26), either the learner is videotaped while being prompted through the task or a model engaging in the task independently is obtained and the video is shown to the learner before he or she is asked to engage in the skill. For video modeling to be effective, it is important that the learner has demonstrated an imitative repertoire.

6. Deliver Reinforcement. It is important to initially reinforce each response as well as the completion of the task. For example, regardless of the level of prompting used to obtain performance of the step, you should praise the completion of each step and make sure the individual earns access to his or her preferred item identified in the preference assessment at the completion of the task (or step, depending on mastery criteria). As the learner makes progress you can gradually fade praise so that you are providing praise only for independent performance and then only for the completion of all the steps along with the terminal reinforcer.

7. Monitor progress. It is important to monitor individual progress along the way. You should frequently review performance to determine if the individual is making progress, what level of prompting should be employed, and whether reinforcers are still working. One way to evaluate the individual's progress is to graph the percentage of independence with the self-care chain (i.e., the percentage of steps completed independently). By monitoring progress it is also possible to identify challenges that would warrant adjustments to the training procedure.

8. Revise program/troubleshooting. If the individual is not making progress, revise your procedure. Do the steps need to be broken down into smaller components? Did you move on too fast (e.g., fading prompting too early, reducing reinforcement too soon)? Maybe mastery criteria should be more stringent. Perhaps the amount of prompts wasn't faded appropriately, and you erroneously thought a skill was mastered when it wasn't. Have parts of the chain been adequately conditioned as reinforcers? Maybe some steps in the chain need to be more thoroughly conditioned as reinforcers (i.e., they need to be paired with already existing reinforcers and not just praise). A good place to start is to re-assess the individual's current skill level. See where the skill breaks down and develop a more detailed, individualized plan to move on. You might need to go back a step, demonstrate mastery on the prerequisite skills, and then carefully move on. For example, if you are doing a BC program, go back to the last step that was mastered, and perhaps break down the next step into more steps, develop a more detailed prompting protocol, etc. Similarly, you might be stumped during a TTC program and find that the individual continues to need prompting on a certain step. In this situation you might develop a specific intervention to get over this hurdle, and then continue with training (e.g., include additional prompts and fade more carefully). Remember, acquisition plans almost always require more detail than we think they will, so don't give up on your intervention efforts just because there are some bumps along the way.

ADAPTATIONS AND MODIFICATIONS

There are now several assistive devices that may be used to facilitate the acquisition of independent self-care behavior. For example, an individual might benefit from a larger handle on the toothbrush or one where the bristles automatically spin. Another example might be to use Velcro shoes rather than buckled shoes.

If the task is particularly long, teach one half of the task and then the other half, and then link them together. A lengthy task may be less difficult when all of the behaviors in the sequence are already acquired. It may also be beneficial to re-determine if all of the steps are really necessary to complete the self-care skill. For example, is it really important that a learner clean under his nails during hand washing?

If the individual has verbal/listening skills, consider using rules to enhance teaching procedures. This may especially be useful if the learner is struggling with one specific step in the chain. For example, you could put a Post-it note on the mirror in the bathroom that says, "Don't forget to close the toothpaste cap." In addition, rules may guide some behavior such that it contacts naturally occurring consequences (e.g., "First heat food, then eat").

KEYS TO REMEMBER

1. The objective of the intervention is to have the individual *independently* engage in self-care routines.
2. Develop a functional task analysis of the desired skill and incorporate natural reinforcement. The less complex the task analysis, the better. Don't be afraid to break down the task into smaller components (especially if the individual isn't making progress).
3. Make sure components of the chain get established as reinforcers and signals.
4. Systematically fade prompts and reduce reinforcement.
5. Plan for generalization and maintenance (see Chapter 23).
6. Monitor the effects of the intervention by recording success and the prompting level necessary to complete individual steps. Don't be afraid to revise the protocol or back up and retrain steps as necessary.
7. Be patient. Be sure to set aside an adequate amount of time for training sessions.
8. Let the learner's behavior guide you.

SUGGESTED READINGS

Anderson, S. R., Jablonski, A. L., Thomeer, M. L., & Madaus Knapp, V. (2007). *Self-Help Skills for People with Autism: A Systematic Teaching Approach*. Bethesda, MD: Woodbine House, Inc.

MacDuff, G. S., Krantz, P. J., & McClannahan, L. E. (1993). Teaching children with autism to use phographgic activity schedules: Maintenance and generalization of complex response chains. *Journal of Applied Behavior Analysis, 26,* 89–97.

Matson, J. L., Taras, M. E., Sevin, J. A., Love, S. R., & Fridley, D. (1990). Teaching self-help skills to autistic and mentally retarded children. *Research in Developmental Disabilities, 11,* 361–378.

Rehfeldt, R. A., & Rosales, R. (2006). Self-help skills. In P. Sturmey & A. Fitzer (Eds.), *Autism Spectrum Disorders: Applied Behavior Analysis, Evidence, and Practice* (pp. 103–124). Austin, TX: Pro-Ed.

Stokes, J. V., Cameron, M. J., Dorsey, M. F., & Fleming, E. (2004). Task analysis, correspondence training, and general case instruction for teaching personal hygiene skills. *Behavioral Interventions, 19,* 121–135.

OTHER RESOURCES

http://www.connectability.ca/connectability/pages/lt_tipsheets/using_visuals_care.pdf

CHAPTER 11

AUGMENTATIVE AND ALTERNATIVE COMMUNICATION

Ralf W. Schlosser and Jeff Sigafoos

OVERVIEW: WHAT WE KNOW

Individuals with autism often have difficulties in the areas of speech, language, and communication. In fact, communication is one of the core deficits associated with autism spectrum disorders (ASDs). The difficulties experienced by some individuals with ASD in the area of speech and language are of a mild to moderate nature and can be successfully treated through the behavioral interventions described in Chapter 12, such as those aimed at improving speech or replacing echolalia and idiosyncratic speech. There are, however, a significant percentage of children and adults with autism who develop little or no appreciable functional speech. These individuals cannot rely on speech to successfully function in educational, social and leisure, and employment settings. For these individuals, augmentative and alternative communication (AAC) strategies have increasingly been used to either supplement or replace their natural speech. A variety of AAC modes and systems are available to draw from, including (a) manual signs and gestures, (b) non-electronic communication boards or books/folders, and (c) speech-generating devices.

Manual signs and gestures do not require any external aids and hence are always available for the individual to use—that is why they are called "unaided" approaches. Because communication boards and speech-generating devices are external to a user's body, they have to be made available to the individual, which is why they are referred to as "aided" approaches. Aided approaches are used with graphic symbols and/or traditional orthography (i.e., letters and words), depending on the user's literacy skills. Individuals with autism may access these aided approaches by pointing to a symbol on a board, pressing a symbol on a speech-generating device, or handing over (exchanging) a symbol to a communication partner.

AAC strategies are not a last resort employed only once it is evident that a child is unlikely to acquire functional speech. AAC may help some children meet their communication needs as they struggle with speech on their way to becoming functional speakers. Indeed, research has shown that AAC interventions applied to children with autism and little functional speech do not hinder speech, but often result in modest increases in natural speech production.

When the person shows some speech that is not functional, being able to rely on another (AAC) mode may allow some children and adults to experience communicative success, and perhaps temporarily reduce the pressure to speak. As an intervention, AAC is not, however, primarily a speech-facilitation set of methods—that is, AAC is primarily used to provide a person with a means of communication, not primarily as a means to facilitate speech development. At the same time, AAC does not require one to exclude the person from using and learning speech either; in fact, communication partners are encouraged to use natural speech in conjunction with other modes as they interact with children and adults. Also, people with ASD who use AAC will often receive auditory feedback from their communication partners when they select graphic symbols or when they operate a speech-generating device. This feedback may help the person to learn new communication skills.

The research base on AAC for individuals with ASD has grown considerably, but we are not yet at a point where research clearly supports the selection of one particular AAC method (or combination of methods) over another. In part, this uncertainty is due to very different skill sets present in individuals with ASD, and therefore one size does not fit all. Perhaps a more fruitful approach is to see whether research supports certain intervention principles that could be applied (and adapted as needed) to an individual and his or her current and future communication partners and environments.

GETTING STARTED: BASIC PRINCIPLES AND APPLICATIONS

Strategies for beginning communicators should build on the person's existing communicative skills. For example, many children with ASD have pre-symbolic means of expressing their wants and needs, as illustrated by a child taking his mother's hand and leading her to a particular toy on the shelf, essentially asking to play with this toy. Alternatively, a child may push away a toy after having played for some time, as if to say, "I'm finished with this." To meaningfully build on the existing skills, it is necessary to assess how the individual currently communicates. The practitioner may use an informal interview strategy with individuals who know the target person. One such form, for example, lists a number of communicative functions on the left (e.g., what if the child wants to be read a book?) and a range of communication modalities across the top (e.g., pulling other's hands). Another strategy is to use the same form and observe the child in a variety of settings. Upon completion of the interview and observations one will have a good sense of the child's current communication functions and modes. One of the earliest communicative functions that children with ASD will likely express is requesting preferred objects, albeit through pre-linguistic means, such as reaching or leading. Hence, building on this existing tendency to request, it will make sense to begin an AAC intervention by teaching new communication skills that will enable the person to make requests using AAC. The same rationale and approach applies to adults with ASD who have not acquired functional communication skills.

TEACHING REQUESTING

To teach requesting the following steps may be implemented:

1. **Select a new form.** Communication partners should understand the new form more readily compared to the pre-linguistic behavior currently in use. As well, the learner should be able to associate the form (e.g., graphic symbol) with the referent (e.g., preferred object).

2. **Define the new form.** For the practitioner to know what behavior is expected, the new form has to be defined. Using manual signs presumes that communication partners understand signs. If that is the case and manual signs are chosen, the practitioner has to know whether an approximation of the sign will suffice or whether the exact form has to be followed. If it is a graphic symbol, it has to be decided whether the individual will point to the symbol or whether the symbol will be exchanged. If the individual seems to understand that receiving an object is the result of pointing to a symbol, there would be no need to use an exchange-based strategy. On the other hand, an exchange-based approach is a more concrete way to introduce a learner to request preferred objects by handing over a picture or line drawing of the desired object. If pointing is chosen, defining the new form also entails a decision whether to use a non-electronic communication board or a speech-generating device that offers the learner activation feedback and auditory feedback upon activation (exchange-based approaches generally do not call for the use of speech output). Speech output may be beneficial if the learner enjoys the auditory feedback, if the auditory feedback helps the learner solidify the association of the symbol with the object, and/or if communication partners cannot read the label of the symbol or decipher the meaning of the symbol itself. If a speech-generating device is selected, the practitioner would go through a feature-matching process to identify the best possible match between the learner, his or her communication environments, and an AAC device.

3. **Ensure the learner is motivated to request.** Requesting is generally one of the more motivating functions for a learner. compared to, say, labeling. Accordingly, it is best to identify objects and activities that are preferred by the learner (see Chapter 4). Teaching may occur in natural environments when the learner indicates a desire to obtain the preferred object by reaching or leading—that is, by using an existing pre-linguistic communication form. This situation presents an opportunity to pre-empt the old form and model the new form, while making sure that only the new form gains the desired object. Because such opportunities may be infrequent, the practitioner may need to engineer these situations by using one or more motivational enhancing techniques— for example, (a) withholding the preferred objects, (b) delaying the giving of assistance (when assistance is requested through old forms), (c) withholding one or more preferred items, (d) interrupting an activity, or (e) providing incomplete reinforcement, such as by giving only one or a few pieces needed to complete a puzzle.

4. **Ensure the learner experiences success.** Especially in the beginning of the intervention, it is important that the child or adult gets what he or she asks for each time the new form is used. When the learner does not communicate the new form within a reasonable amount of time, prompting may be necessary, followed by prompt-fading, until the learner becomes more independent.

5. **Collect data**. It is critical for practitioners to collect data on the effectiveness of the instruction. Having a clear definition of the new form (see Step 1) will greatly assist in this effort. Sometimes more than one form has to be tested; here it is particularly important to gather data on the relative effectiveness of the interventions.

TEACHING REJECTING

Rejecting is another important early communicative function to teach. The learner probably already has some ways of rejecting, such as pushing away a toy. Some have argued that manual signs may be a more suitable form to use when teaching learners to communicate a "rejecting" response, as it allows for a more emotionally laden expression. In many ways the teaching of rejecting follows the same principles outlined for requesting. Key points to remember include the need for greater efficiency with the new form compared to the old form—that is, the new form must be more effective than the old form in producing desirable consequences for the learner. It is also important to ensure that once the new form occurs, the non-desired object is removed or the non-desired activity is discontinued. Once the person has learned to reject in the presence of a disliked or non-preferred item, the practitioner may focus on teaching discriminative rejecting, whereby the learner rejects only the disliked item and not a second item that is preferred.

BEYOND REQUESTING AND REJECTING: OTHER COMMUNICATIVE FUNCTIONS

While requesting and rejecting are good foundational functions that are motivating to children and adults with autism, there are obviously many other communicative functions that are needed to become a proficient communicator in daily interaction. Subsequent communicative functions include naming objects, commenting on aspects of the environment, initiating a greeting, and engaging in appropriate social conversations involving turn taking.

There are several research-based procedures for teaching naming, greeting, and conversational turn taking to learners with ASD. To teach naming, for example, one can follow these steps:

1. Collect a set of common objects (e.g., cup, crayon, box, glasses).
2. Hold up each item, one at a time, while asking the learner *What is this?*
3. Allow the learner 10 seconds to make a response.
4. When the learner responds correctly, by pointing to the correct symbol or by producing the correct manual sign, then give the learner positive feedback. Positive feedback might consist of praise (*Yes, that's right. Well done!*) and an unrelated preferred item (e.g., sip of juice or a raisin).
5. If the learner does not label the object correctly within 10 seconds, then the practitioner should help the learner make the correct response by giving a prompt. The prompt might be a verbal direction (e.g., *Point to the picture of the cup*) or a gesture (pointing at the correct symbol). If these two types of prompts do not work, then the practitioner would physically guide the learner to make the correct response. All correct responses, even if they had to be prompted, should be reinforced.

6. Over time, the practitioner should eliminate prompts by gradually giving less and less of the prompt. If the learner seems to become too dependent on prompts, then one may even need to start giving reinforcement only for correct responses that occur without prompting.
7. When the learner is correct for 7 to 10 times in a row, then the practitioner can start to add in new items for the learner to name.

ADAPTATIONS AND MODIFICATIONS

The above principles and strategies for teaching requesting, rejecting, and object naming apply to all individuals who need to learn to request, reject, and name through symbolic means. There are, however, some situations that warrant adaptations or modifications. Some learners may accept any object/activity in return for an emitted request as long as the object/activity is preferred. These learners have not yet developed a correspondence between "saying" (e.g., pointing to a specific graphic symbol) and "doing" (i.e., receiving the object that is represented by the specific symbol). In other words, these learners use the symbol to make a generalized request and have not discriminated between different symbols, which are meant to serve as requests for different objects.

Given that the instructional procedure described earlier includes only preferred objects/activities, such a scenario is not far-fetched. To check for this, the practitioner could intentionally provide an object that was not requested. If the learner accepts the object without protesting, he or she has not been taught the correspondence between each symbol and each object. To assist the learner in establishing correspondence, the practitioner can have him or her select an object from an array of objects rather than always providing the correct object. Correspondence checks are somewhat more difficult to implement when exchange-based approaches are involved. Because the exchange requires the partner to provide the correct object when the symbol is handed over, the practitioner has to implement separate correspondence checks outside the exchange.

Some learners may have difficulty generalizing any given symbol to exemplars other than the one used during teaching. For example, if a Tropicana™ carton was used during teaching for the symbol "orange juice," and during the next school cafeteria visit the carton is from Florida Natural™, some learners have difficulty applying the same symbol to this exemplar of orange juice. To minimize this problem, instruction should involve a range of exemplars so that the learner is exposed to the universe of orange juice cartons (and perhaps even bottles or cans) to which this symbol applies. After exposure to multiple variations, the learner is more likely to generalize to yet another variation.

As mentioned earlier, the use of a feature-matching process is imperative when selecting speech-generating devices. Data on the acquisition of a new communicative form (as described earlier) should further inform this feature-matching process. Some individuals will do equally well with each of several devices that are being considered in a trial, leaving the practitioner with a hard decision when it comes down to choosing one device over the other. Here, the preferences of the learner may help sway a decision in a particular direction. There are now several studies where children with ASD have displayed a preference for using one type of AAC system or device over another, even though the children learned to use both AAC options equally well. Hence, practitioners may want to provide access to each of several devices simultaneously and assess whether a learner selects a device more frequently than others.

KEYS TO REMEMBER

1. AAC approaches supplement or replace natural speech and/or handwriting.
2. AAC interventions do not hinder speech production and can often result in modest improvement in speech.
3. AAC intervention should not be viewed as a last resort method.
4. A thorough assessment of existing communication forms and functions can assist in intervention planning.
5. Teaching requesting and rejecting through symbolic means are good starting points when beginning AAC intervention.
6. There are empirically based principles for teaching requesting and rejecting.
7. The new forms that are introduced should be more efficient than the old ones and should meet the characteristics and preferences of not only the learner but also her communication partner and environments.
8. Correspondence checks are critical adaptations if it is unclear whether a child has associated a given symbol with its matching referent.

SUGGESTED READINGS

Blischak, D. M., & Ho, K. M. (2000). School-based augmentative and alternative communication evaluation reports. *Contemporary Issues in Communication Science and Disorders, 27,* 70–81.

Mirenda, P., & Iacono, T. (Eds.) (2009). *Autism Spectrum Disorders and AAC.* Baltimore, MD: Paul H. Brookes.

Schlosser, R. W., & Wendt, O. (2008). Augmentative and alternative communication interventions for children with autism. In J. K. Luiselli, D. C. Russo, W. P. Christian, & S. M. Wilczynski (Eds.), Effective Practices for Children with Autism: Educational and Behavior Support Interventions that Work (pp. 325–389). New York: Oxford University Press.

Sigafoos, J., Drasgow, E., & Schlosser, R. (2003). Strategies for beginning communicators. In R. W. Schlosser, The Efficacy of Augmentative and Alternative Communication: Toward Evidence-Based Practice (pp. 323–346). San Diego, CA: Academic Press.

Sigafoos, J., Green, V. A., Payne, D., Son, S.-H., O'Reilly, M., & Lancioni, G. E. (2009). A comparison of picture exchange and speech-generating devices: Acquisition, preference, and effects on social interaction. *Augmentative and Alternative Communication, 25,* 99–109.

OTHER RESOURCES

Schuler, A. L., Peck, C. A., Willard, C., & Thenner, K. (1989). Assessment of communicative means and functions through interview: Assessing the communicative capabilities of individuals with limited language. *Seminars in Speech and Language, 19,* 391–405.

Sigafoos, J., Arthur-Kelly, M., & Butterfield, N. (2006). *Enhancing Everyday Communication for Children with Disabilities.* Baltimore: Paul H. Brookes Publishing Co.

Sigafoos, J., Drasgow, E., Reichle, J., O'Reilly, M., Green, V. A., & Tait, K. (2004). Teaching communicative rejecting to children with severe disabilities. *American Journal of Speech-Language Pathology, 13,* 31–42.

CHAPTER 12

VERBAL LANGUAGE AND COMMUNICATION

Jeff Sigafoos, Ralf W. Schlosser, Mark F. O'Reilly,
and Giulio E. Lancioni

OVERVIEW: WHAT WE KNOW

One characteristic of people with autism spectrum disorder (ASD) is that they often have diffi-culties learning appropriate speech and language skills. In addition, they often learn inappropri-ate speech and language patterns. Examples of inappropriate speech and language patterns associated with ASD include parroting the speech of others (echolalia) and repeating words and phrases over and over (perseverative speech). Another common language problem is known as pronoun reversal. For example, the person might say "Do you want a drink?" or "Do you want to go outside?" when he really means that he wants a drink or that he wants to go outside. Individuals with ASD may also have problems in learning how to speak with appropriate pitch, loudness, intonation, stress, rate, and rhythm.

Children with more severe forms of ASD generally show much greater delays and impair-ment in their speech and language development than children with milder forms of ASD. For example, a child with autism and intellectual disability might not learn to speak until he is perhaps 4 or 5 years of age. Others may not learn to speak at all unless they receive explicit and intensive intervention to train or shape up their verbal language skills. Even with intensive inter-vention to train speech skills, a significant percentage of children with ASD will fail to learn any appreciable amount of speech and will therefore require augmentative or alternative communi-cation systems (see Chapter 11).

We know that unless these speech and language problems are addressed, the person with ASD will be at a severe disadvantage. It is not for no reason that communication is often regarded as the essence of human life. Specifically, they will be unable to express even their most basic wants and needs or enjoy the simple pleasure of conversing with friends and loved ones. In the absence of effective verbal language and communication skills, many children with ASD develop inappropriate ways of communicating, such as leading others by the hand or communicating through problem behavior, such as extreme tantrums, aggression, or even self-injurious behavior (e.g., head banging, face slapping). These inappropriate forms of communication often persist into adulthood and often become more severe and more difficult to treat as the child ages.

Without good verbal language and communication skills, the person with ASD may also experience difficulties with academic achievement, gaining and maintaining employment, and participating in the community. A further undesirable outcome from inappropriate communication is the possibility of overt rejection by peers and stigmatization by the general public.

DIAGNOSIS AND ASSESSMENT

Communication problems are a defining characteristic of ASD. The *Diagnostic and Statistical Manual* of the American Psychiatric Association (DSM-IV-TR, American Psychiatric Association, 2000), defines autistic disorder as involving "markedly abnormal or impaired development in . . . communication" (p. 70). Similarly, in making a diagnosis of pervasive developmental disorder not otherwise specified or "atypical autism," there must be impairment in "either verbal or nonverbal communication skills" (p. 84). People with Asperger's disorder, in contrast, generally show more subtle communication impairments, such as dominating conversations rather than showing appropriate conversational turn taking.

Because the communication problems associated with ASD can vary widely from one individual to the next, it is important to assess each individual to identify his or her particular communication strengths and limitations. Communication assessment is undertaken for four main purposes:

1. **Screening**—To determine if a person's language and communication problems are sufficiently delayed or impaired to warrant a more detailed and comprehensive assessment. Screening should occur in the early preschool years or even earlier to ensure identified children receive early intervention.
2. **Diagnosis**—To assist in making an accurate diagnosis if the child is suspected of having ASD. Accurate diagnosis is essential for developing appropriate intervention plans and receiving appropriate services.
3. **Selection of intervention goals**—To identify the most important priorities for intervention. Priority should be given to areas where the individual shows the greatest problems or deficits.
4. **Evaluation**—To assist in judging whether the intervention program is working. For this purpose, the same assessments should occur prior to, and at regular intervals during, the intervention.

Several standardized assessment instruments can be used to identify the verbal language and communication impairments of people with ASD. These include numerous screening and diagnostic tests, such as the Modified Checklist for Autism in Toddlers, the Gilliam Autism Rating Scale, and the Autism Diagnostic Observation Schedule. There are also several communication-specific tools that can provide useful assessment information, such as the (a) Inventory of Potential Communicative Acts, (b) Receptive-Expressive Emergent Language Scale, (c) Verbal Behavior Assessment Scale, and (d) Assessment of Basic Language and Learning Skills. It is important that these types of assessments are administered by competent clinicians and used only for their intended purposes.

In addition to standardized rating scales, behavioral assessments are often used to identify the precise communication behaviors or deficits that the person shows in different situations, such as when playing with siblings at home, interacting with peers at school, or attempting to participate in everyday community settings (e.g., buying an ice cream cone or asking for directions). Behavioral assessment involves watching the individual and recording what, if any, communication behaviors occur in relation to specific types of situations or opportunities. For example, how does the person respond when greeted by a familiar person? What behaviors, if any, does the person use to tell you that he wants or needs something? How does this person indicate that he does not like something? Does this person initiate conversations with others? If so, how? Direct behavioral observation can also be used to evaluate the effects of a communication intervention plan.

GETTING STARTED: PRINCIPLES AND APPLICATIONS

Learning theorists view verbal language and communication as a type of adaptive behavior. However, unlike other types of adaptive behaviors (e.g., dressing, playing with toys, or preparing a meal), verbal language and communication represent special types of adaptive behaviors because they require the presence of another person—that is, effective communication requires both a speaker and a listener. This means that effective communication intervention often requires teaching new behaviors or communicative interaction patterns to both the speaker and his or her communicative partners, such as parents, teachers, and peers.

Similar to other types of adaptive behaviors, verbal language and communication skills are also viewed as learned behaviors that occur because they are rewarded (or reinforced) by others. For example, children often learn to ask for help with difficult tasks because they have learned that this is a very good way of getting the help that they need. While children with ASD may also need help with difficult tasks, they may be unable to request help when needed unless they have learned good communication skills. Most children also learn to comment on aspects of the environment to engage others in a purely social interaction. For example, the child might say, "Look at the puppy," to which the parent may respond with acknowledgement and praise: "Yes, clever girl! That is a puppy." The function of this latter type of communicative commenting seems to be solely aimed at gaining a positive social response from the parent. Unfortunately, compared to their typically developing peers, individuals with ASD often seem less motivated to make such purely social comments even when they have the skills to do so. The communication problems of individuals with ASD can consequently be viewed as either a failure to learn appropriate communication skills (can't do) or lack of motivation to engage in communication (won't do). Whether related to lack of skills or lack of motivation, the resulting communication problems can rarely be addressed without carefully planned intervention.

GUIDELINES FOR INTERVENTION

One of the most effective strategies for developing verbal language in individuals with little or no spoken communication is to gradually develop the person's ability to imitate speech. This general strategy is known as speech imitation training. Speech imitation training makes use of three main behavioral techniques: (a) shaping, (b) differential reinforcement, and (c) discrimination training. *Shaping* refers to the process of rewarding or reinforcing successive approximations of the desired response—that is, gradually closer and closer approximations are rewarded. *Differential reinforcement* refers to the process of reinforcing some responses (e.g., desired ones) but not others (undesirable ones). *Discrimination training* refers to teaching the person to say different things in different conditions.

To illustrate the application of these three techniques, the interventionist should begin by giving the person a highly preferred reinforcer (e.g., praise, a highly preferred snack, or access to a preferred toy) for any type of vocalization. To do so effectively, one has to first find out what the person likes and dislikes. The aim of this initial step is to simply increase the frequency of speech-like vocalizations. Once the person is vocalizing at a high rate, reinforcement is differentiated—that is, reinforcement is given only for vocalizations that closely follow the interventionist's model. Specifically, the interventionist should instruct the person to say something (e.g., "Say 'mama'") and then provide reinforcement for any vocalization that the person makes within about 6 seconds of this instructional model. The aim of this step is to teach the person to vocalize in response to (or contingent upon) the interventionist's model. Once the person is showing such contingent vocalizations, the next step is to further differentiate reinforcement by withholding reinforcement until the person's contingent vocalizations sound more and more like the prior model—that is, the person is now reinforced for making contingent vocalizations, but only when those vocalizations sound more and more like the model (e.g., only for saying "ma," then "mama"). In this way, the person's speech-like vocalizations are gradually shaped into recognizable words. This shaping process should continue until the person consistently imitates a single word (e.g., "mama") within a few seconds of the interventionist modeling that word.

At this point, the interventionist should implement discrimination training. Discrimination training begins by introducing a second sound or word. Specifically, on about one third of the learning opportunities the interventionist says "mama," but on the other learning opportunities during a teaching session, the intervention should model a new word for the person to imitate, such as "ball" or "bottle" or some other relevant word. This second word should be about the same length as, but quite different in sound from, the first word to make it easier for the person to hear the difference between the two words. The aim of discrimination training is to teach the person to pay attention to (or discriminate) the interventionist's model and then imitate the word spoken by the interventionist.

Initially, when the second word is introduced, the person is most likely to simply repeat the first word that he or she learned. If this happens, the interventionist must withhold reinforcement, repeat the model, and give reinforcement only when the person imitates the new word with a sound that is close to the model. Learning this initial discrimination can often take hundreds of learning opportunities. However, once the person learns to discriminate two words, subsequent new words tend to be learned much more quickly. At some point, the person will often learn to imitate new words and phrases after only three to four trials. When this is observed, it is appropriate to conclude that the person has learned imitative speech. More importantly, the person can now be taught new words and phrases by modeling the correct words or phrases once or twice.

In summary, the following steps are used to teach imitative speech:

1. **Reinforce any vocalizations.** Begin imitation training by providing reinforcement for any speech-like vocalizations made by the person. Continue this step until the frequency of speech-like vocalizations has increased to a high rate (e.g., 5–10 times per minute).

2. **Reinforce contingent vocalizations.** Provide reinforcement only if the person's vocalizations occur closely after the interventionist's model. It is important that the person learns to vocalize in response to the interventionist's model.

3. **Reinforce contingent vocalizations that increasingly sound like the model.** Now ensure that reinforcement is provided only for contingent vocalizations that sound more and more like the word that was modeled by the interventionist.

4. **Introduce a second word.** After learning the first word or sound, the interventionist should introduce a second word or sound. The person is now reinforced for saying the first word when that is modeled and for saying the second word when that is modeled. Initially, the interventionist may have to accept approximations of the second word, but over time the interventionist should provide reinforcement only for contingent vocalizations that sound more and more like the second word.

5. **Continue to add new words and phrases.** Once the person has learned to imitate two words, new words and phrases can be modeled and reinforcement provided for correct imitation. When the person has learned to imitate several words, modeling can be used to teach the person to use speech for requesting wanted/needed items and actions and to name objects or actions. For example, if the person requires help with a task, the interventionist can model the correct phrase ("Say 'I want help'") and then provide help when the person has imitated the phrase. Similarly, to teach the person to name objects, the interventionist might hold up an object (e.g., a cup), ask "What is this?" and then model the correct response (i.e., "Say 'cup'"). The person will most likely imitate by saying "cup," and this correct response is then reinforced ("Yes, that's right. It's a cup"). The interventionist should then repeat this sequence, but delay giving the model for 5 to 10 seconds. Eventually, the person should learn to give the name of the object without requiring the model.

ADAPTATIONS AND MODIFICATIONS

This type of imitation training is appropriate when the person has either very little or no spoken language but can still make some speech-like sounds. Some individuals may fail to make progress in learning to imitate speech. In some cases, their failure may be due to the lack of motivation. In these cases, the interventionists should undertake a preference assessment to verify that the reinforcers being used in the intervention are actually highly preferred by the person. Initially, it may be necessary to use contrived reinforcers, such as food, drinks, and toys, to motivate the person to imitate. Over time, however, the goal would be to try to discontinue the need for such contrived reinforcement and make use of more natural consequences (e.g., praise, access to requested objects).

In some cases motivation is not the problem, but rather the person does not seem to make many speech-like vocalizations to begin with and so there is not much for the interventionist to reinforce during the first step of imitation training. In these cases, the interventionist could attempt to use a procedure known as stimulus–stimulus pairing. With this procedure, the interventionist first gains the person's attention and then repeats a simple speech-like sound (e.g., *ah, ah, ah*). At the same time that this sound is being repeated, a highly preferred reinforcer, such as a favorite snack food, is delivered to the person. The intention of this procedure is that it will eventually teach the person that vocalizations are reinforcing and thus the person's tendency to make vocalizations should increase. However, it may take anywhere from 300 to 400 such pairings before the person begins to spontaneously produce any speech-like sounds.

A third reason for lack of progress during speech imitation training is that the person might lack important readiness skills. Specifically, some individuals may first need to be taught to sit in a chair, refrain from tantrums, remain on-task, and attend to the interventionist, for example, by looking at the interventionist and watching his or her mouth when he or she models a word. In many cases, these readiness skills can be taught during the initial stages of imitation training. In other cases, however, it may prove necessary to develop these readiness skills before beginning imitation training. Even when such adaptations are made, some individuals will fail to make any appreciable progress in learning to imitate speech. As mentioned before, these individuals may be better suited to the use of augmentative or alternative communication systems (see Chapter 11).

A problem of many individuals with ASD is not that they cannot learn to imitate speech, but rather that they imitate too much. This problem, as mentioned before, is called echolalia. When a person simply repeats the speech of others, the goal of intervention is to replace this echolalia with more spontaneous and functional speech. Echolalia can be replaced by using a procedure known as transfer of stimulus control. For example, the interventionist holds up an object (e.g., an apple) and asks, "What is this?" A highly echolalic person is of course likely to respond to this by simply repeating the question. To replace this echolalic response, the therapist should prompt a correct response by immediately saying, "apple." To increase the chance that the person will imitate the final spoken word ("apple") and not the entire question, it may be helpful to prompt the person to remain silent before, during, and briefly after the instructional question (e.g., "What is this?") and also place greater stress on the word "apple." By doing so, the person is more likely to repeat only the response "apple," which the therapist can reinforce as a correct response to the question. Once this occurs, say, three to four times, the interventionist should try to gradually eliminate the need for the model and leave the response solely under the control of the object. This can be done by gradually delaying the model, giving less and less of the model (e.g., "app," "aa") or speaking with progressively less volume over successive opportunities. This so-called transfer of stimulus control process continues until the model is no longer required.

Finally, some variation of imitation training may be applicable to situations where the person presents with unusual or inappropriate speech and language patterns, such as (a) unusual voice tone and inflection, (b) pronoun reversals, (c) lack of variety in sentence structure, and (d) immature grammar (e.g., simple noun–verb formats). For example, the interventionist could model appropriate speech patterns and reinforce the person for correct imitation. In addition to imitation training, the development of more appropriate communication interaction patterns might also be achieved by using some of the social skills training techniques described in Chapter 13.

KEY POINTS TO REMEMBER

1. The objective of intervention is to improve the person's verbal language and communication skills.
2. A useful starting point for achieving this objective is to focus on teaching the person to imitate speech.
3. Begin intervention by reinforcing any speech-like vocalizations. Doing so will lead to an increase in the frequency of speech-like vocalizations, which can then be gradually shaped into words and phrases.
4. When the person consistently imitates a single word, add in a second word and continue to provide imitation training until the person imitates new words after only three

or four trials. At this point, you can conclude that the person has acquired imitative speech.

5. Monitor the effects of intervention by assessing progress using direct behavioral observation.

6. Modify the intervention if the person does not make adequate progress. Consider the need to increase motivation by using highly preferred reinforcers. If the person shows little tendency to vocalize, it may help to start with the stimulus–stimulus pairing procedure. Some individuals might also benefit from an initial intervention phase that aims to teach readiness skills.

7. To develop more advanced communication interaction patterns, a combination of an intervention to teach imitative speech and the use of more general social skills training may be helpful.

SUGGESTED READINGS

Fitzer, A., & Sturmey, P. (Eds.) (2009). *Language and Autism: Applied Behavior Analysis, Evidence, and Practice.* Austin, TX: Pro-Ed.

Goldstein, H. (2002). Communication intervention for children with autism: A review of treatment efficacy. *Journal of Autism and Developmental Disorders, 32,* 373–396.

Lovaas, O. I. (2003). *Teaching Individuals with Developmental Delays: Basic Intervention Techniques.* Austin, TX: Pro-Ed.

Matson, J. L. (Ed.) (2008). *Clinical Assessment and Intervention for Autism Spectrum Disorders.* New York: Elsevier.

Miguel, C. F., Carr, J. E., Michael, J. (2002). The effects of a stimulus-stimulus pairing procedure on the vocal behavior of children diagnosed with autism. *Analysis of Verbal Behavior, 18,* 3–13.

Sundberg, M. L., & Partington, J. W. (1998). *Teaching Language to Children with Autism or Other Developmental Disabilities.* Pleasant Hill, CA: Behavior Analyst, Inc.

ADDITIONAL RESOURCES

Partington, J. W., & Sundberg, M. L. (1998). *The Assessment of Basic Language and Learning Skills (the ABLLS): An Assessment, Curriculum Guide, and Skills Tracking System for Children with Autism and Other Developmental Disabilities: The ABLLS Protocol.* Pleasant Hill, CA: Behavior Analysts, Inc.

Striefel, S. (1998). *How to Teach Through Modeling and Imitation* (2nd ed.). Austin, TX: Pro-Ed.

Sigafoos, J., Arthur-Kelly, M., & Butterfield, N. (2006). *Enhancing Everyday Communication for Children with Disabilities.* Baltimore: Paul H. Brookes Publishing Co.

C H A P T E R 1 3

INTERACTIVE SOCIAL SKILLS

Mark F. O'Reilly, Amanda Little, Terry Falcomata, Christina Fragale,
Vanessa Green, Jeff Sigafoos, Giulio E. Lancioni,
Chaturi Edrisinha, and Hayoung Choi

OVERVIEW: WHAT WE KNOW

Poor social skills are probably THE defining characteristic of the autism spectrum disorders (ASDs). For many persons with ASD both cognitive and language abilities may not be adversely affected, leaving social skills the predominant difficulty. This is particularly true for individuals with high-functioning autism (HFA) and Asperger's syndrome (AS). In Chapters 11 and 12 interventions to treat verbal language and communication were discussed. Indeed, it can be difficult to differentiate what we mean by communication skills versus social skills for individuals with ASD. Communication in its most rudimentary form involves at the very least an initiation or response with one or more partners. Hence, there is a social element inherent in all forms of communication. In this chapter we will therefore focus on social skills interventions with individuals with ASD who have relatively sophisticated communication and verbal language skills (i.e., individuals with HFA and AS). The content of this chapter should therefore complement and not overlap with that of Chapters 11 and 12.

We must first begin by defining what we mean by the term *social skills*. Social skills are all those behaviors, both verbal and nonverbal, that are necessary for successful social exchange and interpersonal communication. Social skills can sometimes mean very specific behaviors such as greetings ("How are you today?") or responding to initiations ("Yes, I would like some of the pie. Thank you"). Social skills can also involve more complicated cognitive and behavioral phenomena such as accurately interpreting a social context, behaving according to contextually and culturally appropriate mores, and evaluating one's own behavior in the light of the responses of others.

The primary social skills deficits exhibited by individuals with ASDs are described in the *Diagnostic and Statistical Manual of Mental Disorders* (DSM-IV-TR) and include difficulties in expressing and interpreting the nonverbal body language of others, including facial expression, eye gaze, and body postures. Individuals with ASD also exhibit difficulties developing peer relationships. They also have difficulty interpreting and demonstrating emotional and social empathy.

Such social skills deficits can have a negative impact on the overall development of a child, including his or her academic success, social networks, and psychological well-being. For individuals with HFA or AS these social difficulties may be particularly acute. Students with HFA or AS are predominantly included in regular classrooms, where they may experience ridicule, rejection, and bullying from peers. They typically fail to establish friendships in school. Most are motivated to make friends and are painfully aware of their social difficulties. These difficulties do not get better with adulthood. Many of these adults are unemployed, have little positive social support, and suffer from resultant mental health issues such as depression. There is a need for comprehensive social interventions for this population. Such social interventions need to begin at an early age, should be comprehensive, and should persist into adolescence and adulthood if needed.

GETTING STARTED: PRINCIPLES AND APPLICATIONS

Social skills deficits of the ASD population encompass both observable behaviors (e.g., poor eye contact, failure to initiate or terminate interactions, invasion of personal space) and cognitive skills (e.g., difficulties in decoding a social context or evaluating the effects of a social interaction). This constellation of social difficulties probably has its origins in some combination of biological factors associated with ASD coupled with a learning history where current social patterns have been strengthened through reinforcement contingencies.

There are a variety of intervention strategies designed to teach social skills that are based on the principles of operant learning or cognitive behavior therapy. For example, operant learning strategies might be used to prompt appropriate social skills and then provide positive reinforcement to strengthen these new responses. Cognitive behavior therapies can be used to teach people new ways of interpreting social contexts and adjusting their social behaviors accordingly. Many comprehensive social skills interventions include combinations of operant learning strategies and cognitive behavior therapies.

Social skills interventions for persons with HFA or AS should address both observable social skills and how the person understands his or her own social behavior and the social behaviors of others. Persons with HFA or AS need to have extensive opportunities to practice these skills and receive accurate and constructive feedback on their performance.

GUIDELINES FOR INTERVENTION

Comprehensive intervention involves an initial assessment of social deficits, selection of appropriate intervention strategies, and ongoing monitoring of changes in social skills. We will describe a select number of interventions that have some level of empirical support in teaching social skills to this population. This set of intervention strategies is by no means exhaustive. It is important for clinicians to be aware of the selection of intervention strategies available and to match the interventions with the individual, the skills to be taught, and the ultimate context in which the skills need to be performed. Ultimately an intervention will be judged to be successful if and only if it ameliorates social skills deficits.

ASSESSMENT OF SOCIAL DEFICITS AND SELECTION OF SOCIAL SKILLS FOR INTERVENTION

Getting a clear picture of the person's social deficits is an essential first step. This precedes and in a sense determines the types of social skills interventions to be selected. The social deficits exhibited by persons with HFA or AS are usually complex and involve verbal, nonverbal, and cognitive difficulties. These social patterns may manifest themselves in different ways across different social contexts. For example, a child may experience difficulties in attempts to enter peer social groups during break time at school (e.g., failing to initiate any interactions with peers or responding to initiations inappropriately). He may also have difficulty accepting feedback from teachers, especially when they try to redirect him from his favorite topic of conversation (e.g., dinosaurs) to the current lesson. This same child may also blurt out hurtful comments about strangers (e.g., "I've seen fat, but I've never seen that!") in public gatherings.

Before any intervention is attempted it is critical to get a comprehensive picture of the person's social difficulties across all relevant contexts. An informal assessment process can be used to gather this information. Informal assessment typically involves observation of the person in real-world social contexts. Observations should be conducted in those contexts where social skills are problematic. Observations can be conduced by parents, teachers, and therapists. In addition, parents, teachers, and the person with HFA or AS can be interviewed to identify social skills difficulties. Care should be taken to identify social difficulties across all relevant social contexts. We recommend that social behavior in community, school or work, and home be explored. A list of social difficulties in each of these contexts can then be compiled and prioritized. In some cases it may not be possible to intervene in all social difficulties, so intervention should initially address those that are producing the greatest barriers to social inclusion.

Once social skill difficulties have been prioritized, they need to be described using objective and clear language. This allows for ongoing measurement of changes in social behavior when the intervention is implemented. An intervention can be deemed useful only if it makes positive changes in the person's social skills in real-world settings. Think about what social behaviors you want to see the person use in that specific context. For example, the child should initiate a conversation on an appropriate topic when interacting with a peer in the playground (e.g., "Want to play on the swings with me?"). The child should typically maintain at least 1 meter of distance when interacting with a peer (i.e., he tends to be too much "in their face" when interacting). The child should make eye contact (i.e., look at the faces of the other children) when interacting. These clear descriptions of social skills become the skills that the therapist, mother, or teacher will teach using the social skills interventions. And again, these are the social skills that you will monitor for change as the intervention is implemented.

INTERVENTION STRATEGIES

One or two meetings per week should be scheduled with the therapist or teacher to learn social skills. These can be individualized or small group sessions. Each session should last 30 minutes to 1 hour. Intervention strategies that could be used in these sessions include discussion/reflection, video models, social problem solving, and goal setting. Strategies such as priming can be used in natural settings to help promote generalization of the skills taught during social skills training sessions.

1. Discussion and reflection. Sessions can begin with a brief discussion of the importance of social skills. This discussion can be led by the therapist or teacher. The discussion should focus on the social skills that are being targeted, why they are important, and the positive outcomes that can occur if the student performs them properly (e.g., get to play with peers, make friends). Students should then be encouraged to discuss some of their successes and failures with these social skills since the previous session (we suggest that each student describe a success story and a situation that might have been handled better). Of course this is a general rule of thumb–some students may be shy and not want to discuss failure. This discussion phase helps set the stage for the teaching activities to follow.

2. Video models. A series of video vignettes demonstrating positive plus negative examples of the targeted social skills can be developed prior to training. Each video vignette can be very brief (e.g., 30 seconds). The vignettes typically feature individuals who are unknown to the student. The therapist begins by drawing the student's attention to the video. Following the vignette the therapist asks a series of questions that guides the student to determine if the vignette represented a positive or negative example of the targeted social skill. Approximately three positive vignettes and one negative one should be used during a session.

3. Social problem solving. Students then get a chance to practice social skills and receive feedback on their performance. In addition to practicing observable social behaviors, students should have an opportunity to practice cognitive strategies that are designed to teach them to interpret the social context, to decide how to behave, and to evaluate their behavior in terms of the social reactions of others. This type of intervention can tackle some of the fundamental social difficulties (e.g., poor self-awareness, lack of empathy) that typify HFA and AS.

The therapist begins by describing a target social situation (usually a situation that has been shown in one of the video vignettes). Next the therapist models a series of questions and answers that help to guide social behavior in this context. The therapist then models the appropriate overt social behavior. Finally, the therapist models a series of questions and answers that are designed to provide feedback on social performance.

In the next phase, the student is asked to role-play the social skills with the therapist. For example, the therapist may play the part of a peer and the student must verbalize the questions and answers used to guide his social response, perform the social behavior, and then evaluate his own behavior and the reaction of the therapist. The therapist prompts the student to use the appropriate responses if an error is observed and praises correct performance.

Using this social problem-solving process, the student is first taught to discriminate the salient aspects of the current social context by asking, "What's happening here?" The student is then guided to describe the social context. Next, the student must decide how to behave in this social context: "What should I do?" The student is prompted to generate a series of alternative avenues of social action and then to choose the most appropriate behavior. Now the student actually performs the social skill (e.g., greeting, responding, initiating) and the therapist responds. Finally, the student evaluates the social interaction by asking, "What happened when I [description of how the student behaved]?" The student describes the responses of the therapist and evaluates whether these responses were positive or negative. Finally, the student gives an overall evaluation of whether the social interaction was successful.

We suggest that students have multiple opportunities to practice these social problem-solving skills across several targeted social skills during each session. Problem-solving strategies can be adapted based on the student's abilities and learning style. For example, students can be taught to discriminate the salient social cues initially during sessions. Once they have mastered this skill, then decision, performance, and evaluation skills can gradually be introduced. Students can also use written or picture cues to help guide them through the problem-solving skills.

4. Goal setting. At the end of each session the therapist and student review the skills practiced during that session. The importance of using appropriate social skills is reiterated (e.g., to make friends). The therapist and student then discuss upcoming natural social contexts where the opportunity to perform the targeted skills will occur. The student confirms that he will use his skills in these upcoming activities and will report back to the therapist the next session. Some students may find it helpful to use a diary to record their successes and challenges between sessions.

5. Priming. This strategy helps to bridge the gap between intervention sessions and performance of the social skills in real-world situations. In its simplest form, priming involves cueing the person to perform the social skills immediately prior to a social context where the skills will most likely be needed. For example, as the student is leaving class to go to the schoolyard on break, the teacher might discreetly pull her aside and mention, "Remember how we practiced initiating and responding to your peers during break? Now try to use those skills."

We have a couple of final points about assessment and intervention with social skills. There needs to be continuous monitoring of social skills in real-world settings. Assessment of social skills is an ongoing and not just a formative process. Make a point to assess the targeted social skills on a weekly basis. The therapist or teacher should try to observe interactions in naturalistic settings. It is very important to recognize that the social skills targeted may rapidly change in priority, again emphasizing the need for continuous assessment. For example, we once taught a middle-school student to initiate and respond to peers during leisure activities at school. He quickly made progress in these skills and one day received a phone number from one of his peers. He proceeded to call his peer 19 times the following day, beginning at 6 a.m. As certain social skills develop, other and perhaps unforeseen social skills may need to be addressed. Also, if social behavior is not improving, then intervention strategies may need to be re-evaluated. Last but not least, it is important to be cognizant that social skills can differ across cultural groups. Certain social behaviors, such as making eye contact or being assertive, while valued in Anglo-American culture, may be seen as aggressive or offensive in other cultures. It is very important for therapists and teachers to be aware of their own cultural context and to seek to understand the cultural context of others and adapt interventions and social skills goals accordingly.

ADAPTATIONS AND MODIFICATIONS

In a sense the methods for adapting and modifying the social skills interventions described above are inherent in the protocols themselves. Social skills interventions should target current social deficits, and these deficits are identified and operationalized through informal assessment. The social skills targeted should be immediately relevant for the person and should promote social inclusion.

Intervention strategies should also be adapted to the person. Individualized learning styles can be supported through using written and/or picture prompts to help guide the person through the social problem-solving process. Discrete components of the social problem-solving process (discriminate salient social cues) can be taught until the person reaches mastery, at which point the next component can be introduced (decide what behavior to perform). Additional intervention strategies can be incorporated to promote generalization, such as teaching in settings where the social skills are to be performed or involving peers in training.

KEYS TO REMEMBER

1. Interventions designed for individuals with HFA or AS focus predominantly on social skills instruction.
2. Social skills consist of observable social behaviors and cognitive rules of social engagement. Both observable social behaviors and cognitive rules should be targeted as part of the intervention.
3. Begin with a comprehensive informal assessment of the person's social difficulties across all relevant environments, including home, school, work, and community.
4. Then identify and prioritize key social skills for instruction. The social skills targeted for intervention should maximize the person's social inclusion in regular life settings. Define these social skills in terms of specific observable behaviors.
5. Measure the person's performance of the targeted social skills in naturalistic settings on an ongoing basis (we suggest once per week). Use these measures to make decisions about the effectiveness of the intervention and whether targeted social skills need to be changed. Also, if social skills are not changing in the desired fashion, then re-examine the targeted social skills and interventions being used.
6. Be aware of cultural and linguistic diversity when selecting social skills and designing intervention programs.
7. Intervention sessions should be held regularly (once or twice per week). They can be conducted with an individual or in small groups.
8. Interventions should provide the opportunity to practice observable social behaviors plus the rules of social engagement. Social problem-solving interventions teach the person to interpret social situations, make decisions about the most appropriate social behaviors, perform those behaviors, and evaluate the consequences of his or her behavior. These skills are practiced through modeling, role playing, and feedback. Priming techniques can also be used to enhance generalization of the social skills to naturalistic settings.
9. Interventions may need to be implemented for extended periods. Many individuals with HFA or AS will need ongoing social skills interventions.

SUGGESTED READINGS

Chan, J., & O'Reilly, M. F. (2008). Using Social Stories™ plus modelling to teach social skills to students with autism in regular classrooms. *Journal of Applied Behavior Analysis, 41,* 405–409.

Matson, J. L., Matson, M. L., & Rivet, T. T. (2007). Social skills treatments for children with autism spectrum disorders: an overview. *Behavior Modification, 31,* 682–707.

O'Reilly, M. F., & Glynn, D. (1995). Using a process social skills training approach with adolescents with mild intellectual disabilities in a high school setting. *Education and Training in Mental Retardation and Developmental Disabilities, 30,* 187–198.

Rao, P. A., Beidel, D. C., & Murray, M. J. (2008). Social skills interventions for children with Asperger's syndrome or high-functioning autism: a review and recommendations. *Journal of Autism and Developmental Disorders,* 38, 353–361.

White, S. W., Koenig, K., & Scahill, L. (2007). Social skills development in children with autism spectrum disorders: a review of the intervention research. *Journal of Autism and Developmental Disorders,* 37, 1858–1168.

OTHER RESOURCES

Baron-Cohen, S. (1995). *Mindblindness: An Essay on Autism and Theory of Mind.* Cambridge, MA: MIT Press.

Klin, A., Volkmar, K., & Sparrow, S. (eds.). (2000). *Asperger Syndrome.* New York: Guilford Press.

Myles, B. S., Trautman, M., & Schelvan, R. (2004). *The Hidden Curriculum: Practical Solutions for Understanding Unstated Rules in Social Situations.* Shawnee Mission, KS: Autism Asperger Publishing Company.

Winner, M. G. (2007). *Thinking About You Thinking About Me* (2nd ed.). San Jose, CA: Michelle G. Winner, Think Social Publishing, Inc. www.socialthinking.com

CHAPTER 14

SELF-MANAGEMENT

Mark R. Dixon and Autumn N. McKeel

OVERVIEW: WHAT WE KNOW

The term "self-management" may initially seem to suggest autonomy from the environment because the word "self" places the potential manipulation of antecedents and consequences within the person and not under external control. As a result, self-management strategies within the behavioral community have been unfortunately limited. However, there are some good empirical demonstrations of self-management altering problematic behaviors of people with autism and also allowing new positive skills to be acquired. Caregivers should consider putting a self-management program into place whenever possible. Doing so will promote additional independence on the part of the learner, decrease time demands on the caregiver, and eventually lead to greater inclusion in the natural environment by the learner.

Self-management is a system of implementation. It is not a basic concept or principle of science. It is not a philosophy or a personality characteristic. Typical behavioral management approaches require the caregiver to arrange learning opportunities, prompt and encourage positive (or reduction of negative) behaviors, and deliver appropriate consequences for task completion. When self-management is implemented, these caregiver responsibilities are transferred to the learner—that is, the learner now seeks out the conditions under which a behavior is to occur, responds within the current repertoire, and then self-reinforces appropriate behavior. The role of the caregiver is altered from managing contingencies to supporting successful implementation of the self-management system. Over time, both caregiver supervision and self-management programs can be faded so that naturalistic contingencies sustain the behavior of interest.

GETTING STARTED: PRINCIPLES AND APPLICATIONS

Behavioral researchers and theorists have considered self-management a skill that can be taught by following several basic learning principles. The first principle is stimulus control: the learner must successfully identify the environmental conditions under which the targeted response is to occur. In fact, the first step in training a learner to self-manage is his or her detecting the antecedent conditions that signal the behavior of interest.

The second basic principle is operant conditioning, by which planned consequences strengthen or weaken the probability of a response in the future. Reinforcing consequences will strengthen and punishing consequences will weaken a self-managed response. Most self-management applications are described in the literature as reinforcement procedures. However, self-managed punishment procedures—for example, skipping desert or donating money to a non-preferred political party—can be used to reduce undesirable behavior.

The third basic principle is stimulus generalization. The typical self-management program is often considered a temporary step toward more naturalistic control by environmental contingencies. As a result, it is hoped and expected that a history with self-management in one context will produce successful behavior change in non-trained/self-managed contexts or untrained behaviors. For example, a child who learns to control aggression in school using self-management checklists may not need such contrived materials at home. Or, after self-managing (reducing) aggression, an adult is able to control another behavior without self-management training.

A fourth behavioral principle is maintenance, and similar to generalization this principle deals with expansion beyond the current, and maybe somewhat artificial, self-management activity. The difference between generalization and maintenance is that in the latter, a person continues to demonstrate a trained behavior without self-management. Take, for example, a child who receives coins in school for completing group activities. He puts the earned coins in a can and later exchanges the coins for time on a computer (a preferred free-time event). Maintenance is evident when the child no longer needs the coins, can, or computer but instead engages in the group activity for the natural reinforcement that participation brings in the classroom community.

While these four principles are at the core of self-management procedures, a variety of other terms and concepts may come into play, given the unique conditions under which a self-management program is constructed. They may include, but are not limited to, observational learning, stimulus equivalence, shaping, fading, the matching law, responding under specific schedules of reinforcement, and extinction.

GUIDELINES FOR IMPLEMENTATION

STEP 1: IDENTIFY AN OBJECTIVE MEASURE OF THE TARGETED BEHAVIOR

It is important to measure the frequency with which a target behavior occurs. For example, a child may have difficulty staying on task. An objective measure could be recorded as the number of minutes the child performs behavior such as doing homework. For measurement purposes, the child could self-monitor his on-task behavior by checking a box on a recording sheet. The definition of the behavior should be reliable across observers, especially between the learner, who will be self-managing this behavior, and the caregiver, who also monitors the child's responding.

STEP 2: SELECT THE APPROPRIATE CONDITIONS UNDER WHICH THE BEHAVIOR SHOULD OCCUR

Select the specific location, time of day, and stimulus materials under which the behavior should be displayed. For example, you would not address an essentially school-dominant behavior when the child is at home. To better discover the appropriate conditions under which the behavior occurs, you should directly observe the learner. Also, teachers and family members should be interviewed to collect relevant information from each setting in which the child spends time each day. A substantial part of self-management training is teaching the leaner to discriminate between and among antecedent conditions. By doing so, he or she will be able to identify the likelihood and the conditions of the behavior.

STEP 3: IDENTIFY POTENTIAL REINFORCERS FOR THE EMISSION OF THE TARGET BEHAVIOR

Prior to the intervention, it is critical to identify preferred items and activities that can be used as reinforcers during self-management training. Empirically validated stimulus preference assessments (see Chapter 4) should be used whenever possible, especially for learners who have limited verbal language. For example, the reinforcer could be a favorite food, access to a favorite toy, or the opportunity to take a break for a few minutes. Since self-monitoring is a self-reinforced procedure, the reinforcer should be readily available for the learner to access. Also, the self-monitoring procedure allows you to ascertain whether the checklist is self-reinforcing without completion of the task. While the checklist is available, it can lend itself easily to reliability checks between the learner and the instructor.

STEP 4: DESCRIBE THE SELF-MONITORING CONTINGENCIES TO THE LEARNER

This step may require the use of modeling and performance feedback to teach self-monitoring, such as checking a box when the learner has been on task every 5 minutes. It may be best for the instructor to demonstrate on-task behavior and then check the respective box on the self-monitoring sheet in front of the learner. As this behavior is modeled, immediate feedback should be given to the learner.

STEP 5: ALLOW THE LEARNER TO ATTEMPT THE SELF-MONITORING PROCEDURE INDEPENDENTLY

While the learner attempts the procedure, it is appropriate to give him or her immediate feedback and to verbally praise appropriate self-monitoring. The key here is to ensure that the learner follows and does not deviate from the self-management program in order to receive positive reinforcement.

STEP 6: EVALUATE CORRESPONDENCE BETWEEN SELF-REPORTED PERFORMANCE AND INDEPENDENT CHECKS OF PERFORMANCE

Compare the self-monitoring checklists between the instructor and the learner to determine whether he or she records behavior accurately. Clearly, self-management is likely to be effective when the learner's self-report checks match the instructor's data. If the checks are not accurate, it may be necessary to review the training procedure again by modeling and giving feedback. Also, the reinforcer selected by the child or adult must be strong enough to make a self-management intervention successful. Although it is important to have a strong reinforcer, it is just as important that the successful completion of the self-management is socially reinforcing to the individual.

STEP 7: FADE ARTIFICIAL MATERIALS

Fading consists of gradually removing the self-monitoring materials and reinforcers so that desirable behavior is maintained in their absence. One approach to fading is increasing the time between each self-report on the checklist until self-monitoring occurs less frequently. This strategy helps to realistically generalize the desirable behavior to another setting. Should maintenance not occur when the recording materials are faded, it may be that the learner is self-reporting inaccurately or falsifying the reports. Furthermore, some children and adults who have autism are sensitive to different contexts and stimuli, which will minimize generalization across settings. Conducting training in these settings is the recommended strategy for overcoming this difficulty.

ADAPTATIONS AND MODIFICATIONS

Adaptations and modifications are sometimes needed when designing a typical self-management program. First, the learner's age may influence the type of program you design. For example, a young child will have a minimal understanding of the future and no history of recording his or her performance or arranging programmed reinforcers. An appropriate adaptation might be eliminating most of the language used by a caregiver when implementing self-management training. The self-recording sheet could include "smiley faces" that the child circles when he or she completes a programmed task (see Worksheet 14.1 at the end of the chapter). Once all the faces on the sheet are circled, the child gives it to the teacher or parent in exchange for a reinforcer. Over successful trials, the role of the caregiver could be eliminated and the child simply places the completed sheet in a "bank" or mail slot before selecting a preferred item or activity as the reinforcer. Similar adaptations might be needed with a learner of any age who has minimal verbal behavior skills.

Second, a learner with limited cognitive functioning may not understand the passage of time. This situation is significant because as noted earlier, a core concept of self-management is being aware of the future and relevant behavior contingencies. Caregivers should take extra care in explaining how "real-time" performance affects outcomes later. Teaching the concept of the future can be implemented by gradually fading the delay components of the self-management

Worksheet 14.1 Example of Basic Self-Management System Recording Form

Classroom Activity	Learner Record Here	Staff Record Here
Math	☺ ☺ ☺	☺ ☺ ☺
Reading	☺ ☺ ☺	☺ ☺ ☺
Art	☺ ☺ ☺	☺ ☺ ☺
Science	☺ ☺ ☺	☺ ☺ ☺
Physical Education	☺ ☺ ☺	☺ ☺ ☺

Instructions: Learner should complete on-task behavior (in seat, working on assignment, and no disruptions) during lesson and record at three intervals: beginning of lesson, during lesson, and at completion of lesson. The face should be circled if the behavior of "on task" has occurred. Staff should obtain this sheet at the end of the lesson and record performance as well. Correspondence between learner and caregiver should be reinforced. Non-correspondence should be discussed and learner should be instructed how to remediate.

SMILEY CASH-OUTS

Smiles Required	Available Reinforcers
1	5-min break from any task
2	10-min break from any task, access to computer, small candy
3	Extra recess minutes, read preferred book, watch cartoon for 5 min
9	Listen to CD
12	Computer game, trip to sensory room
15	End-of-day 1:1 time with coach, extra dessert at lunch next day

system. For example, the learner may begin with the need to complete a word search problem correctly before delivery of a self-managed reinforcer. Over successive days, weeks, or months, more work would have to be completed before he or she receives reinforcement.

Third, learners who are minimally responsive to social reinforcement may be more prone to "cheat" the system. As an illustration, although a caregiver may reinforce adherence to the self-management program by giving praise, unless that caregiver reinforcement is powerful (perhaps more powerful than the programmed reinforcer in the self-management system), the learner may lie about progress. Here the caregiver should take additional steps to monitor the program and lend a hand in the construction of the system if possible. For example, a child who self-reinforces with cookies for completing math problems could be assessed for compliance by checking the number of problems completed AND the remaining cookies in the classroom or kitchen.

Finally, memory deficiencies may affect the self-management program. Obviously, the program would be ineffective if the learner cannot remember the steps that must be followed. It also is important for the individual to be able to identify the target behavior. Depending on the severity of the memory impairment, repetition of the training procedure can better instill the concepts and process of the program.

KEYS TO REMEMBER

1. The goal of self-management is having the learner initiate programmed contingencies that produce desirable changes in behavior.
2. Self-management does not imply autonomy from the environment. Instead, it involves a series of antecedents, behaviors, and consequences, with the latter being delivered by the learner.
3. When teaching a self-management program, reinforce successful self-recording of behavior.
4. Reinforce adherence to the self-management program as well as the desirable behavior it produces.
5. Important procedural elements for teaching a self-management program include self-recording, promoting, tolerating delays to reinforcers, reinforcing alternative behaviors, and enhancing stimulus control.
6. Monitor the learner's adherence to the self-management program to evaluate procedural reliability. Having another person check the learner's self-management skills will increase confidence that the self-management program is being conducted correctly.

SUGGESTED READINGS

Christian, L., & Poling, A. (1997). Using self-management procedures to improve the productivity of adults with developmental disabilities in a competitive employment setting. *Journal of Applied Behavior Analysis, 30,* 169–172.

Cuvo, A. J., Lerch, L. J., Leurquin, D. A., Gaffaney, T. J., & Poppen, R. L. (1998). Response allocation to concurrent fixed-ratio reinforcement schedules with work requirements by adults with mental retardation and typical preschool children. *Journal of Applied Behavior Analysis, 31,* 43–63.

Dixon, M. R., Hayes, L. J., Binder, L. M., Manthey, S., Sigman, C., & Zdanowski, D. M. (1998). Using a self-control training procedure to increase appropriate behavior. *Journal of Applied Behavior Analysis, 31,* 203–210.

Mithaug, D. K., & Mithaug, D. E. (2003). Effects of teacher-directed versus student-directed instruction on self-management of young children with disabilities. *Journal of Applied Behavior Analysis, 36,* 133–136.

Tiger, J. H., Fisher, W. W., & Bouxsein, K. J. (2009). Therapist- and self- monitored DRO contingencies as a treatment for the self-injurious skin picking of a young man with Asperger syndrome. *Journal of Applied Behavior Analysis, 42,* 315–319.

C H A P T E R   1 5

COMMUNITY LIVING SKILLS

Raymond G. Miltenberger and Rachel Shayne

OVERVIEW: WHAT WE KNOW

Often, individuals with autism spectrum disorders (ASDs) lack certain skills that are essential for survival in community settings. For example, a child may not be able to display the behaviors needed to cross a street safely, or an adult may not be able to make purchases from a grocery store. As individuals with ASD grow older, they often are provided with the opportunity for more community activities and freedom. To prepare these individuals for a successful and autonomous life in the community, community living skills need to be taught. If community living skills are not acquired, individuals with ASD may be faced with more restrictive placements and fewer opportunities as they mature. Researchers have found that individuals lacking skills such as money management, apartment cleanliness and maintenance, meal preparation, and purchasing skills sometimes must leave independent living placements and return to more restrictive environments. These skills typically are complex sequences of behaviors that need to be taught in a systematic way to individuals with ASD.

Deficits in community living skills can decrease a person's quality of life by decreasing his or her independence, ability to meet new people and experience new things, ability to maintain a steady job, and ability to survive and thrive in a non-restrictive environment. Furthermore, for individuals with ASD, the absence of essential community living skills, such as ordering from a fast-food restaurant, riding a bus, or purchasing groceries, can result in stigmatization from those in the community.

We know that most people, including individuals with ASD, can learn new skills and use those skills in the appropriate context through systematic training. We also know that simply telling a person what to do is not likely to result in skill acquisition. Rather, individuals need to (a) see others perform those skills (modeling), (b) have an opportunity to practice those skills in simulated (role-play) or real situations, (c) receive reinforcement for correct performance and feedback to correct errors during training, and (d) have the opportunity to use the skills and receive reinforcement in the context of the natural environment.

GETTING STARTED: PRINCIPLES AND APPLICATIONS

Community living skills consist of a chain of behaviors that usually occur in a sequence until the final outcome is achieved. Behavioral skills training in combination with in situ training is often used to teach skills to individuals with ASD. Behavioral skills training combines instructions, modeling, rehearsal, and feedback. In situ training involves further practice and reinforcement of the skills in the natural environment. A detailed task analysis of the steps involved in the skill and additional prompting strategies also are sometimes needed for individuals with ASD to acquire the skills.

The many skills needed to live and thrive in the community need to occur under precise circumstances (under appropriate stimulus control). For example, an individual not only needs to know how to engage in the steps of riding a bus in the training setting but also needs to know how, when, and where to engage in these steps in the natural environment. Because skills must generalize from a training setting to the natural environment, in situ training is a particularly important aspect of training. The individual should be given a chance to engage in the skill where the skill would be occurring in the community (the natural context), and should then receive praise and feedback. More prompting and opportunities to practice should be provided if the skill did not adequately generalize from the training environment to the natural environment.

During training, the steps of the skill should be performed in the correct sequence and in the presence of the S^D (or a simulation of the S^D) that is found in the natural environment. Furthermore, the skill should be practiced in response to variations of the S^D (multiple training examples) until it occurs with consistency across a range of relevant situations. Attention to these training components will increase the chances that the behavior will come under appropriate stimulus control and will make it more likely that the behavior will be performed accurately in the natural community environment.

GUIDELINES FOR INTERVENTION

Some of the most successful procedures for teaching community living skills are those that start with a clear delineation of the skills (task analysis) and incorporate instructions and modeling, rehearsal with necessary prompting, and feedback, also known as behavioral skills training (BST). In addition, interventions that take place in the natural environment where the skill is to be performed have been shown to increase acquisition and promote generalization. Although different variations of BST have been conducted with individuals with ASD, substantial research supports the effectiveness of BST procedures. Guidelines for implementing BST are listed below.

DEFINE THE SKILL/CREATE A TASK ANALYSIS

Training always starts with a clear definition of the skill to be learned. Defining the community living skill as "purchasing a meal from a restaurant" or "riding the bus" is not adequate to facilitate a successful intervention. Rather, the key to defining the skill properly is to create a task analysis of the skill that clearly specifies each of the component behaviors and S^Ds associated

Table 15.1 Task Analysis for Purchasing Milk from a Store

	S^D	→ Response
1.	At the front of the store	→ Enter the store through the entrance.
2.	Once in the store	→ Look above the aisles at the labels.
3.	Once the dairy aisle is seen	→ Walk to the aisle labeled "milk" or "dairy."
4.	Once at the aisle labeled "milk"	→ Locate the correct size of milk.
5.	Once in front of correct size	→ Pick up the carton of milk.
6.	Once milk is in hand	→ Walk to an open register.
7.	Once at the register	→ Place the milk on the counter.
8.	Once milk is on the counter	→ Get money out of wallet.
9.	Once money is in hand	→ Hand the money to the cashier.
10.	Once cashier offers change	→ Take change, receipt, and bag with milk.
11.	Once items are in hand	→ Walk to the nearest exit and leave the store.

with each behavior. One way to create a task analysis is to have someone familiar with the skill (i.e., a trainer) complete the entire sequence of the skill and write down each component involved. See Table 15.1 for an example of a task analysis. This task analysis shows the components (S^{D}s and behaviors) that make up the skill of purchasing milk from the store. Defining the skill in this way allows the trainer to see which components of the skill need to be taught and to train these components in order to teach the overall skill.

CHOOSE THE SETTING AND CONDUCT ASSESSMENT

After defining the skill properly by creating a task analysis, the setting for assessment of the skill needs to be decided. Identifying the setting in which the skill will naturally occur is important. Appropriate and socially valid settings in which the skills are likely to be used need to be chosen. For example, if you are teaching purchasing skills, possible settings could be grocery stores, convenience stores, department stores, or restaurants. It is important to identify all situations in which the skills must be or might be used. A training setting also needs to be chosen. Training can be conducted in the home or classroom setting, but to aid in generalization, training sessions also should be conducted in the natural environment.

Once you have determined the setting, baseline assessments of the skill need to be conducted. Baseline assessments will aid the trainer in determining what components of the skill the individual can complete before training and which components still need to be taught. During baseline assessments, instruct the individual to do the task (e.g., "Buy a half-gallon of skim milk") and record the number of steps of the task analysis completed correctly. Continue to record until the individual fails to initiate or complete a step within a reasonable time (e.g., 30 seconds).

IMPLEMENT TRAINING

Following completion of baseline assessments, training should begin. Numerous studies have shown that BST is an effective way to teach community living skills to individuals with ASD. During training, you may decide that all the components of the task analysis can be taught at once, or for more complex skills or for students with more profound disabilities, you might decide to break the skill down and teach each component of the task analysis separately. The steps involved in BST are described below.

Instructions and Modeling

First, describe the behavior you expect from the learner and the appropriate context for the behavior. Make your instructions clear and precise. Next, provide a model. Have a trainer engage in the steps of the skill in the appropriate context. The student needs to have an imitative repertoire for modeling to be effective. Modeling can be live or via videotape, but the model should perform the skill in the natural setting or a simulation of the natural setting. For example, when teaching cooking skills, the model should complete the steps of the skill in the kitchen, and when teaching bus-riding skills the model should complete the steps at an actual bus stop and bus, or on a simulated model of a bus and bus stop. The model should be someone with high status (e.g., a teacher) or characteristics similar to the student (if the student is a teenager, the model should be a teenager). The model can conduct the entire sequence of the task analysis at once or individual steps of the task analysis at a time; the complexity of the model's behavior needs to match the developmental ability level of the student. In addition, the student needs to pay attention to the model. It can be helpful to have the student describe the model's behavior to guarantee the student was paying attention.

Rehearsal with Prompts

Once the student has received instructions and seen the behavior modeled, it is important that he or she gets an opportunity to engage in the behavior and receive reinforcement. Immediate rehearsal with reinforcement will increase the likelihood that the individual will engage in the behavior in the future under similar circumstances. Simulate the appropriate situation for the skill to occur in a role-play scenario and allow the student to practice the skill. It is especially important for this role-play scenario to be in the proper context in order to promote generalization when training is complete. For example, when training an individual to order from a fast-food restaurant, if you cannot go to an actual restaurant, you can set up a mock checkout counter and simulate the restaurant situation. Correct behavior during the role play should be followed immediately by descriptive praise and possibly other reinforcers. Incorrect behavior during the role play should be followed by corrective feedback (further instruction for improvement). The behavior should be rehearsed until the student engages in the appropriate behavior at least a few times.

With the rehearsal component of training you will most likely need to provide prompts for behaviors that are not occurring. Use the least intrusive prompt first and more intrusive prompts only as necessary to get the learner to engage in the correct behavior. For example, if an individual does not engage a component of the skill during the role play, first prompt by stating the desired behavior again (verbal prompt or instruction). If the student does not engage in the behavior after the verbal prompt, model the behavior again. If this prompt fails to evoke the desired behavior, move to physical guidance with hand-over-hand prompting. Once the learner engages in the behavior, provide praise and/or other reinforcers.

Feedback

During training, follow all correct responses with descriptive praise; tell the learner exactly what he or she did that was correct. Even if the behavior in the rehearsal was not completely correct, it is important to provide praise for some correct aspect of the performance. Following instances of incorrect responding, provide the learner with corrective feedback; tell the learner exactly what to do next time. Then, give the learner an opportunity to rehearse the behavior and use the necessary prompts to make sure the correct behavior occurs.

Fading

Once the correct skill has been performed several times, the prompts need to be eliminated to transfer stimulus control to the S^Ds in the natural environment. Over the course of a number of training trials, the trainer will want to use less and less of the prompt to get the learner to engage in the correct behaviors. In addition, the trainer can provide a greater magnitude of reinforcement for unprompted responses than for prompted responses to facilitate prompt fading. The training is not complete until the learner can exhibit the skill in its entirety in the correct situations without any prompts.

PROMOTE GENERALIZATION

Several strategies can be used during and after training to promote generalization and make it more likely that the individual will respond correctly in all relevant situations, including novel ones. One way to promote generalization during training is to incorporate a variety of real life role-play situations into training. Another way to promote generalization is to simulate the natural environment as closely as possible or include stimuli from the natural environment in training.

Perhaps the surest way to promote generalization of the community living skill is to use in situ training after BST. During in situ training the trainer sets up the assessment scenario in the natural environment and then provides on-the-spot training if the learner fails to engage in any of the components of the skill. For example, if the community living skill was purchasing food from a store, the trainer would set up assessments at a local store. The trainer could then take the client to the store, tell the client to buy a half-gallon of milk, and observe whether the learner engages in the correct behavior. At any time during the assessment, if the learner does not engage in the correct components of the skill, the trainer must step in and turn the assessment into a training session. The trainer will have the learner rehearse the skills in the natural setting and provide praise and corrective feedback when necessary. If necessary, the trainer will use additional prompts to get the behavior to occur. Once the learner engages in the behavior, the trainer provides descriptive praise and possibly other reinforcers. Reinforcing the behavior in the natural environment will make it more likely that this behavior will occur in similar circumstances. The trainer repeats these assessments and training sessions in the natural setting until the learner displays all the components of the skill in one or more relevant natural situations.

PROMOTE MAINTENANCE OF THE SKILL

Following mastery of the skill, maintenance of the skill needs to be assessed. It is important that the person continues to engage the skill in the correct circumstances weeks, months, and years after training. One way to ensure maintenance of the skill is to arrange for the individual to have the opportunity to engage in the behavior frequently.

Follow-up assessments need to be conducted to ensure that the learner is continuing to engage in the skill correctly. During these assessments, if the learner is not able to engage in the skill, the trainer needs to step in and prompt the appropriate behavior using the least to most prompting method described earlier. Following an assessment in which the behavior is not performed correctly, booster training assessments should be administered. These booster training sessions should follow the training method outlined in this chapter and should include follow-up assessments in the natural setting.

ADAPTATIONS AND MODIFICATIONS

For the most part, BST procedures can be used with all individuals who need to learn community living skills. However, it is important to consider the age and ability level of the individual and the setting in which training occurs. In terms of age, some skills may be more or less relevant for children versus adults. For example, teaching pedestrian skills is important for all ages and can be especially beneficial at younger ages. However, a skill such as apartment maintenance would be more appropriate for an adult. In terms of ability level, individuals with more severe deficits may require more training trials, more prompting, or more strategies for promoting generalization than individuals with less severe deficits.

You also need to take the setting of the intervention into consideration. For children, the initial training setting may be in the school, after-school program, or home. For adults, the training setting may be a group home, apartment, or work setting. However, for all ages, assessments (and further training when needed) should be conducted in all relevant community settings.

KEYS TO REMEMBER

1. The goal of training is for the individual with ASD to engage in the community living skill independently in the natural environment where the skill is to be performed.
2. Create a task analysis of the skill so that the skill is divided into multiple component behaviors that will occur in sequence.
3. Choose settings that are appropriate for the individual and the skill to be learned.
4. Use behavioral skills training to teach the community living skill.
5. Incorporate the natural setting into training sessions and assessments.
6. Monitor the individual's ability to engage in the community living skill and conduct in situ training as needed to promote generalization and booster sessions as needed to promote maintenance.

SUGGESTED READINGS

Alcantara, P. R. (1994). Effects of videotape instructional packaging on purchasing skills of children with autism. *Exceptional Children, 61,* 40–56.

Cihak, D. F., & Grim, J. (2008). Teaching students with autism spectrum disorder and moderate intellectual disabilities to use counting-on strategies to enhance independent purchasing skills. *Research in Autism Spectrum Disorders, 2,* 716–727.

Graves, T. B., Collins, B. C., Schuster, J. W., & Kleinert, H. (2005). Using video prompting to teach cooking skills to secondary students with moderate disabilities. *Education and Training in Developmental Disabilities, 40,* 34–46.

Haring, T. G., Kennedy, C. H., Adams, M. J., & Pitts-Conway, V. (1987). Teaching generalization of purchasing skills across community settings to autistic youth using videotape modeling. *Journal of Applied Behavior Analysis, 20,* 89–96.

Neef, N. A., Iwata, B. A., & Page, T. J. (1978). Public transportation training: In vivo versus classroom instruction. *Journal of Applied Behavior Analysis, 11,* 331–344.

Taylor, B. A., Hughes, C. E., Richard, E., Hoch, H., & Coello, A. R. (2004). Teaching teenagers with autism to seek assistance when lost. *Journal of Applied Behavior Analysis, 37,* 79–82.

Williams, G. E., & Cuvo, A. J. (1986). Training apartment upkeep skills to rehabilitation clients: A comparison of task analytic strategies. *Journal of Applied Behavior Analysis, 19,* 39–51.

PART 3

HOW TO REDUCE PROBLEM BEHAVIORS

C H A P T E R   1 6

STEREOTYPY

John T. Rapp and Marc J. Lanovaz

OVERVIEW: WHAT WE KNOW

Individuals who are diagnosed with autism spectrum disorders (ASDs) and other developmental disabilities often display repetitive and invariant motor movements such body rocking, hand flapping, object flicking or spinning, and acontextual vocalizations that we categorize as "stereotypy" or "stereotyped movements." Behaviors that result in self-injury are usually excluded from the category. Behavior that is categorized as stereotypy generally occupies a considerable amount of an individual's time. Thus, one individual could display body rocking for 50% of a 2-hour observation period and another individual could display an identical form of behavior for 4% of the same period. In this example, the former individual's behavior would be correctly described as stereotypy, whereas the latter individual's behavior would not.

Repetitive behavior is often informally referred to as "self-stimulation" or "stimming," but we prefer the formal term "stereotypy" as it provides a clear reference to both the form and function of the behavior in question. Although many of the behaviors that we categorize as stereotypy are frequently displayed by typically developing infants and toddlers, individuals with ASDs may engage in stereotypy for inordinately lengthy periods of time. Moreover, individuals with ASDs may continue to engage in stereotypy as they age, whereas their typically developing peers do not. In this same vein, one of the noted problems with stereotypy is that it competes with an individual's engagement in social activities with peers, as well as with academic and vocational training. Furthermore, individuals who display repetitive behaviors are often perceived negatively by same-aged peers, further decreasing the probability that individuals who exhibit stereotypy will engage in appropriate social interactions.

Individuals with ASDs and other developmental disabilities often display multiple forms of stereotypy. These behaviors may be displayed as a part of a chain or sequence (e.g., an individual may flap his hands for 30 seconds then vocalize for 10 seconds, and then repeat the chain) or may be exhibited simultaneously (e.g., an individual may rock his body while flapping his hands). For some individuals, providing treatment for one form of stereotypy may decrease an untreated form of stereotypy, whereas for other individuals a novel form of stereotypy may emerge when treatment is provided. A variety of antecedent- and consequence-based interventions have been used to decrease individuals' engagement in different forms of stereotypy. As a whole, the interventions that are typically the most effective for decreasing stereotypy involve providing alternative sources of stimulation for engaging in appropriate behavior.

GETTING STARTED: PRINCIPLES AND APPLICATIONS

Most stereotyped behavior displayed by humans is operant behavior that is maintained by a consequence. Specifically, stereotyped behavior appears to be maintained by automatic or non-social positive reinforcement. Put simply, engagement in the repetitive behavior produces a sensory consequence that then reinforces the behavior. In addition, stereotypy may be maintained by conjugate schedules of automatic reinforcement—that is, the magnitude or quality of the consequent stimulation may be directly proportional to the magnitude of the behavior. For example, an individual may flap his hands in front of his eyes to produce visual stimulation. In this way, the visual stimulation produced by hand flapping directly reinforces hand flapping. Moreover, faster or slower flapping of the hands will produce a qualitatively different consequent stimulus from moment to moment. Thus, a feature of stereotypy that makes it particularly difficult to treat is that the consequence that reinforces an individual's stereotypy cannot be directly manipulated by the clinician or practitioner. Instead, treatments focus on providing alternative sources of social and nonsocial reinforcement to compete with engagement in stereotypy, disrupting the relation between engagement in stereotypy and the production of reinforcing sensory stimulation, or both. For example, a caregiver may physically block a child from engaging in stereotypy and, thereafter, use access to stereotypy as a reinforcer for engaging in appropriate behavior. Interestingly, permitting an individual to freely engage in stereotypy at one point in time often decreases the individual's engagement in stereotypy at a later point in time. This observation is important because it indicates that stereotypy, like socially reinforced operant behavior, is sensitive to relative changes in motivating operations—that is, individuals may be more motivated to engage in stereotypy after a period of time when engagement in stereotypy has not been permitted and, by contrast, may be less motivated to engage in stereotypy after engaging in stereotypy for a lengthy period of time.

Some individuals are more likely to engage in stereotypy when levels of ambient stimulation are low (e.g., when neither toys nor social interactions are available); however, others will engage in stereotypy regardless of the environmental conditions. Individuals who exhibit stereotypy across a variety of environmental events are often more difficult to treat. Likewise, an individual's engagement in multiple forms of stereotypy may complicate the treatment. In addition, some individuals will engage in higher levels of stereotypy in the presence of preferred objects or other stimuli (e.g., when music is present). Items or objects that increase an individual's engagement in stereotypy may be viewed as establishing operations for stereotypy—that is, some ambient stimulation increases individuals' motivation to engage in one or more forms of stereotypy. In part, treatment should include controlling such stimulation.

GUIDELINES FOR INTERVENTION

Given the diversity of children and adults with ASDs, the variety of forms that stereotypy can assume, and the various factors that can influence levels of stereotypy, no single intervention is likely to be effective at reducing stereotypy for everyone. Although general guidelines for intervention can be provided, a systematic assessment procedure must be implemented to ensure that the intervention is producing the desired behavior change. To this end, both intervention procedures and a methodology to assess the interventions' effectiveness for reducing stereotypy are described below.

1. **Define the behavior and select data collection method.** As repetitive behaviors are typically categorized as stereotypy based on the amount of time for which an individual exhibits such behavior, response definitions are often focused on capturing the dimension of response duration (but responses such a vocal stereotypy and hand flapping may be defined on the basis of response frequency). Thus, definitions should include clear "onset" and "offset" criteria. For example, the "onset" of body rocking may be defined as two or more forward and backward movements of the individual's torso within 3 seconds and the "offset" may be defined as the absence of forward and backward torso movements for 2 seconds or longer. To ensure maximum sensitivity for detecting changes in stereotypy following the introduction of treatment, you should use continuous duration recording (CDR) or momentary time sampling (MTS) with 10-second intervals to measure forms of stereotypy for which duration of engagement is problematic, and continuous frequency recording (CFR) or partial-interval recording (PIR) with 10-second intervals to measure forms of stereotypy for which frequency events are problematic. Data points for duration measures should be calculated by dividing the total number of seconds for which the target stereotypy was scored by the total number of seconds in the observation period and multiplying by 100%. For example, if body rocking is displayed for 300 seconds of a 10-minute (600-second) observation period, the data point would indicate that stereotypy occurred for 50% of the session. Data points for interval measures should be calculated by dividing the number of scored intervals with the target stereotypy by the total number of intervals in the observation period and multiplying by 100%. For example, if body rocking was displayed for 45 intervals of a 10-minute observation period, which contains 60, 10-second intervals, the data point would indicate that stereotypy occurred for 75% of the intervals. Data points for frequency measures should be calculated by taking the count of the occurrence of stereotypy divided by the number of minutes in the session (in this example, 10) to arrive at the responses per minute (rpm) or rate of stereotypy per session. Thus, if stereotypy was displayed 60 times during a 10-minute session, the data point would reflect that stereotypy occurred at a rate of 6 rpm during the session.

2. **Conduct a functional analysis.** To confirm that the behavior is maintained in the absence of social consequences, you should conduct a functional analysis prior to assessing the effectiveness of the intervention. Perhaps the most efficient method for determining whether the behavior persists in the absence of social consequences is to conduct a series of consecutive no-interaction conditions. Behavior that extinguishes during the course of consecutive no-interaction conditions is possibly maintained by a social reinforcer (see Part II for further assessment of socially reinforced behavior). During the no-interaction condition, the child or adult with an ASD should be alone in a room and observed unobtrusively. If one of the two requirements cannot be met, you may remain in the room with the individual, but you should ignore all occurrences of stereotypy. Furthermore, you should not provide access to preferred toys, games, or activities. Each no-interaction session should be 10 to 15 minutes in duration to ensure that the persistence of the behavior is not a function of resistance to extinction for a social reinforcer. At a minimum, you should conduct a series of 6 to 10 consecutive no-interaction sessions.

During each session, measure the behavior with the definition and the methodology that you chose in Step 1. Next, make a graph of the percentage of time (based on measurement with

CDR), percentage of intervals (based on measurement with MTS or PIR), or rate (based on CFR) the individual engaged in stereotypy. Add the data points on the graph on a continuous basis, preferably after conducting each session.

Figure 16.1 depicts two examples of consecutive no-interaction sessions wherein body rocking was measured with 10-second MTS. If levels of body rocking are fairly stable or increasing across the last five sessions, you may conclude that it persists in the absence of social consequence (Fig. 16.1, top panel). If body rocking decreases across the last five sessions or if its levels are very low (i.e., <10% of scored intervals), the behavior is likely to be maintained by social consequences and the behavior should not be treated as stereotypy (Fig. 16.1, bottom panel). As such, conduct a more thorough functional analysis (see Chapter 3); the behavior should not be treated as stereotypy unless the non-social function is confirmed.

3. Conduct a preference assessment. Conducting a preference assessment is a necessary step to identify potential reinforcers that will be used during the intervention. Before starting the preference assessment, select six to eight stimuli that match the putative function of the behavior—that is, the stimuli should match the overt sensory product of stereotypy. For example,

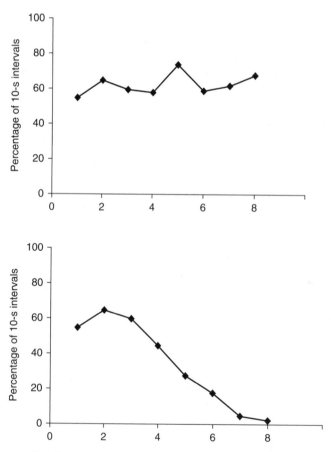

FIGURE 16.1 Two examples of the percentage of 10-s intervals during which an individual engaged in body rocking. The top panel shows that body rocking persisted in the absence of social consequences whereas the lower panel shows that body rocking decreased without social consequences.

if an individual engages in vocal stereotypy, select toys that produce auditory stimulation because they match one of the products of vocal stereotypy. Likewise, if an individual engages in object spinning, assess activities that produce visual stimulation first. Questionnaires and interviews can be used to facilitate the identification of the stimuli that will be evaluated. If you need to use a mild punisher (e.g., reprimands, response cost) as part of the intervention, you should still include empirically identified preferred items as a component of the intervention.

If your intervention involves providing a toy, game, or activity for several short periods of time (i.e., <1 minute), implement a trial-based preference assessment to ensure that the learner engages with the stimulus for brief interactions. If your intervention involves more extended interactions with the stimulus, implement a duration-based stimulus preference assessment. For example, if the individual will be given a piece of food every 10 seconds during the intervention, use the trial-based procedure. Alternatively, if an individual will be given a light-producing toy for periods of 5 minutes, select the duration-based procedure. Several trial-based and duration-based assessments can be used to identify preferred stimuli (see Chapter 4); two of these methods are presented below.

During the *paired-choice* stimulus preference assessment (i.e., a trial-based assessment), present the stimuli in pairs. Each of the six to eight stimuli is presented with each other stimulus once. For each pair presentation, prompt the learner to sample each stimulus for 10 seconds. Then, the individual has 1 minute to select a stimulus. As soon as a stimulus is chosen, record the selection and remove the other stimulus. The individual can engage with the selected stimulus for the rest of the 1-minute interval. Present all possible pairs in a random order. The most preferred stimuli are those that were selected most often.

During the *free-operant* stimulus preference assessment (i.e., a duration-based assessment), the six to eight stimuli or activities are available simultaneously for a 10-minute period. The individual should be permitted to sample each stimulus for at least 10 seconds prior to the start of the assessment. Measure the individual's engagement with each stimulus or activity using CDR or 10-second MTS. Repeat the procedures twice on different days. Compute the mean percentage of time or 10-second intervals that the individual engaged with each stimulus across sessions. The most preferred stimuli are those with which the individual engaged for the longest durations. As preferences are known to change across time, it is may be necessary to conduct periodic "refresher" assessments of preference.

4. Assess intervention procedures. Preferred items can be used in at least three treatment procedures to decrease stereotypy. First, preferred items can be provided non-contingently, continuously or on a fixed-time basis, to decrease stereotypy. Second, preferred items can be delivered contingent on engagement in appropriate (non-stereotyped) behavior as with differential reinforcement of alternative behavior (DRA). Finally, preferred items can be used in conjunction with mild punishment procedures to decrease stereotypy (described below).

The selection of one procedure over another will depend on the nature and the baseline levels of the behavior, as well as your goals and the context in which stereotypy needs to be reduced. In most cases, providing non-contingent matched stimulation should be the preferred intervention because it is relatively easy to implement, even under dense schedules, and may reduce subsequent engagement in stereotypy—that is, engagement with preferred items or activities may reduce the individual's motivation to engage in stereotypy for a period of time after the preferred item or activity is removed. If engagement with the item or activity is incompatible with other activities that the individual must complete in the intervention context, DRA may be implemented when an alternative behavior to reinforce can be identified. Finally, mild punishment may be necessary if all other interventions fail, or if the behavior must be reduced to near-zero levels in a very short period of time. You should conduct the following steps to assess the effectiveness of the interventions for reducing stereotypy.

Decide on the context and duration of your sessions for the assessment and intervention sessions. The context should be the environment in which you want to reduce the behavior. The duration of the sessions will vary according to the level the behavior; decreases in higher levels of stereotypy will be easier to detect than decreases in lower levels. Thus, you should use sessions of at least 10 to 15 minutes in duration to ensure that you can appropriately assess the effects of your intervention.

Determine an appropriate single-subject design for evaluating the effects of your chosen intervention. In this example, we have opted to use a pair-wise multi-element design. For your first session, randomly (e.g., by flipping a coin) select and conduct either an intervention session or a no-interaction session. For the second session, you will conduct the one that was NOT selected in the initial session. As such, the sessions are conducted in a pseudo-random fashion, but you are ensuring that no-interaction and intervention sessions are conducted a comparable number of times. In sum, every time you are conducting an odd number session, you should flip a coin to decide which one to do. The no-interaction session should be identical to the one described for the functional analysis. The intervention session will vary depending on the intervention being assessed. The preferred stimulus will be the most preferred stimulus as identified in Step 3. Record the target behavior across all sessions with your chosen data collection method.

For matched stimulation, in the problematic context, allow the individual to have continuous access to the most preferred item or activity that is matched to the overt product of the target stereotypy. If the intervention is to be implemented over extended periods of time (e.g., 30–60 minutes), it may be necessary to include multiple preferred items or activities. If an edible item is the most preferred, present it on a time-based schedule, which would be 80% of the mean inter-response time. In other words, calculate the mean amount of time between successive occurrences of the stereotypy during the functional analysis and multiply it by 80%. For example, if an average of 50 seconds separated two occurrences of mouthing, the stimulus should be delivered every 40 seconds (50 × 0.8). If the most preferred stimulus is an object or an activity, provide continuous access to the stimulus.

For DRA, select an alternative behavior that may be difficult to emit while engaging in stereotypy; for example, simultaneously engaging in object spinning and appropriate toy manipulation can be difficult. Next, provide the most preferred stimulus when the individual engages in the alternative behavior.

If continuous access to preferred items or activities does not decrease stereotypy to clinically acceptable levels, you can withhold access to the preferred item or activity contingent on engagement in stereotypy. Alternatively, you can simply block or interrupt engagement in stereotypy whenever it occurs. Punishment procedures are typically most effective when delivered on a continuous schedule (i.e., the consequence is provided following each occurrence of stereotypy).

Make a graph of the amount of time the child engages in stereotypy for each condition (see Figure 16.2 for an example with a multi-element design). Conduct four to six intervention sessions and the same number of no-interaction sessions. If the intervention decreases stereotypy to clinically acceptable levels, continue the intervention sessions and move on to the next step. If the intervention does not decrease stereotypy to acceptable levels, either repeat Step 3 to identify a new preferred stimulus from a different array or Step 4 by assessing a new intervention procedure.

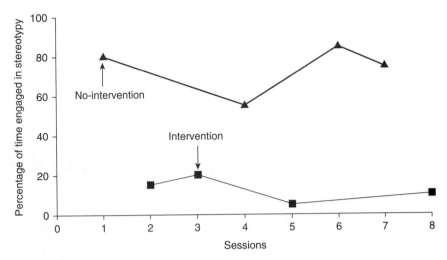

FIGURE 16.2 An example of a multielement design comparing the percentage of time an individual engaged in stereotypy during an intervention condition and during a no-intervention (baseline) condition.

5. Promote generalization. When the behavior remains at clinically acceptable levels for three consecutive intervention sessions, start implementing the intervention in other relevant contexts. Make sure that you also present the stimulus initially associated with the intervention. When you are delivering the most preferred stimulus on time-based (e.g., every 10 seconds) or continuous (e.g., for every alternative behavior) schedules, begin increasing the time interval or the ratio of responses being reinforced. As a general rule, you can increase the interval size or ratio by 50% whenever stereotypy remains at acceptable levels for three consecutive sessions. On the other hand, decrease the interval size or ratio by 50% if the behavior increases at unacceptable levels for three consecutive sessions. As the interval or ratio gets larger, it will also become easier to implement the intervention across longer session durations. Some individuals may revert back to engaging in stereotypy if the schedule of programmed reinforcement is too thin. Therefore, it may be necessary to provide dense schedules of alternative reinforcement on an ongoing basis to compete with the stimulation produced by stereotypy.

ADAPTATIONS AND MODIFICATIONS

Although the interventions described above should be relatively effective, some modifications can be made to adapt the intervention to a variety of settings. For example, the learner with an ASD can be taught to self-monitor. You can provide access to preferred items or activities when (1) the individual accurately measures his or her own stereotypy and (2) levels of stereotypy remain at or below a clinically acceptable level. Make sure the individual is recording stereotypy correctly by measuring it simultaneously until the individual is taking reliable measures of his or her behavior.

A potential problem is that many interventions will interfere with engagement in other activities, especially when access to preferred items is provided on a continuous basis. As such, procedures that decrease engagement in stereotypy when the intervention is withdrawn may be useful. Interventions that reduce subsequent engagement in stereotypy can be implemented

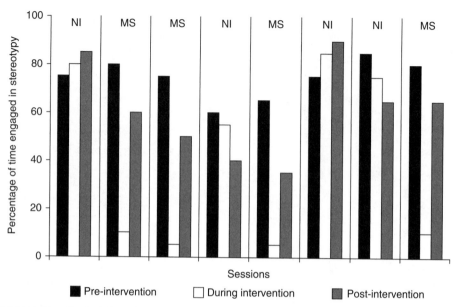

FIGURE 16.3 Hypothetical data showing the percentage of time an individual engaged in stereotypy during periods of pre-intervention, intervention, and post-intervention in the no-interaction (NI) and matched stimulation (MS) sequences.

prior to critical periods of time (e.g., before academic instruction). An adaptation of the procedures is to measure pre- and post-intervention levels of stereotypy during the intervention assessment (see Step 4) for a period of time equal to the duration of the session. Rather than examining the levels of stereotypy only when the intervention is being implemented, stereotypy can be evaluated during pre-intervention (e.g., 10 minutes before the intervention is implemented) and post-intervention (e.g., 10 minutes after the intervention is implemented).

Figure 16.3 gives an example with levels of stereotypy before and after sessions with no-interaction (NI) and sessions with continuous access to matched stimulation (MS). If post-intervention levels of stereotypy are lower after the intervention sequence, continue implementing the intervention. Alternatively, repeat Step 3 when post-intervention levels are higher following intervention sessions. If post-intervention levels of stereotypy are the same after both types of sessions, examine the number of times the pre-intervention levels were higher than the post-intervention levels of stereotypy. Patterns in which pre-intervention levels were typically higher than post-intervention levels of stereotypy (before and after intervention) indicate that a functional match for stereotypy was identified (as in Fig. 16.3). Interventions involving only punishment are likely to produce the opposite effect (i.e., increase subsequent engagement in stereotypy).

KEYS TO REMEMBER

1. No intervention is effective with everyone, so assess the effectiveness of interventions before implementing them on a regular basis.

2. Always confirm that the behavior persists in the absence of social consequences before starting an intervention.

3. Conduct a preference assessment to identify stimuli that will be used during the intervention. It may be necessary to conduct refresher assessments to evaluate changes in preference across time.

4. Select an intervention based on the form and baseline level of the behavior, your goals, and the context.

5. Ideally, measure pre- and post-intervention levels of stereotypy to ensure that the treatment is reducing both immediate and subsequent engagement in stereotypy.

6. In the end, the intervention should decrease stereotypy during critical periods of time and should lead to increased engagement in other behavior (i.e., attending to instructions, learning).

SUGGESTED READINGS

Ahearn, W. H., Clark, K. M., MacDonald, R. P., & Chung, B. I. (2007). Assessing and treating vocal stereotypy in children with autism. *Journal of Applied Behavior Analysis, 40,* 263–275.

Piazza, C. C., Adelinis, J. D., Hanley, G. P., Goh, H. L., & Delia, M. D. (2000). An evaluation of the effects of matched stimuli on behaviors maintained by automatic reinforcement. *Journal of Applied Behavior Analysis, 33,* 13–27.

Rapp, J. T. (2005). Some effects of audio and visual stimulation on multiple forms of stereotypy. *Behavioral Interventions, 20,* 255–272.

Rapp, J. T. (2007). Further evaluation of methods to identify matched stimulation. *Journal of Applied Behavior Analysis, 39,* 73–88.

Rapp, J. T., & Vollmer, T. R. (2005). Stereotypy I: A review of behavioral assessment and treatment. *Research in Developmental Disabilities, 26,* 527–547.

C H A P T E R   1 7

SELF-INJURIOUS BEHAVIOR

SungWoo Kahng, Nicole L. Hausman, and Kathryn E. Jann

OVERVIEW: WHAT WE KNOW

Self-injurious behavior (SIB) is a serious problem exhibited by some individuals with developmental disabilities, including children and adults who have autism spectrum disorders (ASDs). SIB is defined as behavior that produces physical injury to one's body. Head hitting, head banging, self-biting, and pica (the ingestion of inedible items) are common types of SIB. The prevalence of such behavior among individuals with developmental disabilities is estimated to range from 10% to 15%. These estimates vary based on multiple risk factors such as the level of functioning (higher prevalence among lower-functioning individuals), residential setting (higher prevalence among individuals residing in larger institutional settings), and gender (more males engage in SIB).

SIB results in both direct and indirect adverse effects. The most direct adverse effect is bodily injury such as soft tissue lacerations and contusions, permanent scars, callus formations, and damage to the eye (e.g., retinal detachment). In addition to self-inflicted injuries, SIB has numerous indirect adverse effects. For example, some individuals who engage in SIB may have limited access to therapeutic activities, academic instruction, and vocational programming. Furthermore, these individuals may have to reside in more restrictive settings, receive psychotropic medication, and require protective equipment or physical and mechanical restraints to manage them safely.

GETTING STARTED: BASIC PRINCIPLES AND APPLICATIONS

FUNCTIONS OF SIB

Over 40 years of research indicates that SIB is maintained by positive and negative reinforcement contingencies. These variables can further be delineated according to SIB maintained by socially mediated (i.e., environmental) consequences and automatic reinforcement (i.e., the behavior itself produces reinforcement). SIB maintained by social positive reinforcement is reinforced by attention or access to preferred tangible items (e.g., toys or food); SIB maintained by social negative reinforcement is reinforced by escape from undesirable activities (e.g., academics). Research indicates that in a majority of cases, SIB is maintained by socially mediated variables.

SIB maintained by automatic reinforcement refers to behaviors that produce their own reinforcement (i.e., "self-stimulation"). These behaviors occur across contexts, regardless of environmental antecedents and consequences. Although the exact nature of reinforcement is unknown, research has suggested multiple hypotheses, one suggesting that SIB may be a product of a dopamine deficiency. Studies have shown, for example, that the neurotransmitter dopamine may be involved in the manifestation of SIB, particularly among individuals diagnosed with Lesch-Nyhan syndrome (LNS). LNS is a genetic disorder characterized by severe SIB, often in the form of self-biting. Abnormalities in dopamine receptors resulting in a dopamine deficiency have been found among individuals with LNS. As SIB is a behavioral phenotype of LNS, biochemical studies of individuals diagnosed with LNS may provide insight into how dopamine deficiency may be related to SIB.

An alternative hypothesis for the biological nature of SIB is based on some findings of elevated endorphin levels in blood samples from individuals who engage in SIB and stereotypic behavior relative to controls who do not. This opioid hypothesis suggests that (a) SIB may function to release endorphins, resulting in a temporary feeling of euphoria, or (b) individuals with SIB may have decreased pain sensitivity as a result of increased levels of endogenous opiates. Evidence for this hypothesis is based on research showing that drugs that block opiate receptors (i.e., opiate antagonists) such as naltrexone and naloxone can decrease SIB among some individuals.

Finally, SIB may be a product of some injury or illness. Research has indicated that SIB among individuals with ASD may be associated with a painful medical condition such as an obstructed bowel or chronic ear infection. Furthermore, SIB may be exhibited by individuals who suffer from undiagnosed medical conditions that may cause pain. The occurrence of SIB among individuals with painful medical conditions may serve to temporarily attenuate feelings of pain. For example, an individual may begin to engage in hand-to-head SIB after acquiring an ear infection or acute trauma. Based on these findings, it is important to rule out or treat underlying medical conditions when developing interventions for individuals who engage in SIB.

GUIDELINES FOR IMPLEMENTATION

Behavioral interventions are one of the most effective treatments for SIB. To develop an appropriate and effective intervention plan, a thorough functional assessment should be conducted for each client to empirically determine the function of the behavior (see Chapters 2 and 3). The results of these assessments yield vital information about the variables maintaining SIB that can be used to guide the development of behavioral interventions. Determining the etiology of SIB permits you to isolate behavior-maintaining variables, which allows you to (a) discontinue reinforcement for that behavior (i.e., extinction), (b) alter antecedent conditions to reduce the likelihood of SIB, and (c) shape alternative behaviors to access that reinforcer. Effective interventions target both environmental antecedents and consequences of SIB, or events that occur before and after SIB, respectively. Generally, interventions targeting SIB include extinction as well as reinforcement-based procedures. If SIB persists despite these interventions or when the severity of SIB puts an individual at risk for serious injury, punishment may be necessary to further reduce the occurrence of SIB. Several broad categories of interventions are discussed below, along with examples of how these interventions may be used to treat SIB.

EXTINCTION

SIB Maintained by Social Reinforcement

Extinction of SIB is one of the most important function-based components in a behavioral treatment plan. Extinction consists of breaking the behavior–consequence relationship between SIB and its maintaining variable. The procedural form of extinction depends on the function of SIB. An extinction effect (decrease of SIB) will not occur if the contraindicated form of extinction is applied. For example, if an individual's SIB is maintained by access to attention, then caregivers should not deliver attention following SIB. Similarly, if SIB is maintained by access to tangible objects such as food, leisure items, or activities, then caregivers should not provide the individual with these stimuli and events following SIB. In the case of SIB that is maintained by escape from undesirable events such as demands, work, or other situations (e.g., crowded rooms, loud noise, physical attention, remaining seated in a car seat), caregivers should ensure the individual does not escape a task or situation contingent on SIB.

SIB Maintained by Automatic Reinforcement

If SIB is maintained by sensory stimulation, a procedure termed sensory extinction can be implemented by having a caregiver block completion of the behavior. Sometimes, protective equipment such as a helmet or padded glove is applied. For example, if a child engages in hand-to-head SIB, he can wear a helmet to minimize the sensory reinforcement. Alternatively, the child can wear padded gloves or the caregiver can block SIB to attenuate the sensory stimulation.

In some cases, blocking of SIB can be difficult if the behavior occurs at a high frequency or speed or is unpredictable. In these cases, shadowing *and* blocking may be used. For example, if a woman hits her head with her fist, a caregiver can position his hand a few inches above the woman's forearm (i.e., between the arm and the head) so that he is able to block attempts to engage in SIB. At times, shadowing and blocking can be intensive for caregivers, and they may not be quick enough to block SIB. Also, for some individuals, the blocking of SIB may occasion other forms of problem behavior, such as aggression. In such cases, other intervention components, described below, may be indicated.

REINFORCEMENT-BASED PROCEDURES

Differential Reinforcement of Alternative Behavior

A reinforcement-based procedure such as the differential reinforcement of alternative behavior (DRA) teaches an individual appropriate, alternative responses to access reinforcement that previously was achieved through SIB. At times, it may be necessary to teach an individual to tolerate an antecedent that is known to evoke SIB—for example, sharing attention by a child who has attention-maintained SIB and completing a vocational work task by an adult who has escape-motivated SIB. In such cases, DRA can be applied to reinforce an alternative behavior. In the example of an adult whose SIB is maintained by escape from work, a break could be provided when he or she completes a predetermined number of tasks. For the child learning to wait for attention, he or she could receive periodic vocal praise or pats on the back for playing quietly with a preferred toy.

Functional Communication

This is a specific type of DRA procedure that teaches an individual to emit an appropriate response to gain access to the functional reinforcer that maintains SIB. The procedure requires identification of a communicative response such as a vocal statement, sign, hand gesture, exchange of a picture card, or use of a voice output device. Functional communication training (FCT) is conducted by delivering the functional reinforcer contingent on the appropriate communicative response. Typically, the functional reinforcer is only delivered for the communicative response while simultaneously SIB is placed on extinction. For example, if SIB is maintained by escape from schoolwork, a student may be taught to hand a teacher a picture card to request a brief break from work.

Differential Reinforcement of Other Behavior

During differential reinforcement of other behavior (DRO), the functional reinforcer for SIB is delivered for the absence of self-injury. For an individual whose SIB is maintained by access to edible items, the individual could be provided a highly preferred edible item following a period of time during which SIB did not occur. A consideration with this method is that a new skill is not being taught. Whenever possible, DRA should be used instead of or in addition to DRO so that more appropriate behavior increases while SIB decreases.

Noncontingent Reinforcement

Noncontingent reinforcement (NCR) is delivered on a time-based schedule whether or not an individual displays SIB. The procedure has value in reducing the motivation for engaging in self-injury. When possible, the functional reinforcer for SIB should be the one delivered on a NCR schedule. So, for a child whose SIB is maintained by attention, his father could reduce the likelihood of SIB occurring if he provides frequent or continuous attention to the child, even if it is not requested (i.e., noncontingently). Functional reinforcers are not always possible (e.g., the child's father is busy on a work-related phone call), in which case other stimuli can be provided. These situations will be described below in the "Other Interventions" section.

PUNISHMENT-BASED PROCEDURES

The guiding principles of the right to effective treatment mandate that punishment procedures may be warranted when extinction and reinforcement-based procedures alone do not reduce SIB. Generally speaking, punishment procedures are those that, when applied contingently, decrease the future probability of a particular behavior. Punishment is defined solely by its behavior-reducing effect and not whether the punishing stimulus is unpleasant, aversive, or annoying. A punishment procedure should never be the sole intervention component used to treat SIB. Rather, punishment should be used in conjunction with preventive and reinforcement-based procedures. Practitioners have an ethical obligation to ensure that punishment is evaluated only when reinforcement-based and other less invasive procedures have not produced clinically significant reductions in SIB. Practitioners should always closely monitor the use of punishment procedures and fade the use of punishment as early as possible.

Positive Punishment

Positive punishment involves applying an aversive consequence immediately following SIB. For example, you could physically prompt an individual to complete a task for 30 seconds contingent on escape-maintained SIB. Sometimes, a physical hold procedure is used as a contingent consequence for SIB that is maintained by sensory reinforcement.

Negative Punishment

Negative punishment involves the removal of some presumably preferred stimulus (e.g., functional reinforcer) contingent upon the occurrence of SIB. Response cost is a type of punishment in which a preferred stimulus that is already in an individual's possession is removed contingent upon SIB. For tangibly maintained SIB, a child's toy could be removed from his possession for 30 seconds following SIB. Another example of a negative punishment procedure is time-out, which is best applied for attention-maintained SIB by withholding attention contingently or placing the individual in a location that temporarily eliminates attention.

OTHER INTERVENTIONS

Competing Stimuli and Activities

In the case of SIB maintained by sensory stimulation, the functional reinforcer is not socially mediated; therefore, alternative forms of reinforcement that ostensibly compete with SIB may be useful. Also, during times when a socially mediated functional reinforcer of SIB is unavailable, competing stimuli can be provided. A competing stimulus or activity assessment is required to determine what stimuli and activities an individual will engage with and at the same time display reduced levels of SIB compared to times when these stimuli or activities are not available. Once stimuli or activities are identified, they can be provided noncontingently across some or all contexts, or in cases of socially reinforced SIB, during times when the functional reinforcer for SIB is unavailable. Redirection to competing stimuli, blocking, or prompts to engage with competing stimuli may be needed during and following the competing stimulus assessment. Also, for individuals who do not engage with stimuli, additional training (e.g., DRA) may be required to teach methods of interacting with stimuli or to increase motivation to engage with stimuli.

Protective Equipment

When an individual is at high risk for injury as a result of SIB, the use of protective equipment may be necessary. Protective equipment may be used in conjunction with response blocking and shadowing when implementing sensory extinction. Examples of protective equipment include helmets, shin guards, hand mitts, and mouth guards. Canvas arm splints, a form of mechanical restraint, may be used with individuals who target their face or head in the form of self-punching and biting of hands and arms. These splints are soft canvas sleeves with pockets in which metal stays (rods) can be placed to control flexion of elbows. The metal stays are interchangeable and are used to directly affect the degree of elbow flexion permitted. The degree of rigidity necessary to maintain low levels of SIB is highly dependent on individual factors such as strength and restraint history. The use of protective equipment should be closely monitored and steps should be taken to minimize the restrictiveness of the procedure. Clinicians should always plan for the fading and eventual discontinuation of protective equipment. In the case of arm splints, the metal stays may be gradually faded over time such that the arm splints are no longer necessary (e.g., flexible stays → no stays → gradual reduction of the canvas sleeve to a stimulus such as a sweat band or bracelet). Because continuous wearing of protective equipment may have untoward physical effects, we advise consultation with a physician before initiating such intervention.

ADAPTATIONS AND MODIFICATIONS

In reinforcement-based interventions, reinforcer delivery should begin according to a dense schedule—that is, providing frequent access to reinforcement. This arrangement will increase the likelihood that an individual contacts reinforcement for alternative behavior or the non-occurrence of SIB. However, this initial schedule is often so dense that it cannot be supported outside a clinical setting. Therefore, after low levels of SIB are achieved and appropriate behavior is established, reinforcement should be thinned (i.e., reduced) to a practical level while monitoring and maintaining treatment gains.

Time-based schedules used in reinforcement-based treatments (e.g., NCR and DRO) can be thinned by gradually increasing the duration of time between reinforcer deliveries. However, this strategy cannot be used for DRA-based procedures, given the need to reinforce some alternative response. In these situations, one could gradually increase the delay between delivery of reinforcement and the next opportunity for the alternative response to be reinforced. To prevent high rates of the alternative response, you could introduce stimuli that signal the availability or unavailability of reinforcement.

When multiple treatment components are selected for use, a component analysis (i.e., systematic evaluation of each treatment component's effects on behavior) may be useful. Such an analysis can help identify components of a treatment package that are unnecessary or essential or actually worsen the behavior.

Finally, some individuals who engage in SIB also demonstrate self-restraining behavior (SRB). Typical forms of SRB are "hooking" fingers in belt loops, sitting on hands, and wrapping arms in clothing. SRB is inversely related to SIB—high-frequency SRB usually is associated with low-frequency SIB. Accordingly, if confronted by an individual with SRB, your initial treatment goal likely would be reducing or eliminating the behavior before designing a plan specifically for SIB. Often, the treatment approach toward SRB is teaching an individual to perform "acceptable" self-restraint such as holding objects in one's hands or wearing an item such as padded gloves, which would eventually be eliminated through stimulus fading.

KEYS TO REMEMBER

1. SIB is a complex behavioral phenomenon that requires an understanding of physiological and environmental variables, as well as how these variables may interact.

2. It is important for practitioners to understand the function of SIB in order to develop efficacious interventions for each individual client. Each intervention component must be tailored to each function of an individual's SIB, according to context. Interventions designed without an understanding of the function may be irrelevant to the individual's SIB or contraindicated and thus be ineffective or even result in an increase in SIB.

3. In some cases, SIB may be maintained by multiple forms of reinforcement (e.g., attention and escape from demands). Different intervention components targeting these maintaining variables may be necessary to produce significant reductions of problem behavior across contexts.

4. All interventions targeting SIB should be closely monitored by collecting baseline data on the occurrence of SIB and compared to the occurrence of SIB during treatment.

5. Procedures must be evaluated in a controlled manner to identify the most appropriate intervention on an individual basis.

6. There is no single reason for individuals to engage in SIB; therefore, there is no single appropriate intervention for all individuals, at all times, across all contexts, or across all functions.

7. A careful consideration and possible combination of environmental manipulations as well as pharmacological interventions should be evaluated for each individual during the development, generalization, and maintenance of any successful behavioral intervention targeting SIB.

SUGGESTED READINGS

Iwata, B. A., Pace, G. M., Dorsey, M. F., Zarcone, J. R., Vollmer, T. R., Smith, R. G., et al. (1994). The functions of self-injurious behavior: An experimental-epidemiological analysis. *Journal of Applied Behavior Analysis, 27*, 215–240.

Kahng, S., Iwata, B. A., & Lewin, A. B. (2002). Behavioral treatment of self-injury, 1964 to 2000. *American Journal on Mental Retardation, 107*, 212–221.

Matson, J. L., & LoVulla, S. V. (2008). A review of behavioral treatments for self-injurious behaviors of persons with autism spectrum disorders. *Behavior Modification, 32*, 61–76.

Schroeder, S. R., Oster-Granite, M. L., & Thompson, T. (Eds.) (2002). *Self-Injurious Behavior: Gene-Brain-Behavior Relationships.* Washington, DC: American Psychological Association.

CHAPTER 18

AGGRESSION AND DESTRUCTION

Henry S. Roane and Heather J. Kadey

OVERVIEW: WHAT WE KNOW

Severe aberrant behavior problems are broadly defined as behaviors that place an individual or others at risk for physical harm. In some cases, the behavior may be directed toward one's self, as in the case of self-injurious behavior (SIB; Chapter 17). In other cases, the harmful behaviors are directed toward other people (physical aggression) or toward one's property (destructive behavior). This chapter discusses the latter two behaviors.

Common forms of physical aggression are hitting, kicking, or pinching others. In some cases, loud noises, threats of physical violence, and cursing/name calling may be considered aggressive. Destructive behavior typically involves damage to specific objects and may take the form of breaking, throwing, tearing, or knocking over objects. Although both aggression and destruction may be "accidental" in some cases (e.g., knocking over a lamp while playing), in clinically significant cases these behaviors are deemed intentional or purposeful.

It is clear that aggressive and destructive behaviors often occur among individuals with autism spectrum disorders (ASDs), and there are some estimates of the prevalence of these behaviors among individuals with ASDs who have been referred for clinical services. In case reviews of 125 children (aged 3–21) previously referred to our clinic for the assessment and treatment of severe aberrant behavior, aggression was observed in 60.8% of the children and property destruction in 34.4%. Despite this information, it is unclear how accurate these numbers are across large groups of children with ASDs, including those across varying levels of severity and those who do not display clinically significant aggressive or destructive behavior. Thus, greater research is needed on the prevalence of aggressive and destructive behavior among individuals with ASDs.

Although we know little about the prevalence of aggression and destructive behavior in this population, there is some information on the impact of these behaviors. For example, data from an inpatient unit that specialized in the treatment of severe aberrant behavior revealed that aggression resulted in an average of 20 staff injuries, 2 emergency-room visits, and 8 sick days per month. Likewise, caregivers can suffer both physically and emotionally from aggression exhibited by individuals with ASDs. The photograph presented in Figure 18.1 was taken of a

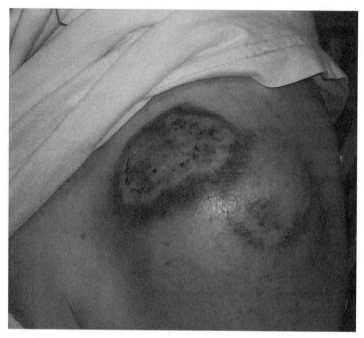

FIGURE 18.1 Physical evidence of aggressive behavior toward a caregiver of a child diagnosed with an ASD.

caregiver who had been bitten by a young child with an ASD. Destructive behavior poses additional concerns, including risks from exposure to harmful substances (e.g., broken glass) and financial effects due to the replacement of items or property repairs (e.g., holes in walls).

GETTING STARTED: BASIC PRINCIPLES AND APPLICATIONS

Some amount of aggression and destructive behavior is considered "normal" in children; however, behaviors are considered aberrant (i.e., different from normal behavior patterns) when they place others at risk for harm or the individual at risk for loss of educational or residential placement. Psychologists and developmental theorists have long attempted to describe the causal factors of aberrant aggressive and destructive behavior, and in many cases, the resulting theories have been influenced by the prevailing psychological zeitgeists. For example, in the 1940s and 1950s aggressive behavior was often viewed to be influenced by internal processes such as a child's unconscious feelings of neglect from caregivers or to incomplete ego development. A related view that emerged in the 1960s stated that humans were instinctively aggressive (and presumably destructive) such that some of these behaviors emerged when there was no other outlet for this instinctual drive. Although these hypotheses led to much debate among theorists, they were supported by little research and have largely fallen from the mainstream.

In contrast, a line of research initiated in the 1960s has influenced views of aggressive behavior to the present time. Albert Bandura and colleagues conducted research that evaluated the role of imitative learning on aggressive behavior. Participants observed an adult model either play with other toys and ignore a doll or engage aggressively with the doll (e.g., punching the doll, hitting the doll with objects), and these two groups were compared to a control group who never observed a model. The participants were later placed in a room with the doll. In general, those children who had observed the model become aggressive with the doll were significantly more likely to aggress toward the doll. Following Bandura's research, the notion of imitative learning (and, more broadly, social learning theory) exerted a great deal of influence on the study of aggressive and destructive behavior. It is from this theory that many of the concerns regarding violence in the media evolved. However, the influence of modeling on aggressive and destructive behavior displayed by individuals with ASDs has not been directly investigated. Nevertheless, research in other areas (e.g., social interaction) suggests that observing models can influence the occurrence of various behaviors in this population. Anecdotally, we have observed a potential case of aggression via imitative learning displayed by a young man whose aggressive and verbal behavior imitated various martial arts and dialogue sequences from *The Matrix*.

The majority of research examining the occurrence of aggression and destructive behavior among individuals with ASDs indicates that different environmental variables influence the behavior (i.e., these behaviors typically occur in certain situations). Consequently, an understanding of the context in which these behaviors occur is tantamount to decreasing their frequency. Said another way, in the majority of published cases involving individuals with ASDs, aggressive and destructive behavior have been shown to be operant behavior.

The notion that aberrant behavior could be operant was first presented by Edward Carr in his account of SIB, which was based on the laboratory research conducted by B.F. Skinner. An operant account of problematic behavior (such as aggression and destructive behavior) simply means that these behaviors operate on their environment to produce consequences that influence their future probability. For example, a child may have a history of receiving attention or toys from others when she is aggressive. Although a caregiver may react in this way with the intention of stopping the aggression, the outcome may be that the behavior is inadvertently paired with attention or toy delivery such that these reactions function to strengthen the behavior via the process of positive reinforcement. Alternatively, a child may become aggressive and destructive (e.g., ripping worksheets) when non-preferred schoolwork is presented. If so, the teacher might move away from the child and wait for him to calm down before presenting the work again. In effect, such a response functions as negative reinforcement for the aggression and destruction in that the behaviors were associated with the removal of an aversive activity (doing schoolwork), which may ultimately serve to strengthen the problem behavior. A final operant contingency that influences the occurrence of aggressive and destructive behavior is automatic reinforcement (sometimes referred to as "self-stimulatory" behavior). In an automatic reinforcement contingency a reinforcing consequence is produced directly by the response in question, independent of the external environment. For example, research has shown that some children with ASDs engaged in destructive behavior (e.g., breaking plastic objects) because it produced smaller pieces of plastic, which the participants incorporated into their stereotypy.

The results of numerous investigations have supported the occurrence of operant aggressive and destructive behavior displayed by individuals with ASDs. This is not to say that operant variables are the only variables that influence the occurrence of these behaviors in this population; rather, these variables have been the focus of the majority of the research, particularly among individuals with ASDs. Thus, the following sections focus on the role of operant variables in the occurrence of aggression and destruction.

GUIDELINES FOR IMPLEMENTATION

ASSESSMENT

Chapters 2 and 3 detail the procedures involved in a functional assessment and a functional analysis. Ideally, any intervention for aggressive or destructive behavior would be preceded by this form of assessment as well as a stimulus preference assessment (Chapter 4). To review, functional assessments involve identifying those variables that occasion and reinforce problem behavior. Using this model, a functional relationship is one in which a behavior is viewed in terms of the events that occur before it (antecedents) and after it (consequences). A functional approach is critical to developing an effective intervention because the results of a functional assessment suggest variables that might be manipulated to bring the behavior under environmental control.

A functional approach to the assessment of aggression and destructive behavior can be compared to a structural approach to assessment. Again, a functional assessment is concerned with identifying the environmental variables (antecedents and consequences) that are associated with the occurrence of behavior, and a function-based treatment is one that is matched to the antecedents and consequences that maintain the behavior. In contrast, a structural approach to assessment involves examining the behavior in accordance with its response form (i.e., its topography) and applying a treatment based on protocols for that specific type of response. To illustrate, a school may have a "zero tolerance" policy for aggression, which results in a suspension from school. Such a structural approach means that the intervention might be effective in some cases but ineffective in others (e.g., if avoiding school is a reinforcer for the child). The relative efficacy of the treatment depends on identifying the reinforcer for the behavior. Understanding that the variables that maintain behavior differ for everyone explains why there is no one treatment that works for everyone. A maximally effective treatment is one that is individualized and based on the antecedents and consequences that maintain the behavior.

INTERVENTION

When an intervention is based on a functional assessment, the variables that maintain the problem behavior can be altered such that the consequences that maintain the behavior are withheld following the problematic behavior and can be presented for some other (alternative) more appropriate behavior. In this regard, interventions for aggressive and destructive behavior share common features with those for SIB and other problematic behavior. In the most basic form of intervention, the rationale is to disrupt the relationship between the behavior and the reinforcer that maintains the aggressive or destructive behavior (i.e., the response–reinforcer relation as identified in the functional assessment).

There are several ways to disrupt a response–reinforcer relation. The most straightforward process is to withhold the reinforcer when the individual engages in aggression or destruction (referred to as *extinction*). For example, if a child's aggression is maintained by caregiver attention, extinction would involve no longer delivering attention following acts of aggression. Because the aggressive behavior would no longer produce the maintaining reinforcer, one would expect a decrease in aggression (i.e., the behavior no longer "pays off"). Extinction differs from the common recommendation of "planned ignoring" even though these terms are sometimes used interchangeably. The distinction lays in the extent to which "ignoring" targets the variable that maintains the aggressive or destructive behavior. In the case of a child whose behavior is reinforced by attention, planned ignoring may well function as extinction. Alternatively, if a child's behavior is maintained by the sensory consequences it produces (automatic reinforcement), then planned ignoring will likely be ineffective. As discussed before, an intervention like planned ignoring is based on the structure of the behavior, not the function.

Extinction is often used as a component of treatments for aggressive and destructive behavior. Although its use is quite effective, extinction is sometimes associated with negative side effects, including an initial worsening of the behavior in terms of frequency or intensity (i.e., an "extinction burst"), the emergence of new forms of problem behavior, or emotional responding. Thus, introducing extinction might produce an increase in problem behavior in the short term. Although such side effects only occur in approximately one third of cases, this possibility may lead some to be hesitant to implement extinction. Thus, it is common practice to combine extinction with other procedures to minimize the risks of such side effects.

A common operant-based treatment approach is one in which the individual can access the reinforcer that maintains the aggressive or destructive behavior, while those behaviors no longer produce the reinforcer (i.e., extinction). This approach can be arranged in two basic formats. In one, the reinforcer is presented, not contingent upon the individual's behavior, but rather according to the passage of time. Such a treatment is referred to as a response-independent reinforcement paradigm, or more commonly *noncontingent reinforcement* (NCR). The rationale for this procedure is that if an individual is receiving access to the reinforcer "for free" (e.g., once every 5 minutes) then he or she should be less motivated to engage in aggressive or destructive behavior to access the reinforcer. Although NCR has been shown to be effective at decreasing the occurrence of aggression and destruction in a number of cases, it is not without possible shortcomings. For example, there have been some cases in which NCR has been associated with the problem of incidentally reinforcing problem behavior, particularly aggression. In previous research, we used NCR to treat aggression displayed by a 13-year-old girl with developmental disabilities. Although the procedure was initially effective, the participant coincidentally aggressed at the same time that reinforcement was being delivered. In effect, her aggression was paired with reinforcer delivery such that aggression increased and the intervention was no longer effective (however, this type of outcome is rare in the use of NCR). The second shortcoming of NCR in the treatment of aggressive and destructive behavior is that the intervention does not teach the individual an alternative (appropriate) method of accessing reinforcement. In other words, behavior reduction relies on the time-based delivery of reinforcement, not reinforcer delivery following an adaptive response.

In contrast to NCR, *differential reinforcement* procedures involve reinforcement of behaviors that are alternatives to aggression or destruction. Broadly speaking, differential reinforcement describes a process whereby one type of behavior results in the delivery of a reinforcer and the targeted problematic behavior no longer produces reinforcement (i.e., extinction). The type of differential reinforcement program varies depending what type of alternative behavior is reinforced. For example, in a *differential reinforcement of alternative behavior* (DRA) procedure, the individual is taught an alternative way to access reinforcement (e.g., completing a task to get a break from schoolwork rather than aggressing). A common type of DRA is a procedure in which the individual is taught an alternative communication response to access reinforcement. This form of DRA is referred to as *functional communication training* (FCT) and is useful because it teaches the individual a novel communication skill that can be recognized across caregivers. For example, a child might be taught a manual sign for "help" during a difficult tasks and destructive behavior is no longer reinforced. Thus, in both DRA and FCT, the intervention targets not only behavior reduction but also response acquisition. A related form of differential reinforcement, *differential reinforcement of incompatible behavior* (DRI), is similar to DRA except that the alternative response is one that is physically incompatible with the targeted problem behavior (e.g., having one's hands on a desk as opposed to another person).

Another common differential reinforcement procedure is *differential reinforcement of other behavior* (DRO or omission training). During a DRO procedure, any behavior other than engaging in problem behavior for a specific amount of time results in reinforcement. In other words, in DRO the important variable is that the individual forgoes problem behavior for a period of time in order to access reinforcement. What he does in that period of time is not necessarily important so long as he is not engaging in the targeted aggressive or destructive behavior.

Noncontingent reinforcement and differential reinforcement procedures (including FCT) are the most common procedures used to treat aggressive and destructive behavior among individuals with ASDs. These programs have been typically implemented with extinction. Although these procedures have proven to be effective in the treatment of aggression and destruction, there are some caveats to their use. First, noncontingent and differential reinforcement are generally most effective when implemented at a relatively high degree of procedural integrity. If a caregiver implements the treatment with imperfect accuracy (e.g., implementing the treatment correctly 50% of the time), the efficacy of the intervention will likely be compromised. Several studies have shown that DRA procedures implemented with extinction are more effective than those implemented without extinction. This suggests that caregivers must be aware of the impact of their behavior on the targeted problematic behavior. For example, if a caregiver sometimes attends to destructive behavior and sometimes does not, extinction is not being implemented correctly. Instead such a situation would approximate an intermittent reinforcement schedule, which might ultimately make the targeted behavior more resistant to treatment.

A second concern with noncontingent and differential reinforcement programs may involve their relative difficulty of implementation. As noted above, NCR is a fairly straightforward process (e.g., a timer goes off and the individual receives reinforcement, regardless of his behavior at the time); however, in some cases this might lead to incidental reinforcement of the problematic behavior. Also, differential reinforcement programs require caregivers or practitioners to monitor the individual's problematic behavior frequently. This might lead to issues regarding procedural integrity (as noted above) or general impracticalities in the implementation of the intervention. For example, a recommended intervention involving FCT might be to reinforce appropriate communication each time it occurs and to no longer reinforce aggressive behavior. This particular recommendation would likely prove extremely difficult to implement under most circumstances because the recommendation essentially comes down to "every time the person asks appropriately for something, give it to him." Although this might well reduce the problem behavior, it is a recommendation that produces high rates of reinforcement, which might be problematic to implement or which might lead to reinforcer satiation. Fortunately, a number of procedures have been introduced to moderate levels of reinforcement delivery during differential reinforcement programs or to decrease the amount of time a caregiver devotes to observing the behavior (i.e., momentary DRO). A final consideration in the use of differential reinforcement procedures is the effect of the process on the targeted individual. Although these procedures are often quite effective and beneficial (particularly when teaching an alternative response), there have been some reports of differential reinforcement procedures being associated with negative emotional behavior, especially when an individual misses the opportunity to access reinforcement (e.g., repeatedly not obtaining reinforcement during DRO). Thus, care should be given to ensure that the initial reinforcement criteria are easily obtainable (e.g., 1 minute) such that the individual establishes a history of success with the intervention before the criteria are increased to something more practical (e.g., 1 hour).

No discussion of interventions for aggressive and destructive behavior is complete without describing the use of punishment (i.e., a process by which a stimulus is presented or removed following a targeted response, which reduces the future occurrence of that response). In the past, the use of restraint/seclusion or other aversive procedures (e.g., water mist) was common in the treatment of aggressive and destructive behavior. The more recent practice is to move away from the application of aversive consequences toward procedures that involve the brief loss of reinforcement (e.g., time-out). Although practitioners have the obligation to avoid punishment procedures whenever possible, it is often the case that reinforcement-based procedures (e.g., DRA) alone are ineffective in reducing the occurrence of aggression and destruction. Under such circumstances, the addition of a punishment procedure has been shown to be effective for producing clinically significant behavior reduction. Given this consideration, there are general guidelines regarding the use of punishment, including (a) an initial examination of least restrictive and reinforcement-based procedures, (b) monitoring the duration of punishment implementation, (c) using empirically derived punishment procedures, (d) assessing for emotional and behavioral side effects of punishment, and (e) assessing for potential negative reinforcement of the punishing agent (i.e., the behavior of the person implementing the punishment is reinforced by the termination of the targeted aggressive or destructive behavior).

ADAPTATIONS AND MODIFICATIONS

In general, the procedures involved in the assessment and treatment of aggression and destruction are similar to those involved in other types of problematic behavior. There are, however, a few special considerations that should be discussed in confronting these behaviors. First, it is often necessary for practitioners and caregivers to wear protective arm guards, hand guards, chest protectors, gloves, and so forth when addressing aggression and destruction. Such equipment can be obtained through a variety of martial arts suppliers available on the Internet. Regarding the individual who displays the behavior, it would often be unsafe to purposefully expose the individual to harmful substances (e.g., broken glass) for the purpose of assessing his or her destructive behavior. Therefore, it is often appropriate to identify safe alternatives (e.g., transparent plastic with no sharp edges) with which to "bait" the assessment environment for conducting such analyses. Alternatively, one could measure attempts to engage in the targeted destructive behavior while blocking completion of the response. Special consideration should also be given to situations in which aggression or destruction occurs under special circumstances. For example, if an individual with an ASD engages in aggressive behavior toward smaller children, it would be unethical to expose a small child to that behavior. Thus, the assessment process must be modified to accommodate this situation by attempting to evoke the behavior under safer circumstances (e.g., toward an adult wearing protective equipment) or by modifying the type of assessment conducted (e.g., using function-based rating scales in lieu of a functional analysis). Also, there have been some cases in which individuals have been found to engage in destructive behavior maintained by automatic reinforcement. Such behavior can be difficult to observe in a functional analysis via the common test procedure for this type of reinforcement contingency (i.e., the alone condition). Researchers have identified alternative test conditions (e.g., the use of an "ignore" condition in which the therapist essentially serves as a target of aggression) or the use of devices that can be used to measure the occurrence of aggression without exposing another individual to a dangerous behavior.

KEYS TO REMEMBER

1. Most research suggests that aggression and destruction exhibited by individuals with ASDs are learned (operant) responses that are often influenced by the reactions of others.

2. A key to developing an effective intervention is to identify the environmental correlates of aggression and destruction and the use of an individual's preferred items and activities.

3. Although effective when implemented in isolation, extinction is often implemented as a component of noncontingent or differential reinforcement procedures.

4. Special consideration should be given to (a) modifying treatments such that they might be easily implemented by others and (b) the use of punishment.

5. When assessing and treating aggressive and destructive behavior, special attention should be given to keeping one's self and others as safe as possible through the use of protective equipment and other environmental modifications.

SUGGESTED READINGS

Fisher, W. W., Lindauer, S. E., Alterson, C. J., & Thompson, R. H. (1998). Assessment and treatment of destructive behavior maintained by stereotypic manipulation. *Journal of Applied Behavior Analysis, 31*, 513–527.

Marcus, B. A., Vollmer, T. R., Swanson, V. A., Roane, H. S., & Ringdahl, J. E. (2001). An experimental analysis of aggression. *Behavior Modification, 25*, 189–213.

Thompson, R. H., Fisher, W. W., Piazza, C. C., & Kuhn, D. E. (1998). The evaluation and treatment of aggression maintained by attention and automatic reinforcement. *Journal of Applied Behavior Analysis, 31*, 103–116.

Vollmer, T. R., & Iwata, B. A. (1992). Differential reinforcement as treatment for behavior disorders: Procedural and functional variations. *Research in Developmental Disabilities, 13*, 393–417.

Vollmer, T. R., Ringdahl, J. E., Roane, H. S., & Marcus, B. A. (1997). Negative side effects of noncontingent reinforcement. *Journal of Applied Behavior Analysis, 30*, 161–164.

CHAPTER 19

NONCOMPLIANCE AND OPPOSITIONAL BEHAVIOR

David A. Wilder

OVERVIEW: WHAT WE KNOW

Noncompliance, defined as the failure to follow a specific command, is a common concern among young children and is particularly common among children and adults with autism spectrum disorders (ASD). Children with ASD, for example, may not comply with caregiver instructions to initiate or complete a task, surrender a toy, or interact appropriately with others. Adults with ASD may not comply with directives to perform a task or engage in social activities or with instructions given by their supervisors, employers, or friends/caregivers. Sometimes noncompliance is specific to one task, setting, or person. In other cases, it is pervasive, affecting numerous aspects of an individual's daily activities. Generally, the more pervasive noncompliance is, the more an intervention is warranted.

Although no studies on the relationship between noncompliance at a young age and problems later in life among individuals with ASD exist, research on the developmental course of noncompliance among typically developing children has been conducted. Generally, noncompliance in young children is related to other, more serious problems and diagnoses later in life. For example, noncompliance at early ages is associated with conduct disorder and oppositional defiant disorder diagnoses in adults.

Noncompliance should be assessed before designing and implementing an intervention. Before beginning a behavioral assessment, physical reasons for noncompliance such as deafness and other hearing problems should be ruled out. In addition, the individual's receptive language skills should be assessed to be sure that he or she can adequately understand what he or she is being asked to do. There is no standardized tool available to assess noncompliance in children with autism, although the Childhood Behavior Checklist (CBCL), which includes a subscale measuring "rule-breaking" behavior, is sometimes used to assess noncompliance in children without a diagnosis of autism. The CBCL is an indirect measure of behavior, meaning that parents or other caregivers report on the child's history of a given behavior. Direct observation of the individual's behavior in a variety of settings is generally the preferred method of assessing noncompliance in children and adults with autism. Assessment should be designed to determine (a) the frequency of noncompliance, (b) the instructions most likely to occasion noncompliance and the consequences most likely to maintain noncompliance, and (c) the individuals with whom the child or adult is most likely to behave in a noncompliant manner.

The frequency of noncompliance should be assessed by delivering at least 10 common instructions to the individual and recording whether he or she complies with each instruction. Allow the individual at least 10 seconds to comply or attempt to comply with each instruction. Record whether compliance occurs on a datasheet similar to one of the sample recording forms provided at the end of this chapter (Worksheets 19.1 and 19.2). Record attempts at compliance as compliance; if the individual tries but cannot complete a task, he or she may have a skill deficit as opposed to a problem with noncompliance. This procedure should be repeated one or two

Worksheet 19.1 Sample Datasheet for High-P Instructional Sequence Intervention

Instructions: Identify three high-p instructions. Present rapidly, immediately before the target (low-p) instruction. Record compliance with each of the high-p instructions and the low-p instruction in the appropriate columns (H1, H2, H3, Target (low-P)). For example, if compliance occurred within 10 seconds after each of the three high-p instructions but did not occur after the target instruction, place a "Y" in the H1, H2, and H3 columns and an "N" in the target (low-P) column.

Trial	HP1	HP2	HP3	Target (Low-P)	Description of Problem Behavior, if any
1					
2					
3					
4					
5					
6					
7					
8					
9					
10					
11					
12					
13					
14					
15					
16					
17					
18					
19					
20					

Worksheet 19.2 Sample Datasheet for Guided Compliance Intervention

Instructions: Present one instruction per trial. Use the verbal (V), model (M), physical guidance (P) sequence. Record compliance in the appropriate column. For example, if compliance occurred within 10 seconds after the model prompt was presented, place a "Y" in the M column.

Trial	V	M	P	Description of Problem Behavior, if any
1				
2				
3				
4				
5				
6				
7				
8				
9				
10				
11				
12				
13				
14				
15				
16				
17				
18				
19				
20				

times (so that a total of 20–30 trials are delivered) to obtain a baseline measure of noncompliance. To score the data, divide the number of trials with noncompliance by the total number of trials and multiply by 100%. Some prefer to measure compliance as opposed to noncompliance (since noncompliance is something that requires no action and is therefore technically not a behavior); if you'd like to measure compliance, simply divide the number of trials with compliance by the total number of trials and multiply by 100%.

To assess the instructions most likely to occasion noncompliance, identify 5 to 10 instructions of different types. Include at least two instructions from each of the following three categories: instructions to initiate or complete an academic, self-care, work, or pre-academic task; instructions to surrender a preferred item or toy or activity; and instructions to interact appropriately with another person. Next, randomly present each of the identified instructions, one per trial. Record compliance to each instruction and calculate noncompliance, as described above, for each of the three types of instructions. It is possible that noncompliance will be greater for a specific instruction or type of instruction relative to another.

To assess the individuals with whom the child or adult is most likely to behave in a noncompliant manner, identify three or more people who routinely deliver instructions to the individual (e.g., mother, father, teacher, work supervisor). Have each of these people present instructions to the individual. Be sure that each person presents the same instructions. Record compliance to each instruction and calculate noncompliance. It is possible that noncompliance will be more common when a specific person delivers the instruction.

GETTING STARTED: PRINCIPLES AND APPLICATIONS

Behavior analysts posit that noncompliance is learned. Individuals with autism behave in a noncompliant manner to get or maintain access to something that they want (social positive reinforcement) and/or to avoid or escape something that they don't want (social negative reinforcement). For example, parents and teachers commonly ask children to stop doing something preferred such as playing with a toy. A child may be noncompliant because it enables him to maintain access to that preferred activity or toy. It is also likely that noncompliance produces attention from caregivers (in the form of repeated prompts or reprimands), and it is possible that this attention maintains noncompliance. Finally, it is also common for parents and teachers to ask children to do something they may not want to do (e.g., clean up). A child may be noncompliant because it enables him to avoid/escape the activity.

Of course, it is possible that noncompliance serves more than one function. Depending on the situation, a child may be noncompliant to maintain access to preferred items, obtain access to attention, and avoid/escape a task. Regardless of the function or reason for noncompliance, formal treatment is often necessary to increase compliance to acceptable levels.

GUIDELINES FOR INTERVENTION

Interventions for noncompliance can be divided into two categories: antecedent-based interventions and consequence-based interventions. Antecedent-based interventions consist of procedures conducted before or concurrent with the instruction delivered and include the use of direct commands, noncontingent reinforcement, advance notice, rationales (i.e., the delivery of reasons for compliance), and the high-probability (high-p) instructional sequence. Generally, direct commands (e.g., "Put the toy on the shelf") should be used as opposed to indirect commands (e.g., "Don't you think it is time to clean up now?") when presenting instructions. This may be particularly important for children and adults who have speech and language difficulties.

Noncontingent reinforcement, or access to preferred items, while delivering an instruction to an individual may also be helpful to increase compliance, although this procedure may not be appropriate in every setting. For example, it isn't very practical to provide individuals with access to a preferred item in a school each time they are given an instruction. Providing advance notice of an upcoming instruction or transition might be useful. Generally, notice of an upcoming instruction or transition is delivered 5 minutes, 2 minutes, and/or 1 minute before the actual instruction (e.g., "In 5 minutes, you'll have to wash your hands"). Rationales or reasons for complying with an instruction (e.g., "Do your homework after school because it is due tomorrow") may also be helpful, although research to date has not supported their use.

The antecedent-based intervention with the most support is the high-p instructional sequence. The high-p instructional sequence consists of delivering a few instructions with which the individual is likely to comply immediately before delivering a low-probability instruction (i.e., the target instruction). For example, a parent might ask a child to "eat your candy," "play with your toy," and "give me five" immediately before she asks the child to "clean up your room" (the instruction she is trying to get compliance with). The three high-p instructions are presented back-to-back so that there is some momentum to comply with the low-p instruction. Although this intervention has been used and found to be effective to increase compliance in many cases, it has also been found to be ineffective in some cases.

Common consequence-based interventions for noncompliance include differential reinforcement of compliance, time-out, and guided compliance procedures. Differential reinforcement of compliance involves the delivery of preferred items contingent upon compliance with instructions. Although effective, this intervention is also difficult to conduct in many settings. In addition, the item(s) delivered as part of this intervention must be strong enough to overpower the contingency supporting noncompliance. To be practical, this intervention must also be thinned over time—that is, instead of delivering a preferred item every time compliance occurs, the schedule of delivery must be thinned so that the individual receives a preferred item every other time he complies, then every third, and so on. This intervention can be effective but must be carefully planned and implemented.

Time-out has also been used as a consequence-based intervention to treat noncompliance. Contingent upon noncompliance with an instruction, the caregiver requires the individual to go to a designated time-out area. The time-out area should be free from toys, activities, and even fun things to look at (e.g., the television). The individual remains in time-out for a short period and is then allowed to return to the "time-in" setting. Although time-out can be effective to increase compliance, it is not appropriate in every situation. When noncompliance is maintained by avoidance/escape from a task, using time-out is contraindicated. In other words, the use of time-out enables the individual to avoid/escape a task because he or she is given a break (i.e., the time-out period) and doesn't have to perform the task associated with the instruction, at least temporarily. For this reason, time-out should be used only when it is clear that the function of noncompliance is not to avoid/escape a task or instruction.

Guided compliance is one of the most effective interventions for noncompliance. Guided compliance procedures involve the delivery of an instruction in a specific sequence. The final step in the sequence is assisted guidance, in which the individual is guided to comply with the instruction that was delivered. For individuals who have speech or language difficulties, guided compliance procedures often consist of three steps (in fact, they are sometimes called "three-step prompting" or "three-step compliance training" procedures). The first step consists of the delivery of the instruction. If the individual does not comply, the second step—repeating the instruction while modeling performance of the task—is conducted. If the individual does not comply with the second step, the third step is implemented: repeating the instruction while physically guiding the individual to perform the task.

GUIDELINES FOR INTERVENTION

Because both antecedent- and consequence-based interventions have been used and found to be effective to increase compliance, guidelines for one intervention from each of these categories will be provided. However, the first step in intervening, defining noncompliance and compliance, is common to both interventions. Definitions of noncompliance usually involve "failure to do or attempt what is described in a directive delivered by an adult within 10 seconds of the delivery of the directive." As previously mentioned, this definition requires no actual behavior, so it should be accompanied by a definition of compliance. Definitions of compliance are typically the inverse of definitions of noncompliance. For example, a common definition might be "completing or attempting what is described in a directive delivered by an adult within 10 seconds of the delivery of the directive."

GUIDELINES FOR ANTECEDENT-BASED INTERVENTION: THE HIGH-PROBABILITY INSTRUCTIONAL SEQUENCE

1. **Identify high-p instructions.** Identify three to five instructions with which your client is likely to comply. These are likely to be instructions that result in an activity that your client likes. For example, "Eat the candy" is an instruction that, if complied with, enables an individual to engage in a preferred activity. "Give me five" is another instruction that might be preferred for some individuals because it results in attention. If you have difficulty identifying instructions, you might ask someone close to your client for ideas. Be sure to test whether each instruction is a high-p instruction by delivering it and then observing your client. If he complies immediately, the instruction is likely a high-p instruction.

2. **Identify a target instruction.** Initially, it is best to identify one instruction to target for increased compliance. Once you are sure that compliance with this targeted instruction increases, the high-p sequence can be used with other instructions as well. The initial target instruction should be something that your client is asked to do on a regular basis. An example would be "Come here" or "Pick up your toys."

3. **Implement the intervention.** Deliver three high-p instructions immediately before delivering the target instruction. All instructions should be brief and stated in the form of a command (not a question). Praise should be delivered immediately after compliance with each of the instructions (i.e., each of the high-p instructions and the target instruction). Allow your client at least 10 seconds to comply with an instruction before presenting the next one. If your client does not comply with the high-p instructions, simply move on to another high-p instruction. Provide excited praise for compliance with the target instruction. Be sure to collect data on compliance with the high-p and target instructions.

GUIDELINES FOR CONSEQUENCE-BASED INTERVENTION: GUIDED COMPLIANCE

1. **Obtain consent.** This intervention includes hand-over-hand guidance. In some settings, physical guidance is not permitted. Thus, before using this intervention, be sure that the setting you are working in allows it. In addition, you should be sure that hand-over-hand guidance is safe to use with your client; this procedure might evoke aggression or other problem behavior with some clients. For individuals who are particularly large, this procedure may be impossible to conduct.

2. **Implement the intervention.** Whenever you present instructions to your client, do so in the manner described below. Use a neutral tone of voice and deliver the instruction in the form of a statement, not a question. Keep the instruction short; avoid unnecessary words.

After presenting the instruction, wait 10 seconds for your client to comply or attempt to comply. If your client complies, praise him. If he does not comply, get his eye contact and then re-present the instruction in the same way, but this time simultaneously model the appropriate response. Wait 10 seconds. If your client complies, praise him. If your client does not comply, re-present the instruction in the same tone (be sure not to yell) while physically guiding him to comply or begin to comply with the instruction. Use the least amount of force necessary to guide your client to complete or begin the task. It may be some time before this procedure is effective; consistent implementation is key to its long-term effectiveness. Be sure to collect data on compliance.

ADAPTATIONS AND MODIFICATIONS

The high-p instructional sequence described above may need modification, depending on the individual you are working with. For example, more than three high-p instructions may be needed for some individuals. Also, if the procedure is initially ineffective, alternative high-p instructions might be identified and used.

The guided compliance procedure described above may also need to be modified, depending on the setting and client you are working with. In settings that don't permit physical guidance, the third step cannot be conducted. Also, this procedure doesn't work for vocal behavior; it can't be physically guided. Finally, for individuals with good language skills, the second step may not be necessary and can be left out of the procedure.

Of course, these interventions will not work with everyone. If neither of these procedures is effective, differential reinforcement of compliance might be attempted. The details of this procedure are described in one of the suggested readings below.

KEYS TO REMEMBER

1. The objective of the intervention is to increase compliance. However, once improved compliance is achieved, many individuals with autism may need to be taught when *not* to comply. In other words, in some situations it may be unsafe for an individual to comply (e.g., when a stranger presents an instruction). Some individuals with autism may need to be taught to discriminate these situations.
2. Provide particularly loud and excited praise the first few times you get compliance with an instruction that historically has not been complied with.
3. Try to implement the intervention in the actual setting in which noncompliance is most problematic.
4. Monitor the effects of the intervention you use by recording compliance and noncompliance each time an instruction is delivered (i.e., each trial).

SUGGESTED READINGS

Mace, F. C., Hock, M. L., Lalli, J. S., West, B. J., Belfiore, P., Pinter, E., & Brown, D. K. (1988). Behavioral momentum in the treatment of noncompliance. *Journal of Applied Behavior Analysis, 21,* 123–141.

McMahon, R. J., & Forehand, R. L. (2003). *Helping the Noncompliant Child: Family-Based Treatment for Oppositional Behavior.* New York: Guilford Press.

Wilder, D. A., & Atwell, J. (2006). Evaluation of a guided compliance procedure to reduce noncompliance among preschool children. *Behavioral Interventions, 21,* 265–272.

Wilder, D. A., Harris, C., Reagan, R., & Rasey, A. (2007). Functional analysis and treatment of noncompliance by preschool children. *Journal of Applied Behavior Analysis, 40,* 173–177.

Wilder, D. A., Saulnier, R., Beavers, G., & Zonneveld, K. A. (2008). Contingent access to preferred items versus a guided compliance procedure to increase compliance among preschoolers. *Education and Treatment of Children, 31,* 297–306.

C H A P T E R   2 0

FEARS AND PHOBIAS

James K. Luiselli

OVERVIEW: WHAT WE KNOW

Many people with ASD are fearful of certain objects, sensory events, and situations. A child, for example, may have a specific phobia of dogs and other animals. An adult may be afraid of going to locations such as a hospital or shopping mall. Sometimes, particular sounds (e.g., ambulance siren, vacuum cleaner) and activities (e.g., riding in an elevator) may be the source of a person's fear.

We know that unless properly treated, fears and phobias can be debilitating and life-long. By avoiding fear-provoking objects and situations, a child or adult misses opportunities for learning and socializing. Furthermore, being frightened by something or somebody makes it difficult for a person to participate in interactions that can enhance quality of life. The emotional distress that characterizes a fear reaction also is concerning—typically crying, heightened anxiety, and negative thinking. A further undesirable outcome from fears and phobias is stigmatization by peers and the general public when they label a child or adult with ASD as being "weird" or not fitting in.

There is no standardized scale or instrument for diagnosing fears and phobias in the ASD population. The *Diagnostic and Statistical Manual of Mental Disorders* (DSM-IV-TR) defines *specific phobia* as marked and persistent fear of clearly discernible objects and situations. The fear must be manifested by avoidance and anxiety that interfere significantly with a person's daily functioning. Subtypes of specific phobia, as defined by the DSM-IV-TR, relate to animals, the natural environment (e.g., heights, storms), situations (e.g., flying, elevators, enclosed places), and blood/injection/injury (e.g., presence of blood, invasive medical procedures).

Of note, the diagnostic criteria for specific phobia contained in the DSM-IV-TR were not derived from symptoms observed among children and adults with a developmental disability such as ASD. Therefore, behavioral assessments, sometimes called *behavior avoidance tests* (BATs), are better suited for diagnostic purposes. Essentially, behavioral measurement entails recording how a fear or phobia is demonstrated. To illustrate, assessment might focus on the amount of time a person comfortably tolerates proximity to a phobic object or how close a person will approach the condition or situation that is avoided. These direct measures also are used for evaluating the effects of a fear reduction intervention plan.

GETTING STARTED: PRINCIPLES AND APPLICATIONS

Learning theorists have explained the origins and maintenance of fears and phobias with reference to classical (respondent) and operant conditioning. Imagine, as an example, a child with ASD who is bitten by a dog. That experience includes physical pain and emotional discomfort. Accordingly, and resulting from classical conditioning, the child is likely to have a negative reaction anytime hr or she sees a dog or hears one barking.

A second conditioning effect occurs when the child avoids any contact with dogs. Such avoidance would be demonstrated by the child refusing to go to or remain in any setting where a dog might be encountered. The avoidance behavior in this example is said to be *negatively reinforced* because it keeps the child from experiencing an unpleasant event. The combination of classically conditioned fear that evokes operantly conditioned avoidant behavior is called *two-factor learning.*

In the case of a child who was bitten by a dog, there is direct contact with the now-feared animal. Most fears and phobias result from such conditioning. However, fears also can be acquired through observational learning. A child, for example, could develop a fear of dogs after watching a movie or listening to a story in which someone was bitten. Whether a fear or phobia develops from direct exposure to or observing an unpleasant event, the resulting emotional distress and avoidant behavior rarely resolve without carefully planned intervention.

GUIDELINES FOR INTERVENTION

One of the most effective strategies for treating fears and phobias is to gradually expose a person to the objects and situations that frighten him or her. Different terms have been used to describe this approach. *Contact desensitization* refers to the process of a person experiencing less anxiety and reduced avoidant behavior after gradually contacting the source of fear. *Reinforced practice* emphasizes positively reinforcing a person's repeated tolerance of fear-provoking objects and situations. Similarly, *shaping approach responses* describes teaching a person to slowly confront what is feared. Although these labels differ, the actual procedures are similar in function and practice.

1. **Define the presenting fear.** Stating that a child or adult is "afraid of going outside" insufficiently describes what may be a fear or phobia because it does not specify the source of distress and avoidant behavior. Is the person frightened by stinging insects, inclement weather that signifies a thunderstorm, or separating from a parent? If a person fears going to the beach, is it because she is afraid of entering the water or some other environmental stressor? You should consider an intervention plan only after precisely defining the fear and associated context.

The key to defining a fear or phobia is to write it in behavior-specific terminology. Here is an example:

"Bob does not like to be examined by his doctor. He will enter the doctor's office, wait there, and talk to the doctor. Bob even allows the doctor to touch him. However, as soon as the doctor displays a medical instrument, Bob screams, appears frightened, and pushes the doctor away. This reaction prevents the doctor from looking in Bob's ears, eyes, and throat, as well as listening to his heart and lungs."

This description shows that Bob is not afraid to visit his doctor per se. Rather, he is frightened by the instruments required to complete a medical evaluation, showing anxiety, emotional distress, and avoidant behavior as soon as they are displayed.

2. Construct a fear hierarchy. A fear hierarchy essentially is a sequence of steps starting where a person can comfortably tolerate the feared object or situation. As the steps increase, the person moves closer to or is brought in closer contact with the source of fear. Table 20.1 shows the fear hierarchy that was established for an 8-year-old boy who had autistic disorder and a specific phobia of electronic animated figures. In this case, the fear hierarchy was based on the boy's distance from the figures, beginning at 6 meters, with each step advancing in 1-meter increments. As shown in Table 20.1, five steps were required for the boy to reach the terminal criterion of being 1 meter from the figures.

In addition to a criterion such as distance, the steps in a fear hierarchy could be based on time, such as the number of minutes a person handles a feared object or remains in a feared location. There is no formula for constructing a fear hierarchy, notwithstanding the guideline that steps should be small enough so that they don't increase anxiety demonstrably over previously tolerated steps. Also, if avoidant behavior occurs at a step, you should consider adding more steps to the fear hierarchy, in effect slowing down the pace of intervention.

3. Determine the setting for intervention. Intervention will work best in the real-world settings where a person's fear is most common. For example, if an adult man with ASD is afraid of going to a movie theater, the fear hierarchy might begin with him simply standing outside the theater entrance. The next steps could be entering the theater but remaining in the lobby, followed by purchasing a ticket, giving the ticket to an usher, listening to the movie through an open door, and so on. Implementing procedures under natural conditions is sometimes referred to as in vivo intervention.

Table 20.1 Example of a Fear Hierarchy

Step	Behavior Criterion
1	Child remains 6 meters from feared objects
2	Child remains 5 meters from feared objects
3	Child remains 4 meters from feared objects
4	Child remains 3 meters from feared objects
5	Child remains 2 meters from feared objects
6	Child remains 1 meter from feared objects (terminal criterion)

Adapted from Ricciardi, J. N., Luiselli, J. K., & Camare, M. (2006). Shaping approach responses as intervention for specific phobia in a child with autism. *Journal of Applied Behavior Analysis, 39,* 445–448.

Unfortunately, it is not always possible to intervene in the actual setting or in contact with the actual object that is feared. One constraint may be the presence of other people or competing activities that make it difficult to apply procedures accurately. Also, the child or adult may not be able to tolerate intervention that is implemented initially in a natural setting. The alternative is to introduce intervention under *simulated* conditions. Referencing the movie theater example, the man's parents could "pretend" that their living room is the movie theater, with the television representing the movie screen. Other relevant stimulation could be added, such as dimming the lights or arranging chairs to resemble seats in the theater. Although sometimes successful, simulated intervention does not guarantee generalization to the real-world setting; however, it may hasten progress during subsequent in vivo intervention.

4. Assess preferences. Assessing a person's preferences should be performed to identify objects and activities that can function as positive reinforcement. As presented later in this section, intervention requires motivating a child or adult to gradually confront steps in a fear hierarchy. Procedurally, this entails offering the person something pleasurable, either continuously at each fear hierarchy step or contingent on completing each step. Common preferences are food, toys, music, books, or interacting with a friend. Absent the incentive of valued preferences, most children and adults will not respond compliantly with an intervention. Ideally, preferences should be easy to deliver, portable, and of sufficient variety.

5. Implement the intervention. Having constructed a fear hierarchy, selected the setting for intervention, and assessed preferences, you can intervene directly. The person conducting the intervention should be in close proximity to the child or adult, starting with Step 1 of the fear hierarchy. Tell the child or adult what is expected at each step. Referring to Table 20.1 again, at Step 2 you would say, "You're going to move a bit closer now—okay? Remember, I'll be with you and you don't have to go farther." At each step in the fear hierarchy, allow the child or adult access to one or more of his or her assessed preferences. For example, if music is being used, the child or adult could listen to a portable player through earphones. When food is the identified preference, small bites could be given intermittently at each step or when each step is completed (e.g., following 2 minutes of exposure). The key to presenting preferences is to determine precisely what the child or adult must do in order to have them.

Set a criterion for advancing steps in the fear hierarchy. A common guideline is to move ahead when the child or adult is successful during consecutive sessions at each step—for example, three times without demonstrating distress and avoidant behavior. Usually, the convention for dealing with failure at a step is to drop back to the previous step, advancing when the child or adult meets the criterion again. A sample recording form for tracking the progression of steps in a fear hierarchy is presented at the end of this chapter (Worksheet 20.1).

Continue with the intervention until you have completed all the steps in the fear hierarchy. At this point, it is desirable to have the child or adult maintain success without presenting him or her with preferences or having someone in close proximity. Preferences can be "faded" by having them available less frequently or in smaller amounts. You or another person conducting the intervention can slowly reduce your presence, speak less during sessions, or withdraw entirely while monitoring the child or adult from a distance. This phase of intervention is critical because ultimately the child or adult must be able to independently tolerate, and no longer avoid, the previously feared object or situation.

The intervention is completed when you have moved the child or adult successfully through all of the steps in the fear hierarchy. With success, he or she will no longer become anxious and try to avoid the object or situation that was previously feared.

Worksheet 20.1 Sample Recording Form

Steps	Consecutive Sessions									
Behavior Criterion: Child does not scream, cry, or show agitation, and does not move away from the feared object for 120 consecutive seconds.										
Step Criteria: Advance to the next step when child meets the behavior criterion during 3 consecutive sessions at the current step (+). Return to the previous step when child does not meet the behavior criterion during one session at the current step (-).										
1										
2										
3										
4										
5										
6										
7										
8										

ADAPTATIONS AND MODIFICATIONS

With few exceptions, the intervention guidelines can be followed uniformly with children and adults. An adult generally will have a longer learning history than a child, in which case the fear or phobia will be more firmly established, perhaps requiring a longer period of intervention. Adults also may have had more failed treatment attempts.

Another variation is that selecting preferences will most likely be different for children and adults. As much as possible, preferences should be developmentally appropriate and individualized for each person.

Finally, certain setting differences have to be considered. The focus with children, for example, would be schools and recreational locations with similar-age peers. For adults, common intervention settings would be a vocational training program and community sites such as stores and restaurants.

KEYS TO REMEMBER

1. The objective of intervention is to have a child or adult *gradually* confront a feared object or situation without distress and avoidant behavior.
2. Construct a hierarchy of steps that approximate and eventually lead to full exposure to the feared object or situation.
3. Select child-specific and adult-specific preferences that will mediate anxiety and avoidant behavior at each step in the fear hierarchy and positively reinforce coping success.
4. Try to implement the intervention in the actual setting and under the natural conditions in which the fear or phobia occurs.

5. Monitor the effects of the intervention by recording success and failure at each step in the fear hierarchy.

SUGGESTED READINGS

Erfanian, N., & Miltenberger, R. G. (1990). Brief report: Contact desensitization in the treatment of dog phobias in persons who have mental retardation. *Behavioral Residential Treatment, 5,* 55–60.

Jones, K. M., & Friman, P. C. (1999). A case study of behavioral assessment and treatment of insect phobia. *Journal of Applied Behavior Analysis, 32,* 95–98.

Rapp, J. T., Vollmer, T. R., & Hovanetz, A. N. (2005). Evaluation and treatment of swimming pool avoidance exhibited by an adolescent girl with autism. *Behavior Therapy, 36,* 101–105.

Ricciardi, J. N., Luiselli, J. K., & Camare, M. (2006). Shaping approach responses as intervention for specific phobia in a child with autism. *Journal of Applied Behavior Analysis, 39,* 445–448.

Shabani, D. B., & Fisher, W. W. (2006). Stimulus fading and differential reinforcement for the treatment of needle phobia in a youth with autism. *Journal of Applied Behavior Analysis, 39,* 449–452.

PART 4

OTHER HOW-TO GUIDELINES

CHAPTER 21

DISCRETE TRIAL TEACHING

Peter Sturmey

OVERVIEW: WHAT WE KNOW

Discrete trial teaching (DTT) is probably the most commonly used method in applied behavior analysis (ABA) to teach skills to students who have autism spectrum disorders (ASDs). It was the basis for Ivar Lovaas' earliest work in early intervention in the 1960s and is found in almost all of the studies that have systematically evaluated ABA with young children with autism. Although most work with DTT has been done with children, DTT also is effective as a teaching strategy with adults. Thus, DTT is an evidence-based practice in special education and habilitation services. There are now other teaching methods, such as incidental teaching, trial interspersal procedures, and natural language paradigm. Researchers are still investigating the relative merits of these different approaches, but many authorities think that a good education should consist of a combination of methods that includes DTT. Other methods, in particular, might be helpful in programming generalization and increasing teaching opportunities throughout the day (see Chapters 22 and 23). Because DTT remains the most commonly used ABA methods with children who have ASD, everyone working with this population should be able to implement DTT accurately and effectively.

This chapter emphasizes DTT with children. Teachers, classroom assistants, professionals, early interventions therapists, and family members can use DTT to teach many skills. These skills include prerequisites for learning, such as sitting, keeping hands down, and eye contact, and also basic language skills such as imitation, increasing vocalization, and verbalizing in the presence of adults. DTT also is useful for teaching children to discriminate colors, shapes, and sizes. It can also be effective in teaching advanced language skills—for example, answering questions and initiating conversations.

Generalization, by which a child demonstrates skills outside of the teaching setting, is part and parcel of DTT. Instructors should plan for generalization from DTT at the onset of teaching. Do not make the mistake of thinking that generalization is something to consider after a child has acquired a skill. Rather, a good DTT program should include at least one baseline generalization probe. For example, you might teach color discrimination with pieces of paper and probe for generalization with Lego© blocks. Also, plan to assess generalization across people, locations, and time. For example, a classroom assistant might teach a child to point to body parts with a doll at the desk in the morning. Then the teacher might conduct generalization with a puppet in the afternoon. As learning progresses, instructors can program generalization to more natural-istic learning situations by (1) gradually increasing the amount of independent work a child can do, (2) fading instruction from one-to-one teaching to a group of children, and (3) gradually increasing the distance between themselves and the child. In this way a child might eventually learn to work independently in a group with few prompts and reinforcers from the instructor.

When using DTT you should teach functional skills and functional tasks wherever possible. To illustrate, when teaching discrimination of coins, use actual coins and dollar bills, not Monopoly© money. If you use analogue materials, you are hoping that generalization might occur from these artificial materials to the actual materials. Generalization, however, is much more likely if you use materials common to the training and generalization tasks. Selecting functional tasks is also important. For example, having a child point to a picture of a bottle of glue is less functional than getting the glue when the child is working on an art project.

DTT also needs a good curriculum—that is, one that specifies teaching goals in small, achievable steps. The curriculum should place teaching goals in the correct sequence, building incrementally to the final skill. A good curriculum should include all the important curriculum domains, such as social behavior, and should not focus on one domain, such as academics. Finally, a good curriculum should reflect behavior analytical theory, especially in curriculum domains such as language. Examples of good curricula can be found in the suggested readings listed at the end of this chapter.

Another important consideration is that DTT should be evaluated and modified regularly, meaning that instructors must record a child's baseline performance, record teaching progress every day, and present data for visual inspection in the form of a simple line graph. Most impor-tant, instructors or their supervisors must use the data to make smart decisions about teaching. If a child does not progress after a few teaching sessions, the instructors must modify the pro-gram or check that they are teaching correctly. For example, they might change the reinforcer, use a different prompting method, or break the task down further. If a child completes a DTT skill program, the instructor must move on to another program that builds on earlier successes. You should be aware of the child's progress on each program and take action frequently to modify teaching procedures as needed.

Fortunately, DTT is easy and quick to learn—if someone teaches you well! Using brief instruction, modeling, practice, and feedback, teachers, classroom assistants, and parents have learned to implement DTT in two or three sessions that last 10 to 30 minutes. Watching a good video model of how to do DTT is a great start to learning DTT skills. I have also found that instructors who learn to teach one program with one child are usually able to correctly teach many other similar programs and other children without additional training. Furthermore, it is usually the case that when an instructor begins teaching correctly, accurate responses by the child increase rapidly and maladaptive behavior decreases.

GETTING STARTED: BASIC PRINCIPLES AND APPLICATIONS

One of the basic principles of DTT is making learning as easy as possible by breaking down teaching into small, brief, easy units called trials. DTT focuses on teaching only one or a few responses at a time. Other principles are giving children a lot of practice by presenting many opportunities to learn, using powerful reinforcers to motivate responding, prompting correct responses and preventing errors, and minimizing competing behaviors by requiring quiet sitting, attending, and keeping hands down at the beginning of each trial. DTT also works best when the instructor minimizes distractions by presenting only the materials needed for teaching and, when necessary, teaching in a quiet place or with room dividers to reduce distractions.

When selecting goals, it is useful to select only a few and in a small number of curricular domains to get some success early on. This process will make teaching enjoyable for both the child and instructor. If the child does not have eye contact and similar prerequisite skills for learning, you should include these skills early in programming. Typically, a child's first programs might include an attending skill, a receptive language skill, an imitation program, a simple expressive language program, and a matching task. As the child masters these programs, the instructor can add new programs in these domains and then introduce new curriculum areas.

GUIDELINES FOR IMPLEMENTATION

Before initiating a DTT session, the instructor should prepare the teaching area. Preparation includes obtaining all teaching materials, datasheets, and objects that will be used as reinforcers. Another step is removing any distractions and unnecessary materials before teaching begins. Do not make the mistake of starting a session and having to disrupt teaching to get materials. When edible reinforcers are selected for a child, prepare them in bite-size pieces and place them in a handy container.

The instructor begins a trial by ensuring that the child is sitting appropriately, properly oriented, and making eye contact. If necessary, the instructor manually prompts these correct responses before giving an instruction. The instructor then gives a short instruction one time in a low, neutral tone of voice. Next, the instructor waits 3 to 5 seconds for a correct response. If the child makes a correct response, the instructor delivers a reinforcer and enthusiastic praise that describes what the child did correctly no later than 2 seconds after the child's correct response. The instructor then records the data. If the child does not make any response or makes an error, the instructor prompts a correct response. The kind of prompt varies from program to program. Generally, least to most intrusive prompting is best as it ensures the child makes a prompted correct response and gives the instructor an opportunity to reinforce that prompted correct response. The instructor should interrupt and correct errors as soon as possible. It is a good idea to vary the time interval between trials so that the child learns to respond to the instruction rather than the passage of time.

Thus, DTT involves 10 teaching steps, which are listed in Table 21.1 at the end of the chapter. You can use the checklist to observe instructors teaching and to give them feedback on how well they implement procedures. You can also observe your own teaching on videotape using this checklist.

It is easy for teaching to become sloppy because instructors usually are not well trained in the first place or they may drift in their teaching skill over time if their supervisors do not observe them teach frequently and give them feedback. The result of poor teaching is that children may learn slowly, fail to learn at all, or even learn inappropriate behavior. Common teaching errors include (1) not preparing the teaching area completely before teaching; (2) not getting a readiness response at the beginning of every trial; (3) repeating or varying the wording of the instruction; (4) using a lively instead of a neutral tone of voice for the instruction; (5) incorrectly reinforcing an error or partially correct response; (6) using an ineffective consequence; (7) failing to conduct a preference assessment when a child does not work for the consequence provided; (8) failing to prompt, prompting too early or too late, or using the wrong prompt level; (9) providing inadvertent cues, such as pointing or looking; and (10) failing to take data on

Table 21.1 Discrete Trial Teaching Behavior Checklist

Behavior	Definition
Eye contact	The instructor makes eye contact with the student for a minimum of 1 second contiguous to delivery of a verbal instruction.
Readiness response	The instructor gives no verbal instruction until the student's body is oriented toward the instructor and his or her hands and legs are not moving before each verbal instruction.
Delivers instruction once	The verbal instruction is presented only one time per trial. Any repetition of the verbal direction either in full or in part is an incorrect teaching procedure.
Verbal instructions	The verbal instruction is delivered with clear articulation, and matches verbatim the specific verbal instruction designated for that program. Each instruction will be a specific set of words defined in each program as the discriminative stimulus.
Correction procedure	A predetermined gestural, physical, or verbal prompt designated for each program is delivered within 3 to 5 seconds of the verbal direction after a failure of the student to respond. The predetermined prompt should be used contiguous to any incorrect response that is given.
Appropriate reinforcement	Only correct responses will be reinforced with a tangible reinforcer. The tangible reinforcer will be presented simultaneously with verbal praise. No tangible reinforcement will be provided for incorrect responses, or while the student is engaged in inappropriate behavior, even following a correct response.
Specific praise	The delivery of a behavior-specific statement is provided concurrently with delivery of reinforcement. For example, the instruction "Touch nose" is followed by the student making eye contact with the instructor is followed by praise such as "Good, touch nose."
Immediacy of reinforcement	The instructor states the behavior-specific praise within 1 second following a correct response and continues to present praise for the correct response until after delivery of the tangible reinforcer.
Data collection	A plus or a minus is recorded on the datasheet after each trial.
Intertrial interval	Following the end of a trial (usually represented by the presentation of the reinforcer or correction procedure), the teacher pauses for a minimum of 1 second before delivery of the next verbal instruction, beginning the next trial. The duration of the intertrial interval must vary from trial to trial.

every trial. Some instructors also make individual errors in their teaching. For example, I have seen instructors deliver musical reinforcers for 5 minutes instead of 10 seconds or chat with colleagues during DTT. Only careful instructor training using directions, modeling, practice, and feedback ensures that instructors acquire DTT skills. Regular monitoring of teaching ensures that instructors maintain these skills.

ADAPTATIONS AND MODIFICATIONS

Occasionally, instructors must modify DTT for a particular child. For example, a child may not learn because the teaching materials elicit competing stereotypy. Thus, the instructor has to substitute some other teaching material for that child. Another child may not learn because he or she frequently looks out of the classroom window. Here, the instructor may have to teach in another location, put up a barrier so the child cannot see out of the window, or add a new program to teach tolerance of distractions.

A more common problem to watch out for is programming correct-trial consequences that are not reinforcing. If a child does not approach the consequence you offer—or, worse, turns away from it—you probably do not have a reinforcer. A good rule of thumb is to hold out the object and if the child reaches for it, close your hand. Should the child persist in trying to get the object out of your hand, it is probably a reinforcer. If this does not happen, you need to identify a reinforcer immediately. The best way to identify reinforcers, however, is through stimulus preference assessment, ideally conducted on a daily basis (see Chapter 4). Briefly, you can conduct this assessment by offering a child the choice of three or four items, presented two at a time, and waiting for him or her to reach for one. Then, offer another choice of the last item the child took and a new item. The last item taken is probably a reinforcer, and you can use it in your teaching right away. You can also consider using reinforcer deprivation to maximize the effectiveness of reinforcers during teaching. For example, if you have an especially difficult program, you might save special reinforcers, such as a highly preferred toy, for that program. You can ensure that this special reinforcer will be most effective by keeping it away from the child until teaching occurs.

Poor imitation training is another common problem when conducting DTT. Sometimes instructors do not understand the importance of imitation and the correct curriculum for such training. Keep in mind that the purpose of imitation training is not to teach a child specific imitation programs but rather to teach *generalized imitation*. Generalized imitation is the skill of imitating novel models that have not been taught previously. An example of generalized imitation is when you go to a restaurant in Barcelona for the first time and you see people wiping garlic and tomatoes onto bread and you imitate that new response. No one ever taught you to do that before, yet you imitated the behavior without explicit training. So, when a child has acquired four or five gross motor imitation programs, the child has learned nothing important unless he or she imitates novel gross motor models that have not been taught. If generalization probes—which instructors conduct without reinforcement—do not result in correct imitation of novel responses, then the instructor must implement more gross motor training programs until the child acquires generalized imitation (however many it takes!).

Relative to discrimination training programs within DTT, a child must respond only to the items presented during the discrimination trial and not to other stimuli. As an illustration, when teaching discrimination between "big" and "small," an instructor might present a large red block and a small blue block. If a child correctly discriminates between these two stimuli, it is unclear whether he or she is responding to a difference in size or color. An instructor might also inadvertently cue a student by looking at the correct material, leaning towards it, or pointing to it. Another problem is when an instructor allows a child to point to the wrong material and rather than immediately prompting a correct response, permits him or her to point to the correct material while reinforcing this second response. In this way, the instructor unintentionally teaches the child to keep pointing at different things and not accurately discriminate between or among them. Finally, instructors might present directions or cues in the same order—for example, always teaching "stand up" followed by "sit down." Again, if a child responds correctly, it may appear as if he or she has learned to discriminate, when unfortunately it is the instructor's behavior that influenced responding.

KEYS TO REMEMBER

1. Learn to do DTT correctly by watching an experienced practitioner directly or on videotape. A person with similar expertise also can observe you teaching and give feedback. Consider getting yourself videotaped when implementing DTT.
2. Program generalization when you start a DTT program. Ask yourself why you are teaching the child this task, and find the useful contexts for that behavior.
3. Use functional materials and tasks that are of immediate practical benefit to the child.
4. Use a good curriculum such as one of those listed in the suggested readings listed at the end of the chapter. Make sure that you know why you are teaching particular skills to the child and where each program is going to lead.
5. Evaluate and modify programs routinely. If a program is not working after a few sessions, you should change something: use better reinforcers, teach more trials, or reduce interfering behavior. Try something! Do not continue ineffective programs forever.
6. Incorporate a DTT checklist, like the one in Table 21.1, to monitor intervention integrity and fine-tune teaching procedures among multiple instructors.

SUGGESTED READINGS

Dib, N. E., & Sturmey, P. (2007). Reducing student stereotypy by improving teachers' implementation of discrete-trial teaching. *Journal of Applied Behavior Analysis, 40,* 339–343.

Koegel, R. L., Glahn, T. J., & Nieminen, G. S. (1978). Generalization of parent-training results. *Journal of Applied Behavior Analysis.* 11, 95–109.

Sarakoff, R., & Sturmey, P. (2008). The effects of instructions, rehearsal, modeling and feedback on acquisition and generalization of staff use of discrete trial teaching and student correct responses. *Research in Autism Spectrum Disorders, 2,* 125–136.

Ward-Horner, J. C., & Sturmey, P. (2008). The effects of general-case training and behavioral skills training on the generalization of parents' use of discrete-trial teaching, child correct responses, and child maladaptive behavior. *Behavioral Interventions, 23,* 271–284.

OTHER RESOURCES

Lovass, I. O. (1981). *Teaching Developmentally Disabled Children. The Me Book.* Austin, TX: PRO-ED Inc.

Partington, J. W. (2006). *The Assessment of Basic Language and Learning Skills (ABLLS).* Revised edition.

Taylor, B. A., & McDonough, K. A. (1996). Selecting teaching programs. In C. Maurice, G. Green, & S. C. Luce (Eds.), Behavioral Intervention for Young Children. A Manual for Parents and Professionals (pp. 63–101). Austin, TX: PRO-ED Inc.

CHAPTER 22

NATURALISTIC TEACHING

Keith D. Allen and Stacy B. Shaw

OVERVIEW: WHAT WE KNOW

Early behavioral treatments for individuals with autism used basic principles of learning to create highly effective teaching interactions. Their success was largely a result of highly structured training procedures, which were developed specifically to maximize learning potential. Distractions were minimized, prompts were delivered in a precise sequence, practices were massed, and consequences were delivered in a reliable, immediate, and frequent manner. These tightly controlled training procedures were also known as "discrete trial training" and have been found to be quite effective at teaching new and complex skills. Indeed, these intensive teaching procedures led to impressive gains in language, social, and adaptive skills for many individuals with autism.

Unfortunately, these highly structured approaches to learning were not without problems. Of significant concern was the fact that many of the newly acquired skills would be exhibited in the highly structured learning environment but not in the less structured natural environment. In other words, the skills learned in controlled training settings did not automatically transfer, or generalize, to other important settings (e.g., regular classroom, playground), other important people (e.g., peers, parents), or other important tasks (e.g., play, daily living tasks). For example, a child who had learned to say "truck" when presented with a picture of a truck in a tightly controlled treatment setting would not necessarily say "truck" when he wanted access to his toy truck at home. Gradually it became clear that in order for important skills to be used in the natural settings of everyday life, training would need to be systematically planned and implemented in a way that would promote generalization.

Over recent years, "naturalistic" teaching has emerged as a way to address this problem with generalization. Naturalistic teaching promotes generalization of skills to the natural or everyday settings where those skills are required. Recent reviews of the expanding literature on naturalistic teaching have found that the research support for this approach is extensive. (See Allen , K. D., & Cowen , R.J. , (2008) for a review.) Naturalistic procedures have been found to enhance the generalization of language, social, and play skills. In direct comparisons with the more structured approaches, naturalistic procedures have, in many situations, been found to produce better generalization of important skills to the natural environment. In addition, because naturalistic procedures occur within the context of everyday life and activities, they can help make learning more fun and in many cases increase a child's willingness to participate in teaching interactions. As a result, parents and practitioners can feel confident in using naturalistic procedures as part of an evidence-based approach to educating individuals with autism.

GETTING STARTED: PRINCIPLES AND APPLICATIONS

To understand the basic principles of naturalistic teaching, a distinction must be made between two behavioral processes: discrimination and generalization. When an individual exhibits the correct or desired response under certain stimulus conditions and not others, the individual is said to have discriminated. Thus, an individual who selects a truck when asked to select the truck from a choice of options such as truck, cup, and shoe has discriminated between different choices.

Generalization occurs when that same correct or desired response occurs under similar but untrained stimulus conditions. Thus, the individual who can select the truck when the truck looks different (e.g., different size, color, or function) from that which was used during training is said to have demonstrated generalization. In addition, an individual who can make the correct response when the teacher or the setting is different is also said to have demonstrated generalization.

Discrimination training can be a critical part of learning because sometimes it is very important that an individual exhibit certain responses under very specific conditions and only those conditions. For example, it is important that individuals learn "stranger danger" and to not get in the car with anyone other than a parent or guardian. This requires that "coming when called" does not generalize to every adult who is calling. Likewise, individuals must learn that not all four-legged animals are dogs, not all liquids are juice, not all coins are quarters, and not all buses will arrive downtown.

Discrimination is problematic, however, when it leads to an individual being unable to perform certain responses under many different yet important conditions. For example, an individual must learn to ask for help not just from the teacher but also from a boss, a parent, or, at times, a peer. Likewise, an individual must learn to identify a jacket on the coat rack as well as in a picture, to count coins at the store as well as at school, and to recite his or her address to a cab driver as well as a parent. When individuals do not generalize important language, social, and play skills from the training environment to everyday life, difficulties in adaptive functioning may result.

GUIDELINES FOR IMPLEMENTATION

When generalization is the goal, naturalistic teaching can be an important solution. However, there is no single or gold standard naturalistic teaching procedure to guide implementation. Various approaches can be found under a number of different names, including incidental teaching, natural language paradigm, behavioral chain interruption, script fading, and milieu teaching. Each procedure emphasizes slightly different ways to approach learning and generalization.

What follows are guidelines, derived from these different procedures, that represent an integration of the most distinguishing characteristics of naturalistic teaching.

TEACH RESPONSES THAT WILL LIKELY CREATE CONTACT
WITH NATURAL REINFORCERS

Generalization is enhanced when an individual is taught a response for which the natural consequence is a reinforcer—that is, a consequence that strengthens responding. Natural consequences are those that would occur naturally, without needing to be programmed by the teacher. For example, a natural consequence to a request for a "truck" is to hand the individual a truck. Thus, the truck naturally reinforces the individual for saying "truck." The use of praise, hugs, or even candy as a consequence would not be a natural consequence of a request for a truck, and these arbitrary consequences would require specific programming by the teacher. Furthermore, responding in this latter case may be limited to conditions where the teacher has arranged for these types of arbitrary reinforcement. Because naturalistic teaching targets responses that will come into contact with naturally available reinforcers across conditions, generalization is enhanced.

Here is an example. Zach's teacher, Mrs. Cole, has observed that Zach loves playing with cars and trucks during free play. Mrs. Cole has decided to target Zach's expressive language by using natural reinforcers that are available. When Zach shows interest, he will be required to request to play with the cars and trucks and to elaborate by describing features of the ones he wants first (e.g., "Yes, Zach, you may play with the cars and trucks. Which color cars and trucks would you like?" or "How many would you like?"). She will hand him a few and once he is engaged, she will impose the same expectations before Zach can access more or different kinds of cars or trucks (i.e., she will require request + elaboration).

ALLOW AN INDIVIDUAL'S INTERESTS TO DIRECT
AND PACE TEACHING

Given the emphasis on natural reinforcers, there will be times when teaching cannot occur because an individual, for whatever reason (e.g., illness, fatigue, satiation), is not interested in the current activities or materials. Under highly structured teaching conditions, a teacher might try to overcome this disinterest by introducing arbitrary reinforcers—for example, the use of candy to reinforce turn taking with the trucks, praise to reinforce requesting, access to preferred computer games to reinforce following directions. However, because naturalistic teaching relies on natural reinforcers, teaching is not forced when interest has waned.

Here are several examples. During free time, Mrs. Cole has planned to work with Zach on appropriate sharing and play sequences with cars and trucks as well as on expressive language requests and elaborations, but today Zach has followed several children to the kitchen area, where he seems interested in setting the table with plastic dishes, cups, and food. Mrs. Cole realizes that at this moment naturalistic teaching associated with car and truck play is not available. Instead, she follows Zach to the kitchen, takes several plates and pieces of food, holds them within view, and waits for Zach to request them. When he does, she asks him to elaborate the colors, sizes, and categories (e.g., fruits or vegetables) that he wants and then hands them to him. Later, Zach loses interest in the kitchen and begins pacing the room. Although she had hoped to work with him on turn taking, she recognizes that because his interest is currently low, naturalistic teaching is not appropriate at this time.

EMBED TEACHING WITHIN THE ACTIVITIES OF EVERYDAY LIFE

Generalization is enhanced when training conditions are diverse and loosely structured. The goal of this approach is for the individual to be unable to tell where or when training is occurring so that trained responses occur everywhere and with everyone. By embedding teaching within the activities of everyday life, diversity is increased by the inclusion of multiple "teachers" (e.g., paraeducators, parents, peers) across multiple settings (e.g., on the playground, in the hallways, in the backyard at home, during a bath, at the mall) and at various times throughout the day.

Here are some examples. Mrs. Cole has observed that Zach loves playing on swings and slides on the playground. Mrs. Cole has decided to target Zach's expressive language by using natural reinforcers that are available during recess. Zach will be required to request to go outside and to elaborate by describing which activity he wants to engage in first (e.g., "Yes, Zach, you may go outside. Where do you want to play first?"). Mrs. Cole has recruited Zach's parents and his daycare providers to do the same. Mrs. Cole has also recruited several peers to participate as "peer tutors" to assist with naturalistic teaching. When Zach is observed to be engaged with cars and trucks, she prompts a peer to arrive with additional highly preferred cars and trucks. The peers then share the additional cars with Zach contingent upon his appropriate request. At home, Zach's parents also make cars, puzzles, and computers accessible only after appropriate requests and elaborations by Zach. The teacher provides a list of the types of elaborations they are working on at school (e.g., "Sure, you can play with some cars for a while. Which color cars would you like?"). In addition, Zach's parents model pushing the cars, making car sounds, and turn taking, encouraging Zach to imitate. They also arrange play dates with a selected peer who brings preferred snacks and puzzles that Zach can access by asking the peer what he has in his backpack. The peer also models appropriate play sequences and turn taking with toys. Back at school, Mrs. Cole occasionally sends Zach on an errand to the office. She has recruited the office secretary to dispense information about the errand only after Zach queries for that information. The secretary also has a collection of treats Zach likes. Mrs. Cole has recruited the secretary to keep the treats in one of three tins on her desk. Zach must query for information (i.e., "Where is it?"), request access, and elaborate about what color, size, or number of treats he would like.

INCORPORATE PROMPTS THAT CAN BE TRANSPORTED
TO NEW SITUATIONS

Prompts are most often thought of as teaching methods that help promote learning. However, generalization can also be enhanced by including prompts within one training situation that can easily be transported to new situations.

For example, individuals with autism often do not initiate social-communicative interactions in any setting and, as a result, prompting is often required. The mand-model procedure allows a teacher to initiate an interaction by telling the child what is required and then modeling the appropriate response. For example, Mrs. Cole might have some nifty cars, but Zach only looks or grabs and does not request without a prompt. Mrs. Cole might then say, "What do you want?"

and immediately model, "Say, 'I want a car.'" Mrs. Cole might also introduce a time-delay procedure where she gradually increases the time between her request and her model, giving Zach a chance to respond but helping him before he gets frustrated or loses interest. Mrs. Cole could also use a script-fading procedure in which visual and/or auditory cues or prompts are provided in the natural setting. For example, Mrs. Cole wants to teach Zach how to approach a group at recess and request sharing of access to a swing. She decides to teach him to follow a written script of an appropriate interaction. Because this is a new skill for Zach, Mrs. Cole initially prompts and reinforces script following in a tightly controlled, less naturalistic setting. Eventually, as Zach acquires the skill, he might take the script with him to recess (e.g., on a small laminated card in his back pocket), where another teacher prompts Zach to look at and follow the script, as needed.

ADAPTATIONS AND MODIFICATIONS

RESTRICT ACCESS

One of the common obstacles to naturalistic teaching is that too often opportunities for naturalistic teaching are lost because individuals have rather unlimited or only slightly restricted access to the things that interest them most. However, with some increased restrictions and a touch of creativity, many additional naturalistic teaching opportunities can be created.

Here are some examples. Mrs. Cole has taken the time to arrange the classroom so that some of Zach's most preferred activities and objects are visible but not easily accessed. His favorite cars and puzzles are on the top of a cabinet that can be accessed only by adults. When he arrives each day his dessert and drink are removed from his lunch and he is required to initiate additional requests to access them. His coat and boots are also moved and after a request to go outside, he is prompted to ask a classroom aide (or sometimes peer tutor) for their location. At home, computer games he enjoys are locked in a cabinet and the best DVD is always in a novel location, requiring queries and social exchanges with parents and sometimes siblings who are recruited to assist with naturalistic teaching.

INTERRUPT CHAINS

Although much of naturalistic teaching occurs at the beginning of potential interactions, when motivation is high, there are times when naturalistic teaching can occur in the middle of an activity sequence. *Behavior chain interruption* involves an interruption of the chain or flow of purposeful behavior in the midst of a familiar routine. For example, Zach's parents typically require Zach to request to play a computer game, but they have also purchased a timer that attaches to the computer. The timer allows them to limit his time on the computer. When the time elapses, a 60-second countdown warns Zach of impending shutdown. Zach's play is then interrupted and he must immediately find his parents and initiate a request for more time.

Zach's parents have also taught him to make his own peanut-butter-and-jelly sandwich. They did this initially in a more controlled, discrete-trial type of procedure. Once mastered, his parents intentionally arrange for him to periodically discover that there is only one piece of bread or a very small amount of jelly. Solving the problem requires interrupting his activities and asking his parents for help.

KEYS TO REMEMBER

1. Naturalistic teaching promotes generalization of skills to settings where those skills are required.
2. To find good naturalistic teaching opportunities, follow the individual's interests and activities.
3. Learning does not need to occur just in the classroom or in tightly controlled, distraction-free environments. Look for opportunities to teach within the context of everyday events with everyday people.
4. Not all skills can be learned through naturalistic teaching. Some new or complex skills may be better learned in a more controlled setting before taking that skill into the natural setting.

SUGGESTED READINGS

Allen, K. D., & Cowen, R.J. (2008). Using naturalistic procedures to teach children with autism. In J. Luiselli, D. Russo, W. Christian, & S. Wilczynski (Eds.), *Effective Practices for Children with Autism: Educational and Behavior Support Interventions that Work*. New York: Oxford University Press.

Alpert, C., & Kaiser, A. (1992). Training parents as milieu language teachers. *Journal of Early Intervention, 16*, 31–52.

Kohler, F. W., Strain, P. S., Hoyson, M., & Jamieson, B. (1997). Merging naturalistic teaching and peer-based strategies to address the IEP objectives of preschoolers with autism: An examination of structural and child behavior outcomes. *Focus on Autism and Other Developmental Disabilities, 12*, 196–206.

Stokes, T. F., & Osnes, P.G. (1989). The operant pursuit of generalization. *Behavior Therapy, 20*, 337–355.

Sundberg, M., & Partington, J. (1999). The need for both discrete trial and natural environment language training for children with autism. In P. Ghezzi, W. Williams, & J. Carr (Eds.), *Autism: Behavior Analytic Perspectives* (pp. 139–156). Reno, NV: Context Press.

C H A P T E R   2 3

PROMOTING GENERALIZATION

Patrick M. Ghezzi and Valerie R. Rogers

OVERVIEW: WHAT WE KNOW

A well-known milestone in the early development of a child is seen when he or she responds appropriately to a stimulus in the present without the benefit of responding in the same way to the same stimulus in the past. A young child may point to and say "door" upon entering an unfamiliar restaurant, for example, and might even say "hi" to the unknown hostess. That the child has never before encountered the door or the hostess and yet is able to make an appropriate response to them is something that often leads a proud parent to wonder, "How did Junior learn to do *that*?"

A second well-known milestone, and one that a parent may also wonder about, is seen when a young child's responses begin to vary in their form or topography. A child learning to eat with a spoon and drink from a cup may at first struggle with grasping or holding these items properly. A firmer grasp of the spoon or a tighter hold on the cup leads to a succession of additional responses that culminate in eating with a spoon and drinking from a cup with ease. The development and refinement of verbal responses follows essentially the same process, from incipient forms that appear as approximations to the forms that will eventually constitute socially desirable verbal behavior.

Aside from the tendency of parents to wonder about their child's achievements, what these two milestones have in common is that they both are aspects of a process known as *generalization.*

The child just learning to grasp a spoon, hold a cup, or speak the language of his or her culture is the beneficiary of one aspect of generalization, *response generalization.* The child at the door to the unfamiliar restaurant and in front of the unknown hostess benefits from another aspect, *stimulus generalization.*

The process by which stimuli and responses generalize is the subject of volumes of basic and applied research. What this work shows is that the process is responsible for an expanding repertoire of countless responses to an endless number and variety of objects, events, people, and places in a young child's physical and social environment. Owing to this fact, the importance of generalization to a young child's psychological development is immense.

Research on stimulus and response generalization further shows that there are alarming exceptions to how the process normally unfolds. The process is swift and effortless for most young children, and yet it can be slow and arduous for other children, notably children with autism spectrum disorder (ASD). Indeed, many children with ASD spend most of their time and effort learning the same few responses to the same few stimuli in the physical and social environment. The result is a limited repertoire of desirable verbal and nonverbal behavior.

Fortunately, effective strategies are available that can be used by parents and practitioners to actively promote stimulus and response generalization. Understanding the principles that underlie the strategies is vital to their proper application, however.

GETTING STARTED: PRINCIPLES AND APPLICATIONS

The principle of *stimulus generalization* states that whenever a response to a given stimulus in the physical or social environment is reinforced, the capacity for similar stimuli to control the same response is enhanced. When the child says "door" at the restaurant and says "hi" to the hostess, the assumption is that the child had been reinforced in the past for making these same responses to similar doors at home and to similar family members and other people in the child's life. Past experiences of this sort increase the likelihood that a child will respond appropriately to stimuli in the current environment that resemble the stimuli in the presence of which a response was originally reinforced.

The similarity between the two stimuli is crucial: only those stimuli that resemble the stimuli in the presence of which a response was previously reinforced gain control. Said another way, the process is selective and therefore restricts the range of generalized stimuli. Upon seeing the door, the child says "door," and upon seeing the hostess, the child says "hi." It would be most unusual, for example, for the child to say "puppy" upon seeing the door or to say "tugboat" upon seeing the hostess. Were this to occur, the child's parents might step in to correct the error by reinforcing "door" in the presence of the door and "hi" in the presence of the hostess.

Correcting errors of this sort by reinforcing only the right or proper response(s) to a given stimulus is called *differential reinforcement*. What this means is that reinforcements are either presented or withheld contingent on an appropriate or inappropriate response to a specific stimulus. A *discrimination* between stimuli is thereby established, and so, too, are the conditions necessary for stimulus generalization to occur. The child's response to the restaurant door and to the hostess, then, is foremost a function of a history of differential reinforcement with respect to responding to various doors and people, which in turn increases the likelihood that the child will respond properly to other doors and to other people wherever and whenever they are encountered.

The principle of *response generalization* states that reinforcing one response directly results in the appearance of other responses that resemble the form of the original response. Like the stimuli in stimulus generalization, the resemblance between responses in response generalization is crucial: only those responses that are similar in form to the one that is directly reinforced will appear. The child just learning to eat with a spoon and drink from a cup struggles at first with grasping and holding onto these objects. Reinforcing consequences naturally follow from a slightly firmer grasp of the spoon or a slightly tighter hold of the cup. Increasingly firmer and tighter responses appear as generalized variations of these previous response forms and become more prevalent, while weaker grasps and looser holds become less prevalent. The eventual outcome of this process is that the child eats with a spoon and drinks from a cup easily.

The method of successive approximations, or *shaping*, reflects the process. As with stimulus generalization, differential reinforcement is necessary to response generalization. In other words, presenting reinforcements for a specific response and withholding reinforcements for all other variations of the response leaves the reinforced response intact and diminishes the prevalence of other responses, even though they are similar to the final, desired response.

The process of response generalization operates on verbal behavior in much the same way as it does with motor or nonverbal behavior. A young child just learning to say "daddy" makes a vocal response that has some similarity, usually a remote one, to saying daddy. The remotely relevant response is reinforced enthusiastically by the child's father. A rise in other, generalized responses follows. Some of these responses are then selected for reinforcement by the father, while others are not, including the ones that were reinforced earlier in the shaping cycle. Response generalization continues to occur, but now from a new base, the generalized responses now receiving exclusive reinforcement. Still more generalized responses appear, some of which are even closer to saying daddy. Combing through these responses, the father hears a more suitable one to reinforce, one that occurs often enough to benefit from exclusive reinforcement. The cycle begins anew and continues until the desired response occurs, "daddy."

Applying the principles of stimulus and response generalization to the education and treatment of young children with ASD is often the most important aspect of good teaching and good therapy. Indeed, in the hands of a competent behavior analyst providing individualized instruction under rigorously controlled conditions, desirable changes in how a child with ASD responds to stimuli in the physical and social environment come relatively easy. The hard part is to ensure that the child's behavior changes similarly in all relevant settings (stimulus generalization), that related behaviors change in complementary ways (response generalization), and that these changes persist over time.

GUIDELINES FOR INTERVENTION

Before we begin our discussion of promoting stimulus and response generalization, a comment is in order regarding the practice of conducting *generalization probes*. What this means is that a child is placed in an environment where the chances are good that generalization will naturally occur. When it occurs and when the response is appropriate to the occasion, there is no need to spend the time and energy it takes to develop and implement a program for achieving what has already been achieved.

To illustrate the practice of probing for generalization, imagine a young child with ASD that is reinforced for greeting his home-based tutor with eye contact, a smile, and "Hi, Sara." Imagine, too, that these responses occur reliably whenever Sara arrives at the home for a teaching session. The child's tutor and his parents wonder whether he will greet Sara in the same way when he sees her in a different environment—say, at the shopping mall. They decide to probe for this by running into Sara at the mall "accidentally on purpose." To everyone's delight and without anyone's encouragement, he greets Sara with eye contact, a smile, and a spirited "Hi, Sara!" Not content with this one instance of stimulus generalization (from the child's home to the mall) and response generalization (a spirited "Hi, Sara!"), the tutor and parents agree to continue probing in other settings and with other tutors until he greets them in the same way he greeted Sara at the mall.

The advantage of probing for generalization goes beyond saving time and energy. The practice also detects instances where generalization has either failed to occur or occurs incompletely, inconsistently, or inappropriately. For example, our imaginary child might not greet Sara at the mall at all, he might make only eye contact with her, or he might mistake her for someone who resembles Sara. This knowledge should be used as the basis for intervening on problems of this sort.

We turn now to four guidelines for promoting generalization. Bear in mind that there is no one, sure-fire way to promote generalization for all children with ASD or even for the same child as he or she develops and matures. Understanding this important point should encourage practitioners to tailor a program to suit a child's unique skills, abilities, interests, and circumstances of living.

TEACH IMITATION

The ability to imitate the behavior of a model is another milestone in the early life of a child. As with all milestones, imitation comes naturally to most young children. For some children, notably children with ASD, steps must often be taken to augment the process.

Imitation is usually, and rightly, regarded by practitioners as a way to gain instructional control over a child's response, and later, as the child becomes more adept at imitating a model's responses, as a way to teach by showing or telling the child what to say or do. What is sometimes underemphasized is *generalized imitation*. This is seen when a child watches and listens closely to what other children and adults say and do and then imitates some or all of what they said or did, immediately or later, without the explicit reinforcements that have followed these responses in the past.

How to promote generalized imitation is straightforward: (1) Reinforce those responses that duplicate the responses made by a model in the teaching environment, (2) Probe for responses indicative of generalized imitation in multiple environments where the cues for imitation and the reinforcements for imitating are both highly likely, and (3) Use the probe observations as a means of assessing whether generalized imitation is occurring reliably and appropriately, or whether additional teaching is needed to hasten the process.

What is also sometimes underemphasized by practitioners is the role that imitation plays in promoting response generalization. An imitated response seldom if ever duplicates the model's response exactly. In other words, response generalization is responsible for some degree of variability in the form of a child's response to a model. If this variability serves a different purpose—for example, reinforcing approximations to a correct or desirable response, as in shaping—then imitation takes on added significance as a source of novel responses to which reinforcements can be applied.

TEACH MULTIPLE EXAMPLES

Responding appropriately to a given stimulus seldom ensures that the same response(s) will automatically occur to stimuli that bear a likeness to the one in the presence of which the response was originally reinforced. More examples, and more reinforcements for responding properly to them, are needed. The practice of *multiple exemplar training* fills this need by deliberately and systematically expanding the range of controlling stimuli.

Consider a young child who is reinforced by his parents for saying "car" in the presence of the family automobile and yet is unable to make the same response to the neighbor's car, a car parked on the street, or a picture of a car in a book or magazine. Providing reinforcements for saying "car" in the presence of cars of various shapes, colors, and sizes would likely ameliorate the problem. Probing for generalization in the natural environment would determine whether generalization occurs with respect to cars or whether additional examples, and additional reinforcements, are needed to ensure that it is occurring.

Finer discriminations are both possible and desirable. The child may be reinforced for saying "red car" and may consequently identify other red cars and might even identify other red objects—for instance, a red crayon, a red light, or red hair. Responses to additional dimensions of a car—for instance, a big car, a small car, a long car, or a short car—may be reinforced, thereby increasing the chances that the child will identify other objects on the basis of these dimensions. The point here is that the practice of including as many examples of a stimulus as are needed to achieve stimulus generalization can be extended to limitless numbers and variations of stimuli.

One key to this practice is to select stimuli that the child regularly encounters in the every-day, natural environment. Bear in mind that the natural environment is the best place to teach, practice, and probe for generalization, that it is also the best place to detect problems where and when they arise, and that it is in the natural environment where correct or appropriate responses to stimuli matter most.

Multiple exemplar training is also a fertile ground for response generalization. Reinforcements for saying "car" may increase the likelihood that the child will either say or learn more easily to say "carpet," "cartoon," "carry," and a host of other responses that are similar in form to "car." On the occasion of hearing a response or an approximation to a response of this sort, reinforcements should be provided—first as a means of increasing their frequency, and second as a matter of bringing them under the control of the relevant stimulus or stimuli.

TEACH RULES

The education and treatment of young children with ASD has advanced dramatically over the past several decades to a point where a sizable minority of children are capable of following rules given to them by parents and other authority figures. A history of reinforcement for following rules increases the chances that a child will follow additional rules in the future without the explicit reinforcements that have accompanied rule following in the past. This is called *generalized rule following*.

Rules and the responses they influence are regarded together as *rule-governed behavior*, which is commonly contrasted with *contingency-shaped behavior*. The difference boils down to whether the response is affected directly by the environment (contingency-shaped) or is affected indirectly through the mediation of another person (rule-governed). A child may be bitten by a stray dog, for example, and learns as a direct result of this experience to avoid unfamiliar dogs in the future. The same response may be affected indirectly with a rule, as when the mother tells her young child never to approach a strange dog. Despite having never been bitten by a dog, the child with the proper history is likely to follow the rule whenever he or she is in the vicinity of dogs of various shapes, sizes, and colors.

Generalized rule following has two main sources: a history of reinforcement for complying with rules, and a history of punishment for ignoring them. Seeing others reinforced for following a rule, or punished for ignoring it, ordinarily complements the process. Watching a classmate running through the halls at school and getting punished for it may increase the likelihood that an observant classmate will follow the rule that prohibits running in hallways—and perhaps other school rules as well. Seeing another classmate reinforced for walking in the halls may have a similar, complementary effect. Watching others ignore a rule without punishment, or following a rule without reinforcement, may have the opposite effect. The classmate running through the halls with impunity, or the child walking through the halls unnoticed by an authority figure, may decrease the likelihood that an observant classmate will follow the rule and other school rules.

It is important to identify rules that are broken or ignored because they are misunderstood. This is commonly due to a failure on the part of the person dispensing the rule to adequately describe what following the rule entails. A good rule is simple, succinct, and always specifies (1) when and where the rule should be followed, (2) the relevant response(s) involved in following the rule, and (3) the consequences for complying with it, ignoring it, or both. Thus the parent of a child with a tendency to approach stray dogs might be given a rule that states (1) when you see an unfamiliar dog in the neighborhood, (2) stay away from it, (3) because it might bite you. Asking the child to practice reciting the rule, which may include appropriate variations on it (e.g., "and dog bites hurt!"), and providing reinforcements for accurately reciting it would help establish both specific and generalized instances of rule following.

Recitation should be considered supplementary to the best way to promote rule following: teach and practice it in the everyday environment to which the rule relates. For the parent of the child who tends to approach unfamiliar dogs, a walk in the neighborhood or through a park where stray dogs congregate would be a perfect way to practice following the rule, to reinforce compliance to the rule, and to probe for generalized instances of rule following.

Ignoring a rule because it has no basis in the physical or social environment deserves mention. While the tendency may be strong at first to follow almost any rule dispensed by an authority figure, most young children soon learn that some rules describe contingencies of reinforcement that have no basis in the world at large. After all, crossing the path of a black cat or breaking a mirror has nothing to do with bad luck. The child who ignores these types of rules, and is reinforced for ignoring them, is likely to follow and consequently benefit from rules that actually pertain to natural contingencies of reinforcement.

This point takes on special significance for children with ASD. Many of these children are tenacious, inflexible rule followers. Indeed, some children with ASD regard rules in a literal fashion and often struggle with rules that are comical, figurative, or metaphorical. A child who avoids cracks in the sidewalk for fear that he will break his mother's back, for example, may follow this rule and other superstitious rules like it and may be impervious to other rules and personal experiences that contradict them.

Superstitious rule following can be counterproductive to a child's intellectual, social, and emotional development. A child who throws salt over his shoulder at the preschool lunch table to ward off evil spirits, for instance, fails to understand that this has nothing to do with how the world operates. The child may invite ridicule from peers and may be avoided or rejected by them in the future. Moreover, irrational fears and phobias, which are common among children with ASD, may also result from following rules that have no parallel in the physical and social environment.

A derivative of generalized rule following is seen when a child states a rule and then follows it as a means of managing his or her own behavior. A child may say to himself, "If I'm good all day, daddy will take me for ice cream after dinner." To the extent that he was good and that his father held to his end of the contingency, the child's self-stated rule may prevent some of his usual misbehavior, and may also encourage him to state and follow rules that he creates for himself in the future.

Once regarded as unimaginable, children with ASD can learn to generate rules of their own making and can learn to follow them as a means of managing their behavior at home, in the classroom, and in other settings. Since rules of this sort originate from a history of following rules given to, and reinforced by, people and events in a child's life, adhering to the guidelines for teaching those types of rules enhances the prospects for self-generated rule following in the future.

Children with ASD may need assistance in responding to their own behavior, however, and to use those responses as cues to follow a rule that relates to them. To this end, it is helpful to teach children (1) to identify their own responses, (2) to state a rule that relates to those responses, (3) to describe the conditions under which the rule should be followed, and (4) to evaluate compliance with the rule. On this fourth point, it may be necessary in the early stages of teaching to monitor the child's compliance with the rule as a safeguard against false claims made by the child that the rule was followed when in fact it was broken or ignored. Later on, after the child shows good correspondence between what he says and what he does, monitoring for compliance may be turned over to the child, with periodic checks by an adult to make sure that correspondence remains strong. This safeguard is relevant to all rules, of course, and yet it gains in importance, for example, as a means of teaching a child with ASD the difference between honest and deceptive behavior.

TEACH NATURALLY

This fourth and final guideline is the shortest yet most important of all: take full advantage of a child's everyday, natural environment to teach, to practice, and to probe for stimulus and response generalization. Whether teaching imitation, multiple exemplars, or rule following, it is always best to locate or recruit the contingencies of reinforcement that naturally support already-made behavior changes. The natural environment elaborates, refines, shines, and perfects those changes, giving them a permanent or enduring quality that will last a lifetime.

ADAPTATIONS AND MODIFICATIONS

Imagine a young boy who says "girl" when shown a picture of a girl and says "boy" when shown a picture of a boy. The two pictures are then altered, this time showing the same two children not wearing shoes. When these altered pictures are shown to the boy, his discrimination deteriorates, meaning that he no longer distinguishes between the boy and the girl. What has happened is that the shoes worn by the children are exerting control over the child's discrimination, overshadowing far more relevant stimuli such as hairstyle and physique that ordinarily form the basis for differentiating between boys and girls.

Stimulus overselectivity is the term that identifies those instances when a stimulus exerts unwarranted or idiosyncratic control over a response. Children with ASD are prone to stimulus overselectivity, and thus practitioners should (1) be alert to the possibility that a child is responding to irrelevant stimuli in the environment and (2) become adept at modifying their teaching techniques and instructional materials to combat the untoward effects of stimulus overselectivity, which can include generalization with respect to irrelevant stimuli.

Overcoming stimulus overselectivity includes identifying the stimulus that is exerting undue control over the response and then slowly altering or changing the stimulus until it gains the desired control over the response. In the case of the child whose discrimination relied on shoes, the practice might entail gradually fading out the shoes until they are no longer present. Reinforcements would be provided throughout the process for making the proper discrimination. The shoes may then be faded in, with reinforcements given for continuing to make the correct discrimination.

KEYS TO REMEMBER

1. The essence of generalization is variability. Variability with respect to stimuli in the physical and social environment to which the child responds is the essence of stimulus generalization, while variability with respect to how the child responds to these stimuli is the essence of response generalization.
2. Teach imitation to establish instructional control, to promote teaching and learning by observing what other people say and do, and to achieve generalized imitation.
3. Teach multiple examples to increase the range of controlling stimuli.
4. Teach rule following to supplement or supplant contingency-shaped behavior and to foster self-styled, verbally mediated rules.
5. Teach to the prevailing contingencies of reinforcement in the everyday, natural environment.
6. Probe often for generalization in the natural environment, and use the results as evidence for generalization or as the basis for further instruction.
7. Be alert to stimulus overselectivity and follow procedures that eliminate it.

SUGGESTED READINGS

Baer, D. M. (1999). *How to Plan for Generalization* (2nd ed.). Austin, TX: Pro-Ed.

Ghezzi, P. M., & Bishop, M. R. (2008). Generalized behavior change in young children with autism. In J. K. Luiselli, D. C. Russo, W. P. Christian, & S. M. Wilczynski (Eds.), *Effective Practices for Children with Autism: Educational and Support Interventions that Work*. New York: Oxford University Press.

Stokes, T. F., & Baer, D. M. (1977). An implicit technology of generalization. *Journal of Applied Behavior Analysis,* 10, 349–367.

Stokes, T. F., & Osnes, P. G. (1989). An operant pursuit of generalization. *Behavior Therapy,* 20, 337–355.

CHAPTER 24

WRITING A BEHAVIOR SUPPORT PLAN

Joseph N. Ricciardi

OVERVIEW: WHAT WE KNOW

Children and adults with autism spectrum disorder (ASD) are at risk for developing disruptive behavior disorders. The vulnerability stems from delayed development of communication, social, problem-solving, emotional regulation, and self-management skills. In typical development, skills in these domains are applied to navigate contexts where one is required to perform necessary tasks one doesn't immediately care to do, to accept the denial of something one immediately wants, to gain help and comfort from others, and to tolerate temporary discomforts. Without these skills, challenging behaviors emerge as "solutions" (albeit self-defeating ones) to the mismatch between skills and environmental demands.

Disruptive behaviors can become "chronic" and "acute"—that is, there develops a long-term pattern of severe problem behavior often increasing in intensity over time (chronicity), punctuated by periods of severe worsening (acuity) in response to unavoidable changes in the person's life (programs, staffing, and family supports). This waxing–waning course leads to stress in families, service systems, and the individual with ASD. Chronic problem behavior in persons with developmental disorders has been shown to lead to separation from family and friends, interference with education and work opportunities, hospitalization, restrictive placements, and the use of interventions with greater associated risks (e.g., behavior-modifying medications, physical restraint and contingent aversion stimulation).

During the past several decades advancements in behavioral intervention have led to a wider range of options and improved outcomes. Indeed, decades ago, an intervention might be recommended on the basis of topography (e.g., "time-out" for aggression). The most common interventions paid little attention to the "function" of problem behavior (e.g., DRO). Since then, however, the field has developed a more sophisticated understanding of the interaction between skills and contexts, and the influence of learning history, caregiver interactions, setting variables, medical problems, and mental illness, on the occurrence of problem behaviors. As a result, an intervention is now more comprehensive and takes the form of an individualized behavior support plan (BSP) that addresses multiple contributors to the problem behavior in a coordinated way.

Contemporary behavior support planning is "multi-component" and "contextual"—in other words, the BSP combines several interventions (multi-component) and may include procedures applicable in one situation but not another (contextual). For example, a child with ASD who shows aggression in school and home may be treated with a plan that includes token rewards for time on school task, "shaping" increased time on tasks, interspersing high-preference with low-preference school tasks, teaching how to request breaks, extinction (both attention and escape extinction), a preventive seating arrangement, a scheduled nap after lunch, and rewards for absence of aggression to peers applied only during small-group activities. At home, her plan may include a schedule of 1:1 activities with caregivers, access to certain high-preference activities when caregivers must attend to other children, a special seating arrangement while traveling with peers, a later bedtime, and attention extinction.

GETTING STARTED: PRINCIPLES
AND APPLICATIONS

The primary principle behind all behavior support planning is the "functional relation." It is assumed that a behavior of concern is an operant behavior with a discernable function. The functional relation describes how the behavior of concern effects certain reinforcing consequences (at least some of the time, or "intermittently") in the settings where the behaviors occur. Reinforcement is an event that follows a behavior and increases its rate (positive reinforcement), or when removed or avoided, increases the behavior it follows (negative reinforcement). For example, a person with ASD screams when crowded by others and as a result people move away (negative reinforcement). Alternatively, another person with ASD screams when hungry and caregivers give him a preferred food (positive reinforcement). Discernment of function is the product of careful assessment (functional behavior assessment and functional analysis—see Chapters 2 and 3, respectively). So important is the principle of functional relation that a functional assessment is required for all intervention planning.

A second and related principle is "functional stimuli." It is assumed that there are certain events, activities, settings, people, interactions, and tangible materials that occur *before* the problem behavior and are likely to elicit the problem behavior. Essentially, these stimuli have been associated with the consequences of the behavior, and when they are present, the person is more likely to show the problem behavior. Loosely, they might be called "triggers"; however, this term implies an immediacy that is rarely seen. Typically, there are multiple stimuli that combine and interact, increasing the likelihood that the behavior of concern will occur over time. For example, the setting (school classroom), the teacher (a certain teacher who seems most often associated with disruptive behaviors with this student), and certain materials (low-preference work tasks) co-vary. As these stimuli accumulate and persist, the problem behavior becomes more and more likely to occur. Identification of these factors is essential for comprehensive behavior support planning. This occurs during a functional assessment and through careful direct observation.

These relationships are summarized by clinicians as "antecedent–behavior–consequences" (sometimes written as A→B→C). This is the "three-term contingency," a useful rubric for organizing an operant-behavioral formulation of a case, sharing it with others, and designing interventions around the core drivers of the problem.

However, contemporary behavioral intervention includes another set of contributing factors based on a third important principle: the theory of motivating operations. A motivating operation (MO) is a condition that changes the effectiveness of a certain consequence to function as a reinforcer (or punisher). For example, satiation or deprivation would alter the status of food used as a reinforcer. A number of more subtle events have been shown to function in this manner. These include states such as illness, pain, fatigue, boredom, noise, and task effort. The assumption is that when an MO is present, behaviors might be evoked that correspond in some way to the effect of the MO. For example, a person with ASD who is often motivated to avoid social contact through displays of loud outbursts might be more inclined to display outbursts when suffering from an illness. Presumably, the motivation to self-isolate is greater when feeling ill, in pain, or fatigued. Identification of MOs has led to the development of case formulations that can account for the acute changes in behavioral stability. Often, the identification of MOs has led to collaborative interventions (with another discipline, such as physician, psychologist, or occupational therapist), with improvement in the overall quality of care being provided.

In application, these principles form the basis for designing a comprehensive BSP with multiple intervention components. The ideal plan includes at least a summary of the case formulation—the specification of targeted behaviors, the probable function of the problem behavior, and the identification of MOs. The procedures directed will include preventive strategies (antecedent modifications and efforts to ameliorate or manage the effects of MOs); proactive, systematic strategies to teach functionally equivalent alternative behaviors; specific extinction guidelines; and probably some attempt to reinforce behaviors that are adaptive and valuable for the person, and would be incompatible with the concerning, problem behaviors.

GUIDELINES FOR INTERVENTION

While the general intent of a BSP is to reduce some behavior of concern, current research suggests that the most effective behavior support planning is aimed at changing the environments where the problem behaviors occur and teaching functionally equivalent, adaptive skills, and skills that will help the person become more successful at home, at school (or in a work setting), and in important relationships. Intervention design begins with a comprehensive assessment (which is beyond the scope of this chapter but is fully covered in Part I of this volume). Some general considerations are provided below.

GENERAL ASSESSMENT CONSIDERATIONS

First, the clinician will need to operationally define the behaviors of concern so they can be observed and discussed with precision with caregivers, professionals, and all others involved in the process. There is a common tendency to describe problem behaviors in a vernacular that confuses the process. For example, "Jim is out of control. He needs to get his own way, and when he doesn't he blows up." Analyzed objectively, the clinician learns that Jim displays loud outbursts, aggression, periods of crying, and holding his head and rocking. These behaviors may or may not be related, yet reporters call each of these "out of control." Thus, the starting point is a clinical definition that identifies the focus of concern so that it can be discussed, observed, and measured (see Chapter 1).

The clinician designing the intervention plan works from a functional assessment—the presumed relationship between antecedents and consequences (see Chapters 2 and 3). In addition, the clinician will need to consider the possible influence of illness, medical symptoms, medication effects (and side effects), developmental syndromes, fatigue, and myriad events that might function as MOs. The consideration of the effect of MOs helps clinicians identify acute issues that can be corrected with possible immediate benefit. Because many behavioral clinicians are not trained in this form of "differential diagnosis," it is valuable to collaborate with nurses, physicians, and allied health specialists already familiar with the person when conducting this assessment. Often an assessment of this sort can be facilitated by explaining the MO concept, giving examples, and then inviting the specialist to consider any features he or she is aware of that might function as an MO.

Clinicians generally conduct an interview around several major domains or "states" that may function as MOs: (F) fears and anxiety, (A) appetite, (M) mood states, (I) interest level, (S) sleep problems, (H) health concerns, (E) energy and activity, and (D) distractibility and sensitivities (Table 24.1). The mnemonic "FAMISHED" shows several areas to consider when evaluating MOs. A positive finding may suggest a need for consultation by a specialist in the treatment of medical or psychiatric disorders. Identification of these areas can lead to simple but powerful intervention components. For instance, an individual with ASD with severe outbursts prior to meals and a history of having been given food to ameliorate problem behavior is presumed to be more motivated to misbehave when hungry. A BSP may include a protocol for managing hunger and appetite through increased meal quantity, more protein added to snack options, and changes in timing of snacks.

Finally, clinicians should identify contexts of concern. A contextual assessment is a review with caregivers and staff of the normal, day-to-day sequence of recurring activities to ascertain any difficulties unique to each event. The goal is to find discrete contexts of concern that may lend themselves to interventions implemented only in these contexts. The author has found that contextualizing interventions provides a greater range of options. For example, aggression during seated instruction might be addressed in one manner, with aggression during ADL care in the bathroom managed differently. (In this case, seated sessions might be shortened, reinforcements increased, and time on task gradually shaped upward; bathroom incidents could be managed by a task-analysis prompted sequence, with reinforcement contingent on absence of aggression during the discrete event.) Caregivers would then be asked to select the contexts with the greatest immediate concern, and intervention could focus on one or two contexts at a time.

WRITING A BEHAVIOR SUPPORT PLAN

Behavioral intervention settings are accustomed to using differential reinforcement, prompts, prompt fading, and a range of other standard techniques and approaches as issues arise. It would be cumbersome and unnecessary to operationalize every one of these procedures per individual served. However, when an intervention is complex, involving multiple steps and a number of specific procedures and protocols, it must be made in writing. This same standard applies to any intervention that involves punishment or restrictive procedures. This standard has been shown to limit intervention drift and facilitate training and supervision. Below are typical conventions for developing a comprehensive BSP.

1. List all targeted behaviors and definitions. Begin with a list of the behaviors targeted in the support plan. This limits the plan to these behaviors, and none other. Some clinicians begin

Table 24.1 FAMISHED: A Quick Check of Possible Motivating Operations

Domain		Examples of Effects
F	**Fears and anxiety** Assess for the presence of fear reactions	• Fear can increase the motivation to escape certain stimuli, may increase aggression if escape is blocked. • Children with fears and worries may use misbehavior to secure attention (comfort, help) from adult caregivers. • Persistent anxiety and fears can be conditioned to settings and persons.
A	**Appetite** Check for changes in appetite	• Low appetite diminishes the effectiveness of food as reinforcer. • Increased appetite may increase motivation for challenging behaviors that have been reinforced by food.
M	**Mood states** Check for mood changes	• Irritability may increase motivation to escape. • Sadness may increase seeking attention for caregivers. • Individuals with depression often show loss of interest in activities and events that were once satisfying (loss of reinforcing effects).
I	**Interest level** Check for boredom with activities and settings where the problems are observed	• Individuals who are bored may show increased motivation to escape low-preference tasks, or misbehave to cause others to change an activity. • Some bored individuals may misbehave to secure the attention and interactions of others.
S	**Sleep problems** Check for periodic sleep disturbance	• Sleep deprivation may increase motivation to escape or avoid tasks, refuse to transition from break back to more effortful activities.
H	**Health concerns** Check for any ongoing medical problems, signs of medical problems, or symptoms	• Illness has been shown to increase escape-motivated behavior, or to motivate some individuals with ASD to use misbehavior to secure attention (comfort, help) from adult caregivers.
E	**Energy and activity** Check for fatigue or difficulty sitting still	• Fatigue increases motivation to escape or avoid effortful or low-preference activities. • The ability to sit still as required in some contexts might be compromised (e.g., developmental phenomena, neuropathology, medication effects); this may evoke escape-motivated problem behavior.
D	**Distractibility and sensitivities** Check for tolerance for noises, commotion, intrusions into personal space	• Individuals with clinically significant distractibility may find persistent visual/noise distractions frustrating. • Some individuals with ASD seem especially sensitive to intrusive noise and other sensations; exposure to these may evoke escape behaviors.

*Suggested as an exemplar of intervention design that incorporates the principles described in this chapter.

the written plan with the heading "Target Behaviors" and include here operational definitions for all behaviors of concern and positive behaviors being targeted.

2. Include a brief case conceptualization. Provide two or three paragraphs summarizing the case conceptualization (the findings of a functional assessment and the putative impact of any MOs). Professional staff will perform better if they understand the formulation and the rationale for the plan. Some clinicians include this under the heading "Functional Assessment."

3. List any preventive procedures and antecedent modifications. List any specific preventive procedures in this next section, "Preventive Procedures." Some MO-based interventions are preventive and should be specified. Simple headings and brief descriptors are sufficient—for instance: "30-minute nap after lunch. Provide Janet with a quiet space to nap shortly after lunch. Naps are limited to 30 minutes. If she refuses, continue to offer nap periodically; apply no pressure to nap, however." This section should contain any antecedent modifications as well. Referencing the preceding example, one illustration would be: "Intersperse preferred work with non-preferred. Janet loves spelling lists; allow 1 minute of spelling work for every 2 to 3 minutes of seated instruction to improve her motivation for seated schoolwork." Note that the language is carefully constructed: it is precise but casual and without jargon. If there are any specialized safety guidelines that can be stated in one or two succinct sentences, they can go here as well. For example, "Specialized seating protocol during meals. Ryan should be seated out of arm's reach from other students with his 1:1 staff person sitting between him and his peers to prevent/block grabbing foods."

4. Specify when to apply each procedure with a brief heading. Ideally a comprehensive BSP includes interventions applied under some conditions or contexts but not all. Staff and caregivers will need to know when to apply a procedure. Using a heading before all lengthy descriptions of procedures will cue caregivers when to use the procedure. For example, the BSP might include "Procedure for Increasing Completion of Seated Instruction." This makes it clear that during seated instruction, this is what teachers will do.

5. Operationalize procedures. Depict each procedure as a sequence of steps, giving concise directions for each event that might occur. The ability to describe an intervention protocol as a series of brief but specific steps is the hallmark and strength of behavioral intervention and is a defining characteristic of applied behavior analysis. Interventionists should take nothing for granted—specify each procedure much like a competency-based checklist, listing a logical sequence of steps. For example: "(1) Arrange token board and all instructional materials on desk top; (2) Call student to table; (3) Provide one token upon arrival, 'Good job, Janet! Nice listening'; (4) Set timer. Provide one token for every 4 minutes absence of aggression: 'Nice job keeping safe, Janet'; (5) Upon aggression, block/manage and continue with instruction; reset timer upon cessation of aggression for 30 seconds. Continue until four tokens earned. (6) Upon earning four tokens, provide choice of one item from prize box." Note the use of scripted interactions—these are often valuable for cuing the social reinforcement that is a component of many interventions.

6. Include a systematic plan for teaching functionally equivalent alternative behaviors. Based on the case conceptualization, it should be apparent that if the individual had a certain adaptive skill, he or she might be less inclined to display a particular behavior of concern. For example, if a student who is believed to exhibit aggression to escape or avoid seated instruction could communicate a need for an immediate break, she would be less inclined to display aggression. All behavior plans should include a plan for increasing an alternative or adaptive behavior that if acquired would defeat the immediate need for the maladaptive behaviors. In the example given above (Item 5), the student is on a reinforcement plan that combines token reinforcement plus shortened time on task. Adding functional communication training as an alternative, positive behavior treats the problem in a more lasting and beneficial way. It is important that the plan to teach a specific, functionally equivalent alternative be approached in a way that is sensitive to special learning needs. In persons with ASD, this means repeated sessions of discrete learning trials, prompting, reinforcement, prompt fading, and generalization training. Having determined an ideal, alternative behavior, the BSP should include a plan to practice making the new response while fading prompts toward independence (positive practice sessions), plus strategies to cue the alternative behavior when it is likely to be needed (prompting in vivo), and a protocol for redirecting problem behavior and guiding the person to the alternative behavior in vivo (error correction). These procedures are well known to teachers and direct support specialists when conducting discrete trials instruction, and the same principles apply for alternatives to disruptive behaviors. Adding a systematic skills teaching plan to the BSP helps manage "intervention drift" and facilitates training and implementation supervision.

7. **Emergency procedures.** In some cases it may be necessary to specify any emergency procedures should a problem behavior escalate to levels that are severe and pose a risk of imminent harm to the person or others. Agencies and clinicians usually have specific policies for which procedures may be used and how they are to be used in their settings. The prescribed procedures, criteria for implementation, safety guidelines, limits, and monitoring requirements can be described here under the heading "Emergency Procedures."

ADAPTATIONS AND MODIFICATIONS

The behavioral principles and standards for writing a BSP would be applicable across children and adults. Intervention designs and reinforcement selection should be sensitive to age-appropriateness.

The choice of intervention options will depend on where and by whom the interventions will be implemented. Interventions that are successful in a school setting may not be transferable to a home or even a staffed residence. Professional staff may be more comfortable with "attention extinction" than parents, for example. Similarly, the technical proficiencies of staff in a day setting are not always the same as those in a residential program. The choice of interventions must fit the experiences and training of those who will implement the BSP.

Clinicians will have to vary their language and writing style to fit the intended audience. Some researchers have demonstrated improved intervention integrity and acceptability using non-technical "conversational language" versions of BSPs (e.g., using the word "reward" where the word "reinforce" would be more precise). Others have added training in concepts and terminology, and direct observation and feedback as part of consultation in order to improve implementation. The interventionist should periodically observe staff and correct or retrain as necessary.

Another consideration has been called "treatment acceptability"—how the proposed intervention will be "welcomed" by implementing professional staff or caregivers. For families, proposed interventions must be consistent with their attitudes toward parenting, family functioning, lifestyle, and culture. In some cases, families will need counseling to address concerns about a component before it can be prescribed. In most cases, families are open to accepting a plan that recognizes these concerns. With families, BSPs may be more acceptable when written in a language that is sensitive to the parents' concern and love for their child.

Treatment acceptability may take a different turn in clinical systems where punitive and restrictive approaches dominate and behavior plans are the same across all recipients (e.g., "levels systems" and "earned privilege/restrictions" plans). In these settings a BSP proposing an individualized approach featuring positive skills building, greater access to preferences and rewards, and limited punitive consequences might be viewed suspiciously. In these settings the clinician is required to educate about the current standards of practice in behavioral intervention, which includes the "least restrictive model," positive behavior supports, and individualized programming where applicable.

KEYS TO REMEMBER

1. All behavior support planning is multi-component and contextual: combine multiple components and vary the intervention across contexts where applicable.

2. To design a support plan, the clinician will need to determine the functional consequences, the relevant antecedents, and the motivating operations and will need to analyze the contexts where the disruptive behaviors occur (and do not occur). These findings facilitate a comprehensive case formulation and will suggest multiple intervention options.

3. Select one or more functionally equivalent, alternative behaviors to target as well. The key thinking is "if the person could only do this more often, then there would be no need for the problem behavior." This could be an ideal behavior to target for systematic training and increase.

4. The BSP should include a systematic plan to train and increase the alternative behavior. The teaching plan should include all the adaptations known to facilitate learning in persons with ASD, such as repeated practice trials, prompting, reinforcement, prompt fading, and generalization.

5. The BSP should be written in a manner that is sensitive to the characteristics of the setting and audience—plans for parents are written differently than plans for professional service providers. Professional staff will differ in training and background, and intervention selection and writing style will have to be adjusted to accommodate these differences. Using conversational language versus technical language may improve intervention acceptability.

SUGGESTED READINGS

Carr, E. G., Smith, C. E., Giacin, T. A., Whelan, B. M., & Pancari, J. (2003). Menstrual discomfort as a biological setting event for severe problem behavior: Assessment and intervention. *American Journal on Mental Retardation, 108,* 117–133.

Horner, R. H., Sugai, G., Todd, A. W., & Lewis-Palmer, T. (2000). Elements of behavior support plans: A technical brief. *Exceptionality, 8,* 205–215.

Jarmolowicz, D. P., Kahng, S., Ingvarsson, E. T., Goysovich, R., Heggemeyer, R., & Gregory, M. K. (2008). Effects of conversational versus technical language on treatment preference and treatment integrity. *Intellectual and Developmental Disabilities, 46,* 190–199.

Lucyshyn, J. M., Dunlap, G., & Albin, R. W. (Eds.), (2002). *Families and Positive Behavior Support: Addressing Problem Behavior in Family Contexts.* Baltimore: Paul H. Brookes.

Ricciardi, J. N. (2006). Combining antecedent and consequence procedures in multicomponent behavior support plans: A guide to writing plans with functional efficacy. In J. K. Luiselli (Ed.), Antecedent Intervention: Recent Developments in Community Focused Support. Baltimore: Paul H. Brookes Publishing.

CHAPTER 25

EVALUATING INTERVENTION EFFECTIVENESS

David P. Wacker, Jay W. Harding, Wendy K. Berg, Yaniz C. Padilla, Kelly M. Schieltz, and John F. Lee

AUTHOR NOTE

This research was supported by Grants R01-HD029402 and R01-HD042813 from the National Institute of Child Health and Human Development of the National Institutes of Health. The opinions expressed herein do not necessarily reflect the position or policy of that agency. The authors express our appreciation to Agnes DeRaad for assistance with manuscript preparation.

OVERVIEW: WHAT WE KNOW

In developing effective interventions, applied behavior analysts have followed the advice of T. R. Risley to "Do good and take data" (Risley, 2001, p. 267). To know that we are doing good, we not only have to take data but also have to collect data in a way that is interpretable. Interpretable data permit us to determine if the intervention is responsible for the observed effects on target behavior (i.e., to establish internal validity) and to replicate the effects of the intervention in other situations or with other individuals. To better interpret the effects of interventions such as functional communication training (FCT), applied behavior analysts conduct those interventions within single-case designs. Conducting the interventions within single-case designs permits us to determine if a functional relation exists between the application of the intervention and changes in target behavior (i.e., between the independent and the dependent variables). For each individual receiving the intervention, the establishment of functional relations within single-case designs has led to the development of highly effective interventions because these designs permit us not only to demonstrate that an intervention was effective but also to evaluate why it was effective. Knowing why an intervention is effective in one situation helps us to determine the conditions under which an intervention should be effective in other situations and under what conditions a different intervention should be selected. For example, showing that time-out works effectively when problem behavior is maintained by gaining attention or tangible items permits practitioners to determine when to use time-out (e.g., when problem behavior is maintained by attention or tangibles) and when not to use time-out (e.g., when problem behavior is maintained by escape from demands).

GETTING STARTED: BASIC PRINCIPLES AND APPLICATION

Interventions can be considered as changes to the environment, and the goal is to identify whether those changes result in improvement in behavior. Most interventions involve multiple changes to the environment, with each change being considered a component of the intervention package. In some cases, it is sufficient to show that the intervention package produced improvement in behavior. In other cases, we wish to identify which components of the intervention package were responsible for improvement. For all single-case designs, the key is replication. To demonstrate that a functional relation exists between the intervention and the target behavior, the changes in behavior produced by the intervention must be replicated. Replication shows that changes in behavior (the dependent variable) are due to the intervention (the independent variable) and not to other events, such as other changes in the environment. In single-case designs, behavior is shown to change from A (baseline, or the environmental conditions in place prior to intervention) to B (intervention, or the conditions in place during intervention). To validate that B was responsible for the change in behavior, changes in behavior that occurred from Conditions A to B must be replicated at least once. Replication can be achieved sequentially by repeating the AB sequence as in a reversal (ABAB) design. Replication can be conducted concurrently, with rapid and repeated changes from A to B as in a multi-element design. Finally, replication can be conducted by showing that behavior changes when A is changed to B each time it is applied to a new situation (e.g., setting) or person, as in a multiple baseline design. The selection of which design to use is based on the question being addressed (e.g., evaluating a specific component of intervention versus an intervention package), the behavior being changed (e.g., maintenance of behavior is expected following intervention versus changes in behavior will likely occur only when the intervention is in place), and the preference of the practitioner.

GUIDELINES FOR IMPLEMENTATION

In this section, we (a) describe the three most common single-case designs (reversal, multi-element, and multiple baseline designs) used to evaluate interventions and (b) provide case examples to show how to evaluate an intervention within each design.

REVERSAL DESIGNS

Reversal designs, or ABAB designs, are most often used to evaluate the effects of intervention by first introducing and then removing the intervention and measuring its effect on the target behavior. In applied situations, the A condition can also be the intervention currently in place and the B condition can be a new intervention.

This design should be considered when we want to show that changes in behavior continue to occur whenever the B condition is being implemented. This design is not recommended when changes in the target behavior are irreversible, such as with some academic skills. Caution should be taken when using this design if a target behavior, such as self-injurious behavior or aggression, can potentially cause harm.

To implement a reversal design (ABAB):

1. Begin by measuring the target behavior during baseline (A) until a consistent pattern (i.e., steady rate) of behavior is achieved. In most situations, at least three sessions or data points are needed to show steady-state behavior.
2. After demonstrating steady-state behavior in baseline, initiate the intervention (B) and continue the intervention until changes in behavior reach desirable levels and remain steady.
3. Return to baseline (i.e., discontinue the new intervention) to show that the changes in behavior during B occur only with B. When these changes fail to occur (i.e., behavior returns to the levels during the first baseline), re-implement B to again show the same effects on behavior. If desired changes in behavior occur only during B and each time B is implemented, then the intervention is shown to be effective.

Case Example: Decreasing Problem Behavior with Functional Communication Training

In Figure 25.1, a reversal design (ABAB) was used to evaluate the effects of an intervention, functional communication training (FCT), on destructive behavior. Adam, a 3-year-old boy diagnosed with developmental delay, engaged in aggression, self-injury, and property destruction at home. FCT was implemented in the context of demands to evaluate whether destructive behavior decreased during intervention (B) compared to baseline (A).

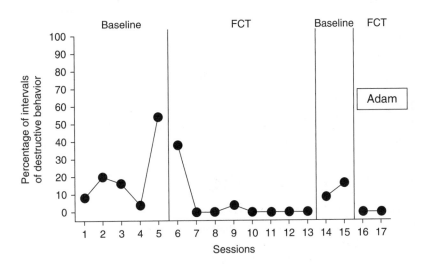

FIGURE 25.1 Example of a reversal design.

During baseline (A), Adam's mother delivered one request (e.g., put the block in the bucket) every 30 seconds during 5-minute sessions. The occurrence of destructive behavior was ignored and task completion received brief praise. FCT (B) consisted of providing reinforcement contingent on independent task completion and appropriate communication (e.g., request for a break). During the initial baseline condition (A), Adam's destructive behavior showed an increasing trend; therefore, FCT was implemented. When FCT (B) was introduced, destructive behavior decreased to zero levels. After multiple sessions with zero occurrences of destructive behavior (steady-state responding) during FCT, the intervention was removed and destructive behavior increased. FCT (B) was reintroduced and destructive behavior again decreased to zero occurrences. These results showed that destructive behavior increased during the baseline condition and decreased during FCT. The return to baseline and reintroduction of FCT provided a replication of those results and showed that FCT was effective in reducing destructive behavior.

MULTI-ELEMENT DESIGNS

Multi-element designs are used to evaluate the effects of two or more independent variables or interventions on target behavior. The independent variables could be two or more assessment conditions (e.g., play alone versus play with parent), two or more interventions (e.g., noncontingent access to reinforcement versus play with parent), or a baseline condition and an intervention. Each independent variable is presented in a rapidly alternating sequence to determine if target behavior increases or decreases with the change in conditions. If consistent changes in behavior occur with the introduction/removal of each condition (e.g., behavior increases during Condition A and decreases during Condition B), then a functional relation between those conditions and the target behavior is shown.

One advantage of using this design is that you can often evaluate multiple interventions in a relatively brief time. Therefore, this design may be helpful in situations in which there is a limited amount of time to evaluate the effectiveness of an intervention. However, this design is limited to behaviors that show an almost immediate response to an intervention and to behaviors that do not persist when the intervention is not in place (e.g., carryover effects). Caution should be taken in determining the order of the conditions to avoid having one condition always precede another. For this reason, A and B should be conducted in either a counterbalanced or a randomized order.

To implement a multi-element design:

1. Assign each independent variable to a condition.
2. Decide if the order of conditions (A and B) will be randomized or counterbalanced. Ensure that there are approximately an equal number of sessions for both A and B.
3. Conduct the sessions until a clear difference in behavior occurs across conditions (i.e., a differentiated and stable pattern in behavior occurs between A and B).

Case Example: Evaluation of Stereotypy

In Figure 25.2, a multi-element design was used to evaluate the occurrence of stereotypical behaviors across two conditions: play and ignore. The participant for this evaluation, Bjorn, was a 5-year-old boy diagnosed with pervasive developmental disorder who engaged in stereotypical behaviors (e.g., hand flapping, toe walking) that interfered with his participation in

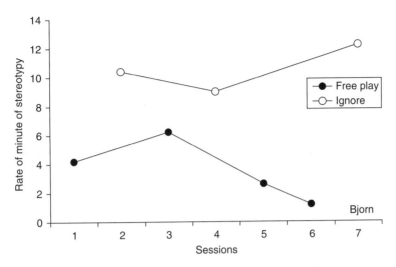

FIGURE 25.2 Example of a multielement design.

age-appropriate activities. The purpose of this evaluation was to determine if Bjorn would be less likely to engage in stereotypy when he had access to preferred toys and parent attention (play condition) than when he had nothing to do and no one to interact with (ignore condition). During the play condition, Bjorn had access to toys that were identified as preferred based on a preference assessment conducted earlier that day and his father's attention. During the ignore condition, all toys were removed from the room, and Bjorn's father diverted his attention away from him. As shown in Figure 25.2, Bjorn engaged in consistently higher levels of stereotypy during the ignore condition than during the play condition, and the occurrence of stereotypy decreased across play sessions.

MULTIPLE BASELINE DESIGNS

Multiple baseline designs are implemented by conducting a baseline condition (A) until steady-state behavior occurs and then sequentially introducing the intervention (B) across situations (people, contexts, settings, tasks, or behaviors). Multiple baseline designs do not require a return to baseline after the intervention is implemented and therefore are useful for evaluating behaviors that are maintained, or for situations when a change to baseline is not practical. To identify intervention effectiveness using this design, there needs to be a change in behavior when the intervention is in place but not when baseline is conducted. Replication is achieved by sequentially showing that changes in behavior occur when the intervention is introduced.

To implement a multiple baseline design:

1. Initiate baseline conditions across different situations.
2. When a consistent pattern of behavior is achieved for at least one situation, implement the intervention in this situation while continuing to implement baseline in the other situations.
3. After observing a change in behavior with the intervention, introduce the intervention in the second situation.

4. Continue this process until the intervention has been implemented across all situations.

Case Example: Evaluating Problem Behavior Across Functional Contexts

In Figure 25.3, a multiple baseline design was used to evaluate problem behavior under baseline and treatment conditions across functional contexts. Al, a 3-year-old boy diagnosed with mental retardation, engaged in self-injury, property destruction, tantrums, and noncompliance at home. Functional communication was implemented in a staggered fashion during the contexts of

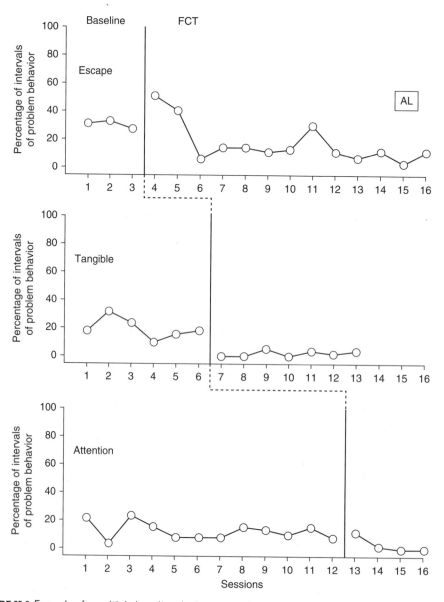

FIGURE 25.3 Example of a multiple baseline design across functional contexts.

demands, restricted access to toys, and diverted attention to evaluate if FCT reduced displays of problem behavior.

In each baseline condition, reinforcement (i.e., escape from demands, access to toys, access to parental attention) was provided contingent on the occurrence of problem behavior. FCT consisted of providing reinforcement contingent on appropriate communication. After a consistent pattern of problem behavior was observed in the baseline demand context, we introduced FCT while continuing to conduct baseline sessions across the other two contexts (restricted toys and diverted attention). Reductions in problem behavior were observed in the treatment demand context, whereas no change in behavior patterns was observed in the other two baseline contexts. Therefore, we implemented treatment in the second context (restricted toys) while continuing to conduct treatment sessions in the demand context and baseline sessions in the diverted attention context. After treatment effects were replicated in the restricted toys context and no change in behavior was observed in the diverted attention context, we implemented treatment in the diverted attention context and again replicated the effects of FCT.

ADAPTATIONS AND MODIFICATIONS

Experimental (single-case) designs provide a rigorous methodology for identifying functional relations. To further show the broad effects of intervention, applied behavior analysts often obtain additional information, such as generalization and consumer satisfaction, when evaluating an intervention. An example of each type of analysis is provided below.

TREATMENT GENERALIZATION: TREATMENT PROBES AND BEHAVIOR RATING FORMS

Function-based interventions such as FCT are often conducted with a specific task within a specific context. For example, a child may be taught by his mother to request a break from a specific activity (e.g., tooth brushing at home) as an alternative to engaging in destructive behavior (e.g., aggression, self-injury). Following intervention, we are often interested in determining if positive behavioral changes generalized across different caregivers, settings, and tasks (e.g., getting dressed, academic tasks). We can evaluate generalization by conducting pre- and post-FCT probes in different situations to determine if changes in behavior occurred across different caregivers, settings, and tasks that are similar to those achieved with intervention with no or substantially reduced training. Thus, the intervention is conducted with one care provider, in one setting, and on one task within a single-case design, and pre/post probes with other care providers, settings, or tasks are conducted to evaluate generalization. An advantage of evaluating treatment generalization via direct observation is the amount of specific information that can be collected. A disadvantage is the amount of time that is required to conduct the additional observation sessions.

A less direct but more efficient approach to assessing generalization is to use a behavior rating form both before and after intervention. The purpose of this form is to evaluate the severity of problem behavior that is occurring prior to and following intervention across persons, settings, and tasks. A form we use asks the child's parent to rate child behavior during multiple home and community activities as (0) *Child never performs this activity*, (1) *Major problem behaviors occur during this activity*, (2) *Minor problem behaviors occur during this activity*, or

(3) *No problem behaviors occur during this activity.* Completing the form prior to and after an intervention can show if the effects of the intervention have generalized.

CONSUMER SATISFACTION: TREATMENT ACCEPTABILITY

Another consideration in evaluating intervention effectiveness is the extent to which the individuals implementing the intervention (e.g., parents) are satisfied with the recommended procedures and treatment outcomes. One approach we use to evaluate consumer satisfaction is to collect ratings of treatment acceptability. Questions on this form are answered by indicating a response between the numbers 1 and 7. For example, for the question, "How acceptable do you find the treatment to be regarding your concerns about your child?" parent ratings could range from (1) *not at all acceptable* to (7) *highly acceptable.* When combined with single-case analyses of the intervention, these ratings show that effective interventions are acceptable to the care providers, which may increase the maintenance or continued use of the intervention over time.

KEYS TO REMEMBER

1. The effectiveness of an intervention must be established in an interpretable and replicable manner so that we know that the intervention was responsible for the changes in behavior that occurred during intervention.
2. Applied behavior analysts have carefully developed interventions by evaluating the effects of those interventions, or the separate components within an intervention, within single-case designs. This has permitted us to show the effectiveness of an intervention for each individual who received the intervention.
3. The range of single-case designs that are available to evaluate interventions makes them a useful procedure in most situations.
4. Empirically valid interventions should be developed for each individual and not established only for individuals who initially received those interventions.
5. By conducting interventions within single-case designs, we can continue the evaluation of behavioral treatment and can continue to honor Risley's advice to "Do good and take data."

SUGGESTED READINGS

Johnston, J. M., & Pennypacker, H. S. (1993). *Strategies and Tactics of Behavioral Research* (2nd ed.). Hillsdale, NJ: Lawrence Erlbaum.

Kennedy, C. H. (2005). *Single-Case Designs for Educational Research.* Boston, MA: Allyn & Bacon.

Risley, T. R. (2001). Do good, take data. In W. T. Donahue, D. A. Henderson, S. C. Hayes, J. Fisher, & L. J. Hayes (Eds.), *A History of Behavioral Therapies: Founders' Personal Histories* (pp. 267–287). Reno, NV: Context Press.

Vollmer, T. R., & Van Camp, C. M. (1998). Experimental designs to evaluate antecedent control. In J. K. Luiselli & M. J. Cameron (Eds.), *Antecedent Control: Innovative Approaches to Behavioral Support* (pp. 67–86). Baltimore, MD: Paul H. Brookes.

Wacker, D. P., Berg, W. K., & Harding, J. W. (2008). Single-case research methodology to inform evidence-based practice. In J. K. Luiselli, D. C. Russo, & W. P. Christian (Eds.), *Effective Practices for Children with Autism: Educational and Behavior Support Interventions That Work* (pp. 61–79). New York: Oxford University Press.

OTHER RESOURCES

Iwata, B. A., Bailey, J. S., Neef, N. A., Wacker, D. P., Repp, A. C., & Shook, G. L. (Eds.). (1997). *Behavior Analysis in Developmental Disabilities, 1968–1995* (3rd ed.). Lawrence, KS: Society for the Experimental Analysis of Behavior.

Iwata, B. A., Neef, N. A., Wacker, D. P., Mace, F. C., & Vollmer, T. R. (Eds.). (2000). *Methodological and Conceptual Issues in Applied Behavior Analysis, 1968–1999* (2nd ed.). Lawrence, KS: Society for the Experimental Analysis of Behavior.

Reimers, T., & Wacker, D. (1988). Parents' ratings of the acceptability of behavioral treatment recommendations made in an outpatient clinic: A preliminary analysis of the influence of treatment effectiveness. *Behavioral Disorders, 14,* 7–15.

CHAPTER 26

VIDEO MODELING

Bridget A. Taylor and Jaime A. DeQuinzio

OVERVIEW: WHAT WE KNOW

The core deficits of children with autism include impairments in social, language, and play skills. If play skills exist, they may be limited or may include stereotyped patterns of behavior, such as a preoccupation with parts of objects. For example, a child with autism may persistently spin the wheels on a toy car as opposed to "driving" the car or engaging in appropriate pretend play with the car. As such, parents and clinicians will often have to implement interventions to teach children with autism how to play with toys.

Video modeling is one type of instructional strategy that has been used to improve play skills in children with autism. Video modeling involves showing the child a videotaped segment of a person (the model) engaging in a specific sequence of responses. The sequence may include both motor and vocal responses. For example, the model on the videotape may place a toy figure in a toy car, move it back and forth, and say, "Vroom, vroom." After the child has viewed the video several times, he is presented with the same play materials that appear in the video. Several outcomes are possible: (a) the child may perform responses that are the same as or similar to those presented on the video, (b) the child may fail to perform the target responses and thus will require additional viewings of the video segments, or (c) the child may require additional assistance, such as prompting, in order to perform the responses modeled on the video.

Video modeling has a number of advantages over live modeling. First, when using video modeling, explicit prompting by an instructor is not always required, particularly if the child has previously demonstrated the skills of imitation or observational learning. Secondly, a video model, unlike a live model, which may vary with each subsequent presentation, consistently presents the exact same model with each repetition. Third, various researchers have reported that video modeling permits better acquisition and generalization of skills than does live modeling. For example, it has been demonstrated that for some learners the number of modeling presentations required for responses to be acquired to a criterion level is higher when using in vivo modeling than when using video modeling. Finally, a child observer may more readily sustain attention to a video model than a live model, particularly if television is among the child's preferred activities.

A variety of model types may be used in video modeling instruction. It is common for adults, such as teachers or parents, to serve as models by performing the target responses on video. Peer models such as siblings or classmates are another common model type, and may include children who are the same age and gender as the learner. Point-of-view models are filmed from the visual perspective of the learner (i.e., as would be seen if the learner was performing the responses). Finally, mixed models employ different combinations of the model types described above. All of these model types have been reported as effective for use in video modeling instruction.

Video modeling has broad applicability. Individuals with autism ranging from ages 3 to 20 have participated in studies using video modeling, and video modeling has been successfully used to increase various skills. As previously mentioned, play skills and pretend play have been a focus of video modeling instruction. Additional repertoires include reciprocal play with peers, perspective-taking skills, affective responding, pro-social skills such as helping others, daily living skills, social initiations, and conversational skills. Although this chapter will focus on the use of video modeling to increase play skills, the strategies outlined are applicable to any skill set.

GETTING STARTED: BASIC PRINCIPLES AND APPLICATIONS

There are three basic principles that are relevant to video modeling: imitation, observational learning, and stimulus control.

Teaching children with autism to imitate the responses of others is important in the learning of language, communication, social, and play skills. Initially, young children with autism are typically taught to imitate live adult models who demonstrate simple one-step responses, such as touch nose, clap hands, and stomp feet. The adult models the response and says, "Do this." The adult may assist the child in matching the model by gently guiding him or her to engage in the response (i.e., prompting) and may also provide rewards for correct imitation. When children demonstrate *generalized imitation* (i.e., they readily imitate new responses that were not previously taught or rewarded) they can more easily acquire complex responses when presented on a video tape, rather than as a live scenario. Video modeling is commonly used to model more elaborate and complex responses, such as long play sequences and social interactions.

In addition to imitation in the presence of a live model, *observational learning* is an important skill that may be related to the successful use of video modeling. Observational learning is learning that results from observing the responses of others, as well as the consequences of those responses, and performing those responses later in time and in the absence of the model. For instance, a child may observe a peer pressing a button on a musical toy (i.e., response), which in turn activates the toy's music and lights (i.e., consequence). Later on and in the absence of the peer model, if the child engages in that same response of pressing the button on the toy, it may be considered a demonstration of observational learning. Often in the use of video modeling, the child is first shown the video and then later provided with the opportunity to perform the target responses. Skills in observational learning may assist in successful performance of target responses presented earlier in time via the video model.

When using video modeling, at first target responses are more likely to occur following the presentation of the video model than in its absence. This discrimination illustrates the principle of *stimulus control* by the video model and occurs because reinforcement for engaging in target responses matching the video model occurs following the presentation of the video model. Reinforcement (e.g., an edible or token) may be delivered by the teacher or access to the toys themselves may serve as reinforcement. Over time, it is important to remove the video model in a systematic process called *fading* and to change reinforcement so that it occurs only in the presence of the play materials themselves, and not the video model. Once target responses begin to occur in the presence of the play materials alone and the video model is no longer presented, stimulus control has been successfully shifted from the video model to the materials in the natural environment.

GUIDELINES FOR IMPLEMENTATION

1. **Assess prerequisite skills.** To benefit from video modeling, the child with autism must have several prerequisite skills. For one, the child should be able to imitate a variety of novel actions with objects when the actions are presented live (not in a video). To assess this skill, model several novel actions with objects in front of the child (e.g., say, "do this," and push a toy car while saying, "Vroom, vroom"). Then, hand the child the object to see if he imitates your action and vocalization. If he is unable to do so across several actions, he may not be ready to imitate actions presented on a video. The child should then be taught to imitate actions when they are presented live rather than in a video. The child should also be able to visually attend to the video. Present an age-appropriate video and observe how long the child visually attends to the video. If the child looks away from the screen often, showing little interest, he may need to be taught to attend to videos before introducing video modeling as an intervention. Thus, children with autism must be able to imitate novel live actions and vocalizations and visually attend to videos if they are to benefit from video modeling.

2. **Assess imitation of simple video models.** Even if the child can imitate a variety of actions when they are presented live, he may still require some instruction on how to imitate actions when they are presented in a video. To begin, make a video of a person performing simple motor actions (e.g., clapping, touching head, bending over, holding arms up). Stand the child in front of the video monitor, play one action on the video, and pause the video after the first action. If the child imitates the action, provide praise and a reward. If he does not, replay the video and guide the child to imitate the action on the video. Play the next action on the video and repeat the prompting procedure if necessary. Over teaching trials, fade prompts by providing less assistance until the child can imitate the simple actions on the video independently. Once the child can imitate varied motor actions, make a video of actions involving objects. For example, record a video of a person moving a car back and forth on the table or banging a hammer on the table. Repeat the procedure described above but have the objects available for the child to manipulate after watching the video (e.g., place the car and hammer on the table between the child and the video monitor). Once the child is able to imitate actions with objects, present videos of actions with objects along with vocalizations. For example, present a video of a person saying "Wee!" as she moves a doll down a slide. If the child imitates the action and vocalization, provide praise and a reward. If he doesn't, replay the video and provide both guidance to imitate the action and a model of the vocalization for the child to imitate. Fade guidance and the vocal model across teaching trials until the child is able to imitate the action and vocalization independently.

3. **Develop video modeling play scripts.** When the child can imitate a variety of single actions and vocalizations with objects, identify more elaborate play sequences to teach. Choose activities

in which the child shows interest. If the child likes cars and trains, for example, incorporate those into the play sequence. You can also recruit information from the child's parents about his available play activities at home and the interests of siblings so that the play sequences incorporate familiar activities. Also, consider the developmental appropriateness of the targeted play actions. For example, if the child is three, preschool-related play actions involving a farm with animals would be appropriate; if the child is ten, actions involving figures and a castle may be more appropriate. Initially, develop play scripts that are fairly simple and short and that involve a single actor. Over time, you can develop more complex play sequences involving interactions between people. To develop both the motor and vocal scripted content for the video, present the toys to a typically developing peer, or a peer with adequate play skills, to see what he or she does and says with the play materials. Record on a piece of paper each action and vocal response made by the peer. You may also present the materials to the child with autism to determine if he makes any appropriate actions or vocalizations in relationship to the objects; these can then be incorporated into the content of the video. For example, if the child makes the horse gallop but doesn't say, "Neigh," you could model galloping on the video and add the vocal response, "Neigh" as part of the play sequence. After observing a typical peer with the play materials and/or the child with autism with the play materials, identify the actions and vocal responses to include in the video model. Several simple sequences involving different play activities can be developed so that the child can be taught several play sequences simultaneously rather than practicing the same sequence every day.

4. Record the video model. Once you have written out the scripted motor and vocal responses to include in the play sequence, make a video depicting each step of the play sequence. In the video, you can use an adult or a peer as the model. It is advisable to begin with an adult as the model since an adult will more precisely model the actions and vocalization on the video. The video should show the model demonstrating each action slowly and clearly. For example, the video would show an adult walking a doll to a car, placing the doll in the car, pushing the car, saying "Vroom, vroom," and removing the doll from the car (for more sample play sequences, see Worksheet 26.1 at the end of the chapter).

5. Make a datasheet. After the video has been made, make a datasheet that includes all the scripted motor actions and scripted vocalizations and movements presented on the video. Also include a section on the datasheet to record any unscripted motor and vocal responses. These would include any appropriate actions or vocalizations related to the play material that were not demonstrated on the video (see Worksheet 26.1).

6. Establish baseline performance and conduct probes. Before showing the child the videotape, present the toys to establish baseline performance. Present the toys along with a relevant instruction such as, "Play with the dolls." Sit at a distance from the child and record on the datasheet any motor or vocal responses, whether scripted or unscripted. After baseline, begin teaching the play sequence using the video model. Prior to showing the video model each day, conduct a probe to assess the child's scripted and unscripted motor and vocal responses with the play materials. Record on the datasheet each scripted motor action and vocalization, as well as any unscripted motor or vocal responses made by the child. Summarize the data on a graph by plotting each recorded performance. This allows for a simple and objective visual inspection of the child's performance (see Worksheet 26.2 at the end of the chapter).

7. Show the video. Immediately following the probe, show the child the video. There are several different recommendations in the literature for how many times to show the video. We suggest that you show the video at least two times in succession before presenting the student with play materials. While the child is watching the video, monitor his visual attention to the video. If he looks away, direct his attention back to the video. After playing the video twice,

Worksheet 26.1 Sample Datasheet for Play Responses

Learner's Name_____ Date_____

Score a plus (+) in the column labeled *scripted* if the child performs the responses exactly as they appear in the video. Score a plus (+) in the column labeled *unscripted* if the child performs novel responses that do not match those presented in the video. Score a minus (-) if the child does not perform any scripted or unscripted responses.

MOTOR RESPONSES			VOCAL RESPONSES		
	Scripted	Unscripted		Scripted	Unscripted
Put Dora in car			"Time for the park"		
Move car to park			"Beep-beep"		
Move Dora down slide			"Weeeee"		
Put Dora on seesaw, move up and down			"Up, down, up, down"		
Stand Dora next to seesaw			"That was fun!"		
Put Dora in car			"Let's go home"		
	Total Scripted Motor	Total Unscripted Motor		Total Scripted Vocal	Total Unscripted Vocal

present the play materials and see if the child imitates any of the actions and vocalizations presented in the video. Again, several different prompting and reinforcement strategies have been outlined in the research. Some studies have documented guiding the responses viewed on the video and providing a preferred reward for imitation of the motor and vocal responses; other studies concluded that there was no need for additional prompts or rewards. Following video viewing, we recommend that you present the play materials, and observe the child to see if he imitates any actions or vocalizations presented in the video. If he imitates an action or vocalization, provide a reward such as a small edible, a token, or praise. If after several days of observing the video and having the opportunity to play with the toys, the child does not imitate any of the actions on the tape (or very few), additional instruction may be necessary (see "Adaptations and Modifications" below).

8. **Fade the video and maintain the skill.** Continue to conduct a probe each day prior to video viewing. If the data collected during at least two consecutive daily probes indicate that the child plays with the toys as modeled in the video, continued viewings of the video are no longer necessary. Nevertheless, continue to monitor maintenance of the play responses by conducting intermittent probes (e.g., present the toys every few days and record data). If performance declines, have the student watch the video every so often. Maintain the play sequence by teaching a parent or care provider to present the play activities or to incorporate the play sequence into other play activities or in the child's daily schedule.

Worksheet 26.2 Sample Performance Graphs

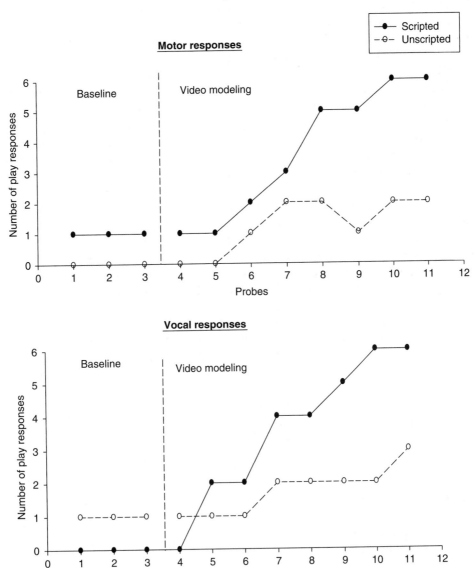

ADAPTATIONS AND MODIFICATIONS

On occasion, specific adaptations of the procedures described above are necessary to enhance imitation of the video. One procedure that may help is a forward chain procedure. When using a forward chain, show the first step in the video and then stop the video and have the child practice that response. Do not show any additional portions of the video until the child can play with the toy as modeled in the first step. Once he can imitate the first step, show the first and second part of the video, and have the child practice both responses in the sequence presented. Add additional steps sequentially as the student masters each new component.

To facilitate varied actions and vocalizations related to a specific play activity, generate multiple play scripts for the same activity. In this case, make several videos using the same play material but vary the motor and vocal responses across the videos. For example, in one video, have the model act out one scenario in which dolls drive the car to the airport and fly to Disneyland. In another video, start with the dolls flying in the plane, landing it, and going home. When using multiple videos, show a different video each day so that the child has exposure to multiple models of play actions and vocal responses. Look for novel and varied actions during probes to assess if multiple videos lead to more varied actions and vocalizations.

To facilitate generalization to novel play activities, present toys that are similar to yet different from the toys shown in the video. For example, if the video depicts a model moving a *car* down a ramp and saying "Vroom," present the child with a *truck* and a ramp. Each day, you could present materials that are slightly different to assess generalization to novel play material (e.g., present a motorcycle and a road rather than a ramp).

To encourage play interactions between a child and his peer or an adult, develop play scripts that involve interactions between two models. For example, you can develop a video model of two adults engaging with one another during an activity, such as one pretending to cook and the other pretending to eat the food that is presented. In this case, present the activity to the child along with another person. Each person then assumes one of the roles modeled on the video. In some cases the child may need to be prompted which role to assume.

The advance of technology increases the efficiency of making video models and of incorporating them across a range of activities. Two examples illustrate this point. First, videos could be embedded in computerized activity schedules and downloaded into portable devices (e.g., an Apple iPod) that can be played anywhere. Second, a video model of a play script could be played on a small portable device right within a classroom in a play area, or a video model of an appropriate greeting response can be viewed by a young man with autism just before he greets his supervisor at work.

KEYS TO REMEMBER

1. Some children may not benefit from video modeling. Generalized imitation and the ability to imitate actions and vocalizations observed in videos are important prerequisites to assess.

2. Use play materials and activities the child shows an interest in. Once several play scripts are mastered, allow the child to choose which play scripts he would like to engage in and incorporate into the scripts the activities and people in the child's daily life.

3. If supplemental prompts such as guidance are used to teach the child to imitate the actions on the videos, be sure to fade these prompts until the child is able to imitate the actions with the video only. Eventually fade the video as well by reducing the number of times the video is shown to the child.

4. Develop video modeling play scripts that are developmentally appropriate and specifically geared to the individualized needs of the child with autism.

5. Record performance so that you can accurately track acquisition, make decisions about modifications, and set new goals when necessary.

SUGGESTED READINGS

Charlop-Christy, M. H., Carpenter, M., Le, L., & Freeman, K. A. (2000). A comparison of video modeling with in vivo modeling for teaching children with autism. *Journal of Autism and Developmental Disorders, 30,* 537–552.

Charlop-Christy, M. H., Le, L., & Daneshvar, S. (2003). Using video modeling to teach perspective taking to children with autism. *Journal of Positive Behavior Interventions, 5,* 12–21.

D'Ateno, P., Mangiapanello, K., & Taylor, B. A. (2003). Using video modeling to teach complex play sequences to a preschooler with autism. *Journal of Positive Behavior Interventions, 5,* 5–11.

Kimball, J. W., Kinney, E. M., Taylor, B. A., & Stromer, R. (2004). Video enhanced activity schedules for children with autism: A promising package for teaching social skills. *Education and Treatment of Children, 27,* 280–299.

MacDonald, R. G., Clark, M., Garrigan, E., & Vangala, M. (2005). Increasing play using videomodeling. *Behavioral Interventions, 20,* 225–238.

Reeve, S. A., Reeve, K. F., Townsend, D. B., & Poulson, C. L. (2007). Establishing a generalized repertoire of helping behavior in children with autism. *Journal of Applied Behavior Analysis, 40,* 123–136.

OTHER RESOURCES

When creating video models, it is best to individualize the videos to accommodate the particular needs of each learner. These websites offer additional information and pre-made videos:

1. http://www.neccautismplay.com
2. http://www.dttrainer.com/jos/index.php
3. http://www.modelmekids.com/video-modeling.html

CHAPTER 27

TRAINING PARENTS AND OTHER CARE PROVIDERS

James K. Luiselli

OVERVIEW: WHAT WE KNOW

Professionals in the field of autism spectrum disorder (ASD) frequently are responsible for training other people to implement teaching procedures and behavior support interventions. Parents, for example, should be able to conduct instruction with their children, perhaps teaching them a self-help skill, daily living routine, or leisure activity. A staff person at a vocational center may have to learn procedures for supervising adults during assigned tasks. And classroom teachers, residential counselors, and respite-care providers frequently must be taught methods for preventing and managing problem behavior.

Training parents and other care providers has been accomplished in several ways. Sometimes, professionals conduct training by having trainees follow instructional manuals, read information about a specific topic, or attend workshops. Generally, this kind of training does not produce favorable results. The main reason is that although trainees may learn about teaching methods during a lecture or by reading a relevant publication, they may be unable to implement them correctly when called upon to do so—that is, knowledge by itself does not necessarily translate to performance.

Another approach to training parents and other care providers is having them interact with a surrogate during simulated sessions. Essentially, the surrogate plays the role of a child or adult with ASD while the trainee is instructed and prompted to perform certain behaviors. Training under these conditions has the advantage of being "hands on" because the skills to be acquired are taught as they should be performed. The chief limitation is that learning effects may not, and usually do not, generalize to "non-trained" environments.

Research suggests that competency-based training is the best approach with parents and other care providers. Defined broadly, a competency is a set of behaviors that when performed properly produces a desired outcome—for example, playing a musical instrument, driving a motor vehicle, delivering a speech, or hitting a golf ball. Relative to the training of ASD practitioners and paraprofessionals, various competencies would be carrying out discrete trial instruction, teaching alternative and augmentative communication, and implementing a behavior support plan. As with any approach to training, procedures should be adjusted to the specific demands of the people being trained—this qualification, in fact, is a strength of competency-based training.

GETTING STARTED: PRINCIPLES AND APPLICATIONS

Competency-based training represents an empirical methodology that has been employed successfully in a number of areas, including industry and human services organizations. One of the basic principles underlying competency-based training is behavior shaping. Consider the example of training a parent to teach her son how to brush his teeth. Tooth brushing is a skill comprising several smaller behaviors (grasping toothbrush, applying toothpaste, bringing toothbrush in contact with teeth) that must be performed fluently. A parent learning to teach this skill would be instructed on each component behavior, gradually chaining the behaviors in sequence using physical guidance, verbal prompting, positive reinforcement, and similar procedures. Through the process of behavior shaping, the parent acquires a competency in a step-by-step progression that accommodates each person's pace of learning.

Another feature of competency-based training is that it targets skill acquisition in the natural setting. So-called in vivo training has the objective of building skills under the conditions of ultimate functioning. Training a teacher to conduct discrete trial instruction should occur in the classroom. Training residential care staff to support an adult in the community should take place in stores, restaurants, banks, and municipal buildings. As noted previously, training that occurs in context avoids the limitation of weak generalization when procedures are applied in an artificial environment.

Although other training methodologies include practice, it is a key element of competency-based approaches. Practice, sometimes referred to as behavior rehearsal, entails repeated demonstration of responses within a skill sequence. With repetition, a person's responding becomes more fluent, a prerequisite for skill mastery. Practice occurs under the direction of a trainer and is encouraged outside of formal training sessions.

Performance feedback is an additional defining characteristic of competency-based training. A trainer provides feedback to a parent or other care provider after observing him or her interacting with a child or adult. Positive performance feedback consists of the trainer praising and approving behaviors the trainee implements accurately. When delivering correction, the trainer points out behaviors that were not implemented accurately and instructs the trainee in how the behaviors should be performed. Performance feedback is most effective when it is presented immediately following an observation and contingent on measurable behaviors. Typically, performance feedback is delivered verbally but may also include visual reference to data or graphs.

The control exerted by performance feedback is unclear. For most people, praise and approval from a trainer function as positive reinforcement. However, acknowledgement itself may be sufficiently reinforcing and capable of motivating desirable behavior. Others have speculated that receiving correction from a trainer may be an unpleasant consequence that can be avoided by performing behaviors accurately. Whatever its source of control, performance feedback is integral to conducting competency-based training.

GUIDELINES FOR INTERVENTION

As noted, competency-based training requires that you observe a parent or other care provider interacting with a child or adult. The purpose of observation is to document objectively how the trainee performs. Your data-based measurement is then used to shape performance.

1. **Identify the target skill or implementation objective.** Competency-based training begins by selecting a target skill or implementation objective. For example, a skill could be having a parent or in-home care provider conduct a toilet training protocol with a young child. Or, the focus could be training a classroom teacher to follow the steps of a student's behavior support plan. Although you may identify several skills and objectives as the focus of training, it usually is best to address them one at a time and not simultaneously.

2. **Train in the natural environment.** Choose the relevant context to conduct competency-based training. A simple guide is to train in the settings where the target skill and intervention objective are relevant. For example, if the goal is to teach behavior support procedures to classroom staff, training ideally should be applied at school. If parents are the recipients of training, introduce procedures in their home.

3. **Design a training checklist.** After identifying the target skill or implementation objective, you should design a training checklist. Worksheet 27.1, which concerns the training of discrete trial instructional skills, illustrates the general format for such a checklist (it is at the end of the chapter).

Worksheet 27.1 Training Checklist: Discrete Trial Instruction

Date of Training:
Setting:
Trainee:
Trainer:

Step	Definition	Competency Rating	
		Accurate	Requires Correction
1	Trainee has instructional materials present: objects, student's teaching plan, datasheet		
2	Trainee positions student in proper location		
3	Trainee sits oriented toward student		
4	Trainee initiates trial by eliciting eye contact from student		
5	Trainee displays Sd (if warranted) and/or gives appropriate verbal command		
6	Trainee prompts student appropriately as per teaching plan		
7	If student responds correctly, trainee reinforces within 3 seconds		
8	If student responds incorrectly, trainee applies correction one time		
9	Trainee records data for preceding trial		
10	After recording data, trainee waits 3 to 5 seconds before initiating next trial		
11	Trainee conducts total trials specified on the student's teaching plan		

Terminal Criterion: Trainee receives 100% accuracy rating on all steps during three consecutive training sessions.

a. List the behaviors that make up the training target as "steps" and in the order of implementation.

b. Write a concise, behavior-specific definition for each step by describing how the step should be implemented and how it will be measured.

c. Include an "accurate" and "requires correction" competency rating for each step. "Accurate" means that the step was performed according to the behavior-specific definition. "Requires correction" means that the step was not performed according to the behavior-specific definition.

d. Indicate a "terminal criterion"—that is, a measurable standard verifying that the trainee has accomplished all steps on the checklist. For example, a possible criterion could be that the trainee was rated "accurate" for all steps on the checklist during five consecutive observations.

4. Preview. Begin each training session by reviewing the checklist with the trainee. You should highlight each step, the respective behavior definitions, and the sequence of implementation.

5. Rehearse. Training can be enhanced by rehearsing the checklist behaviors. So, after reviewing the checklist before each training session, have the trainee practice implementation with you once or twice. In effect, these practice opportunities function as a "warm-up" for the trainee.

6. Set up. At the start of each training session check to see that all required materials are present. Position yourself so that you can clearly observe the trainee and the child or adult but without causing distraction.

7. Observe. Observe the trainee and the child or adult. Record the trainee's performance, step by step, on the checklist.

8. Deliver performance feedback. When the training session concludes, spend 3 to 5 minutes with the trainee to deliver performance feedback. Feedback should be presented while referencing each step in the checklist.

a. Praise the trainee for each step that was implemented accurately. Your praise should include a positive, descriptive statement such as, "Terrific: you established eye contact with Bob before giving him the instruction."

b. Correct inaccurate performance steps by pointing out what was missed and describing how the steps should have been implemented. An example would be, "Remember, you have to wait 5 seconds before starting another trial."

c. After reviewing all of the checklist steps, have the trainee run through the sequence once or twice with you, again praising accurately implemented steps and correcting inaccurately implemented steps.

9. Terminate the session. Conclude the training session by allowing the trainee to ask questions. Clarify any issues or concerns. Then schedule the next training session.

10. Follow up. Continue training sessions until the trainee achieves the terminal criterion specified on the checklist. Training, however, should not end abruptly. Instead, arrange one or more follow-up observations to ensure that the trainee continues to perform accurately. These follow-up sessions can be a few weeks after formal training was terminated or, if possible, even months later. Trainee implementation at these times should be reinforced and/or corrected according to the performance feedback procedures that have been described.

ADAPTATIONS AND MODIFICATIONS

Not all parents and other care providers need the same intensity of training. For example, some staff at a habilitation services setting may have participated in a training program. Other staff may not have had a similar experience. Parents, too, are likely to have different training histories. With competency-based training, you will be able to measure each trainee's performance ability and adjust procedures accordingly. Thus, your time will be relatively brief with a trainee who is able to perform some of the steps in the training checklist accurately before training is initiated. Conversely, a longer course of training should be expected with people who are less proficient.

One modification that can be made when training does not progress smoothly or requires more time is to simplify the steps in the training checklist. This adjustment entails dividing one or more steps into smaller behaviors. Even though this process adds steps to the checklist, a target skill or intervention objective may be acquired more rapidly when the relevant behaviors are easier to implement.

KEYS TO REMEMBER

1. Focus training on the competencies required for a parent or other care provider to effectively teach and provide behavior support.
2. Conduct training in the actual settings where children and adults live, go to school, work, and play.
3. Work with trainees on implementing behaviors that are described and sequenced on a competency training checklist.
4. Review the competency training checklist with trainees before observing them during a training session.
5. Conclude each training session by giving performance feedback to the trainee: praise the behaviors that were performed accurately and correct the behaviors that were performed inaccurately.
6. Make your performance feedback remarks positive and supportive. Avoid harsh and punitive language.
7. Establish a terminal criterion signifying that a trainee is "fully competent." Schedule post-training observations to determine whether additional training is needed.

SUGGESTED READINGS

Gilligan, K. T., Luiselli, J. K., & Pace, G. M. (2007). Training paraprofessional staff to implement discrete trial instruction: Evaluation of a practical performance feedback intervention. *The Behavior Therapist, 30,* 63–66.

Lavie, T., & Sturmey, P. (2002). Training staff to conduct a paired-stimulus preference assessment. *Journal of Applied Behavior Analysis, 35,* 209–211.

Ricciardi, J. N. (2005). Achieving human service outcomes through competency-based training. *Behavior Modification, 29,* 488–507.

Stokes, J. V., & Luiselli, J. K. (2008). In-home parent training of functional analysis skills. *International Journal of Behavioral Consultation & Therapy, 4,* 259–263.

Wood, A. L., Luiselli, J. K., & Harchik, A. E. (2007). Training instructional skills with paraprofessional service providers at a community-based habilitation setting. *Behavior Modification, 31,* 847–855.

INDEX